"As a therapist, success trainer ~~~ ~~~
ing books to improve my skil ~~~ ~~~
While most of them have given me insights, there are only
books in my library that are dog-eared from constant use. Soon
the fourth dog-eared copy will be Michael Hall's book, *Secrets of
Personal Mastery*. He ingeniously weaves together theory and
application while thoroughly explaining how one might utilize
the thirteen secrets of personal mastery in a manner that is
incredible, inspiring and revealing. Buy this book; you do want
to achieve personal mastery, don't you?"
—Rob McCarter, M.S., LPC, NCC

"In the search for meaning, the study of semantics, and the field
of Neuro-Semantics, Michael Hall's Meta-States, is a most
significant and critical contribution … In my view, [*Secrets of
Personal Mastery*] is a book that is the best to be a standard for
every medical student, student of psychology, philosophy
student and their respective professional graduates."
—Dennis Chong, M.D.

"This material can spare people years of useless, expensive effort
with traditional therapeutic modalities."
—Craig Johnson

"What Dr Michael Hall is presenting is truly a new area of NLP
that solidly integrates with the rest of NLP; it brings a completeness to NLP that's greatly needed."
—Tommy Belk, M.A., M.Div., LPC

"Dr Hall masterfully explains, demonstrates, and models
Meta-States so that from newcomers to masters in this field,
people effectively learn to use the model to make a difference
in life."
—William P. Glaros, DDS

"In Meta-States, a seemingly complex theory actually provides
simple techniques for producing effective results. The model
gives one the processes for increasing personal effectiveness."
—Hugh Yamashiro, Trainer

Secrets
of
Personal
Mastery

Awakening Your Inner Executive

Advanced Techniques for Accessing
Your Higher Levels of Consciousness

L. Michael Hall, Ph.D.

Crown House Publishing Limited
www.crownhouse.co.uk

Published in the UK by

Crown House Publishing Ltd
Crown Buildings
Bancyfelin
Carmarthen
Wales
www.crownhouse.co.uk

First published 2000; reprinted 2001, 2002, 2004.

British Library Cataloguing-in-Publication Data
A catalogue entry for this book is available
from the British Library.

ISBN 189983656X

LCCN 2003113102

Printed and bound in the UK by
Gomer Press
Llandysul

Table of Contents

Appendices

Preface

"No man is free who is not a master of himself."
(Epictetus)

Julie didn't think she had any *personal power*. And from what I could see from the way she lived her life and her everyday feelings, I wouldn't have connected her with the idea of "personal mastery" either. I soon discovered that she didn't even know about her *executive powers*.

"What do you think, Julie; do you want to live out of your own values and visions and let them guide you as your executive powers?"

"Yes, I do," she said in a soft voice.

"Really? I don't think so," provoking her a bit, "I think you ought to be a mirror for the values and visions of others and that you should spend your energy on living up to what others prescribe for you!"

"You do…? No, I don't want to do that. I've spent too much of my life already living that way and I'm tired of it."

"You have chosen up until now to live your life to please others, to conform to their values and visions about life?"

"Yes, I have. That's really the story of my life."

"Up until now?"

"Yes, up until now."

"And what do you say, at this point in your life, does that express *your uniqueness* and specialness? Is that what Julie is about?"

"No, definitely not."

i

"So it sounds like you're clear that in order to more fully experience and express your own personal power, you will need to push out the opinions of others so that you can give yourself a chance to actualize your own dreams and passions."

"Right. But I don't know how to do that."

"Really? You sound definite about what you don't want to tolerate any more. Or, were you just pulling my leg?"

"No, I wasn't kidding, I really am tired of trying to please others."

'Well, isn't that the starting point for you then? That is, to push away and refuse to tolerate being a slave to the values and visions of others, then you'll be able to identify your own."

"I guess so. Is that how it happens?"

"Then have you accessed your *executive power* to establish that as your pathway? ... Would you like to?"

"My executive power? I don't understand."

"You don't know about the higher levels of your mind, those executive levels where you set intentions and purposes, where you establish your passions about who to be and what to experience?"

"You mean 'will power'?"

"No, it's not that at all. It's the higher levels of your mind, the part of your mind where you establish your life direction and then build processes for activating that vision in your way of being in the world."

"That sounds nice ... but ..."

"Julie, suppose ... just for the sake of this discussion that you woke up tomorrow totally free from being dominated by the opinions of others and totally free to choose your own way. Just imagine that ... go ahead, be wild in your imaginations about this ... Good. What would that be like?"

"What would that be like?"

"Yes. Suppose you woke up with all of your executive powers of mind and emotion so that like any empowered, informed, and decisive CEO, you awoke ready and able to live in a way that's fully congruent with your values.... How would you know that you're truly free from the opinions of others and that you get to choose to live by your own values?"

"Well, I would be breathing easier ... and I'd be focused on what *I* want to do ... and I'd just act on my goals to make them come true."

"What would you be doing?"

"I'd be feeling confident enough about myself to call on some people in my field and setting up some contacts."

"How would that be different?"

"I'd not be worrying about what others would be saying. I'd be focused on what I can do and taking one step at a time to make it happen ... Oh, I'd not be overwhelming myself by expecting my goals tomorrow."

"Any difference in how you'd be presenting yourself?"

"I'd be speaking with more confidence, more firmly, you know, with a sense of strength in my voice."

"With the tone of voice that you're now using? Julie, perhaps you have awoken that executive within. Perhaps the journey has begun ... What do you think?"

Discovering Your Executive Powers

I have written this book to invite you to embark on *an adventure of discovery* so that in the end, you will access your executive powers. Along the way, we will awaken and utilize the higher levels of your mind. The journey will take us into realms of:

- mind and emotion
- the excellence of expertise
- the tragedy of complacency
- identity and existence
- madness and genius
- language and semantics
- procedures and magic
- personal and interpersonal development

and

- the mind-muscle connection that enables us to translate "concepts" into everyday actions.

This book has been designed to facilitate your personal adventure in discovering and using *the secrets that govern your executive power so that you can cultivate the personal mastery over your mind and emotions that you desire.* Upon making *that* discovery, you will enter into the higher management, the management of your own mind at all of its levels. And that will enrich you for the ultimate development of excellence—accessing your personal genius. And from there? Well the sky is the limit. You can apply your executive powers to your career and business, to mastering your health and fitness, your relationships, or wherever you'd like to apply that mastery.

A big order indeed!

Regarding this kind of a thing, many books, programs, and trainings promise that the pathway to wealth, health, success, and mastery will be "quick and simple." You will find no such promise here.

Personal mastery does not come easily, quickly, or even naturally.

If the secrets for accessing your executive power and developing personal mastery came easy and quick, would we not see more people at that level? No, the truth is that *mastery* necessitates effort. We have to give ourselves to it. Do Olympic athletes reach the Olympics without effort? Do they obtain medals easily and without training? No, there's a price for mastery.

At the same time working toward mastery can feel like an exciting journey. It does *not* demand a nose-to-the-grindstone kind of self-denial. The *Flow* researcher, psychologist Csikszentmihalyi, has documented that the majority of those who do reach optimal levels of human excellence do not find it "work." Instead, as they become so absorbed in their passion, they get lost in it. What may appear to an outsider as "work" or "struggle" is experienced by the master as part of the fun, part of the challenge.

So it is here.

The mental mastery involved in "running your own brain" involves a discipline of understanding and skill. As in any other field where people master a set of competencies—to access your *highest executive states* involves learning the principles (secrets) and applying or practicing the operational dynamics. And as with other disciplines, those who enter into the process more often than not become so fascinated and caught up by the challenge of discovery, that they primarily experience it as fun and exciting. The *flow* of their optimal experience transforms the very quality of their adventure as a discipleship.

The content of this field focuses on mind, consciousness, subjective experience—hence, *"personal"* mastery. This also includes both physical and mental mastery. If you choose to accept the pathway to your own mastery by means of identifying, accessing, and utilizing *executive states,* you will adventure "inside" to explore the very structures that now organize and govern the very basis of your life. This exploration will take us on a search for *the dynamics* of mind at all of its higher levels, the dynamics at those levels which set the frame for how we think, feel, speak, and behave. Knowing this, in turn, gives you an insider's knowledge about how to run your own brain and body, and how to take charge of your own experiences. It offers to transform you into the World's Best Expert for bringing the best out of yourself.

Secrets of Personal Mastery aims to facilitate your own personal discovery of specific secrets—secrets about executive power. This will enable you to become a competent explorer as you discover and take charge of your own inner executive states. The secrets create a whole new level of empowerment. It puts into your hands the mechanisms by which you can effectively leverage control over your mind, emotions, body, experiences, and destiny.

To do that I will first provide a *model of mind*. It does help to have a good workable model of mind if you want to manage it, especially its higher levels. But a caveat. The way you will come to think about *mind* will differ from how you have typically learned to think about it.

Here you will be offered a brand new way to think about your thinking and feeling, your beliefs and values, and your memories and imaginations. Traditionally, psychology has treated mind too much as a *thing* and its *contents* as its most important features. You will not find those assumptions here. Instead we treat *mind* as an emergent process of our entire mind-emotion-body system and *structure* as more determinative than content. In the chapters to come you will discover that it is not so much *what* you're thinking that controls your destiny and experiences, but *how* you are thinking—*your frames of references*. This theoretical model of mind (*the Meta-States Model*) is briefly sketched here.

Also, I will provide coaching via a set of exercises and technologies. Why? To give you practical experience in "running your own brain." So along the way you will find various *Thought Experiments* and processes (exercises, experiments, patterns) for accessing your executive powers.

When you come upon these *Thought Experiments*, stop ... in your mind, put the book down and immediately *run the experiment* (the ellipses of three dots ... provide a signal to do this).

What scientist wouldn't put his or her theories *to the test* by using their lab equipment to see if the hypothesis can stand the crucial test of an experiment? So refuse to allow yourself to buy into the ideas of this work without trying the processes out for yourself. We know they work. We have lots of testimonials to their effectiveness. Yet the best way for you to know that lies in your own experiences of the processes.

Is it possible to think and work through Thought Experiments and thereby experience significant transformations?

Yes, you bet it is!

How? This can happen because all thoughts are not on the same level. We not only experience "thoughts," we experience *all kinds and qualities of thoughts*. The "thoughts" we experience on a day to day basis come in a wide range of assorted forms that we call beliefs, values, understandings, knowledge, intuitions, decisions, ideas, etc.

These "thoughts" can take the form of images, pictures, movies, diagrams (*visual* representations), sounds, music, noise, beats (*auditory* representations), body sensations, movements, touch, intuitions (*kinesthetic* representations), smells (*olfactory* representations), tastes (*gustatory* representations), balance, orientation in space, movement (*vestibular* representations), words, language, mathematics, music, metaphor, story, narrative (*symbolic and linguistic* representations), etc.

Our "thoughts" can also become very rich and intense by involving many kinds of representations simultaneously. We can also jump levels and *think "thoughts" about our "thoughts"* (meta-cognition). When we do, we layer one level of thinking *upon* another level. This creates the levels of our higher frames of mind—our executive states and it reflects our executive power.

This highlights one of the secrets:

> *All of our thinking-and-emoting* (which creates states and frames of mind) *do **not** work on the same level.*

We begin with the regular thoughts that make up our *primary* states of mind and emotion. Then we move to higher level frames of mind that involve more complexity as we layer thought upon thought. With each feedback loop, we build up *Conceptual States*.

With these executive levels of mind, we build *attitudes* that we then carry with us through life. Yet often these higher level thoughts of our attitudes do not serve us very well. They may be toxic thoughts and states. They may poison our very existence.

What conceptual states do you have and "never leave home without?" What *attitudes* do you seem to take everywhere you go? Do you tend to think optimistically? Do you tend to see the dark side of things? Do you expect people to be warm and friendly? Or do you expect people to be out for their own gain at your expense?

When we move to such high level states of mind, we access a "place" or "attitude" that has more influence, more power, and more extensiveness than just a regular, everyday frame of mind. These states-upon-states, or Meta-States, of layered thoughts-and-emotions then govern experience. We experience these meta-level structures or executive states, as more complex and stable. As a result, working with, communicating with, and relating to these states will require higher level understandings.

Getting to the Boss

Would you like to get to your boss? What about the boss in others? As you discover how to effectively speak and relate to our own (or another's) *executive states of mind-and-emotion*—you discover how to go right to **"the boss."**

So what?

This will provide immediate access to the processes that actually govern our experiences. With this access, we can now go right to "the boss" who runs the show over our emotions, behaviors, reference systems, and our model of the world. Wouldn't you find that kind of executive power valuable?

By accessing the executive power of *the boss* we can cut through all of the lower-level experiences, states, ideas, and frames-of-references that can blind and delude us with regard to what's really going on. Having access also empowers us to communicate directly to *the governing influence* in our own thinking, valuing, and believing or another person's. With this, we then experience greater effectiveness in:

- Communicating: being able to quickly recognize the level of thought and to tune in to that level.
- Mind: recognizing our own levels and the levels of mind-and-emotion in others.
- Understanding: being able to more thoroughly understand ourselves and others.

- Relating: being more able to support, validate, and assist others.
- Persuading: by recognizing the governing influences at the higher levels.
- Skills: by learning how to use the *executive level technologies* as guidelines for effectively managing and influencing our states.

Every time we try hard to make ourselves go to sleep, we use an *ineffective* method for attempting to manage one level (facilitating sleep) by another level (order, commanding—"trying hard"). This introduces paradox into our mind-body system. After that, the more we do this, the more we worsen the problem. The *attempted solution* increases the problem.

This example gives birth to the *relational question* about how *one level of mind interacts with another level*.

"What happens when I bring one thought or representation, at one level of mind, to bear upon another thought at another level?"

All kinds of things! *The Meta-States Model* specifies at least sixteen different possible results. Out of the *interface* of one state of mind upon another, numerous systemic complexities can emerge. Sometimes one state interfacing with another amplifies the two. Sometimes it reduces the first state. At other times it can completely nullify it, soften it, create paradox, interruption, amnesia, etc.

In reading and experiencing the *Thought Experiments* and *Meta-State Patterns* in this work, you will exercise your own ability to "run your own brain." This will provide you with practice in directing the operations of your mind. With each move you will be "stepping back" from your *thinking-and-feeling* to observe the products of your consciousness. Doing this self-reflexive shifting involves what we call *"going meta,"* or taking a meta-position, to your own consciousness. You will be using your *reflexive awareness* to become aware of your awareness. At first, you may feel dizzy, even disoriented. At first it may feel weird and "not like me." You may even feel tempted to fear this level of awareness, thinking that you'll get caught up in a loop or that others will think you've "lost your mind." Well, you won't get caught up in a non-existing loop. About the charge of your friends and family thinking that you've "lost it," well, they may have a point ... for a while ... until you emerge as *a master of your mind*. Then you'll get the last laugh.

As you move up (conceptually, of course) in your mind and identify higher level managers, you move to a higher perceptual position. You begin by first simply observing something in the world. Then you observe your own observing, then you observe your observing of the observations. With each move, you attain (conceptually) a higher logical level as each level operates above, and about, the lower level (that's what the word "meta" means). At each level, you reflect back onto your previous thinking or experiencing.

Owning Your Executive Power

Mind is like a wild and powerful force, like a stream of water in which we navigate in a canoe, raft, or kayak. To do this effectively, we need both skills and an understanding of the structure and nature of the craft. We need to know certain principles of navigation. We need to know how to use a compass, a paddle, and to learn to calibrate to the movements of the river. This also applies when we explore the art of learning to navigate your inner stream of consciousness—which, as you access and develop your executive power will become "a piece of cake!"

Summary

- Because we have a consciousness that operates on many levels, our executive power lies at the higher levels of mind. So that's where we will go. Our brain's ability to *reflect back* on itself enables us to toy with our own brain and to even learn to direct its operations to a great extent.
- Accessing our executive levels will allow us to take charge of our mental-emotional programming. Then we will not default on the programs of our genetics, culture, family, etc. This will enable us to take a much more intentional stance in life as we choose to "run our own brain" and develop personal mastery.

- If our current "programs" for thinking, feeling, speaking, and acting do not make *life a party*, we have only to access our executive states, get to the boss, and from there establish new goals, games, and values.
- The secrets of accessing our executive power provides us with the way to truly take charge of our mind, meta-mind, and everyday actions.
- So on to the game—turn the page to begin the journey toward your own *Personal Mastery.*

L. Michael Hall, Ph.D.

The First Secrets
of
Executive Power
and
Personal Mastery

Secret #1

The road to mastery begins when we appreciate our "thoughts" as neuro-linguistic programs.

The foundation for personal mastery lies in "thought." What you think determines what you feel, how you perceive, your internal reality, in a word, your states. They also give you your initial road maps for navigating life.

Secret #2

Mastery occurs when you discover your higher states as your executive operations.

We humans never just think— we think about our thinking, and then think about that thinking. Our thoughts-and-feelings forever and inevitably reflect back onto themselves to become more and more layered. Therefore the secret of personal mastery lies in discovering our higher thoughts-and-feelings and choosing those that serve us well.

Chapter 1

Taking Charge

Foundational Tools for Mastery

Secrets for Personal Excellence

- Who (or what) *controls* your thoughts and feelings?
- *To what extent* do you feel in charge of your mind, your emotions, your body, your talk and language use, and your behaviors? To what extent would you like to?
- *How often* do you *wonder why* you entertain the thoughts that you do or experience the emotions that intrude, whether negative or positive?
- *To what extent* can you get yourself to actually **do** the things that you know you should do and want to do to succeed?
- *How much more resourceful* would you feel and *how much more productive* would you be if you could access and activate your inner executive?

Robert felt that he had nothing going in his life that could be classified as *personal mastery.* Though he was quite knowledgeable in his field, skilled, and personable, though he had made a decent living from it, enjoyed a good relationship with a special lady in his life, and though he wasn't officially "depressed," he felt discouraged, frustrated, and disillusioned about himself and his career.

I asked him, "So, Robert, what stops you from getting on the highway of life and moving on down the road with a sense of vitality and passion?"

He shrugged his shoulders.

"What would you have to have so that you could wake up tomorrow morning feeling a sense of personal mastery?"

3

"I'd have to get over my procrastination. If I didn't keep putting off things … That's what holds me back."

"Ah, procrastination. And how do you know to call what you're experiencing 'procrastination'?"

"Well, I know what I need to do, but when I think about doing it, it seems too overwhelming and I tell myself that I'll never get it right enough, so I put it off."

"Then what? What do you do when you're putting these pieces of effective activity off?"

"Well, I might end up at the office just fiddling around, or at the donut shop."

"And how often do you do this?"

"Daily. I waste lots of time every day just fooling around."

"It sounds like you really have this down to a highly developed skill that you can pull off regularly and consistently. You never forget to procrastinate? You never just put it off till later?"

(Laughing) "Well, yeah, sometimes."

"Tell me about those times. What's different during those times? What messes you up from this effective skill of procrastination so that you blow it by just getting out there and taking effective action?"

"Usually I just tell myself that I can do it, and that I can't make any more of a mess of it than it's already in."

"Robert, it sounds like you have a frame of perfectionism wherein you torture yourself by demanding that you do things *just right* so it is easy to feel overwhelmed. And that when you release that frame, it frees up your psychic energies. Does that ring a bell with you?"

"Yes, that's exactly the way it is."

"Ah! So personal mastery lies just around the corner for you. All you need to do is establish a frame of being kinder and gentler with yourself so that you can apply your knowledge and skills."

Well, it actually took more than that, but that was the beginning. From there Robert took off. As we flushed out his higher frames of mind, his belief frames about taking action, risk, how much he had to know, what others thought of him, his value frames that he applied to himself and others, his frames of identity, decision, etc., I simply coached him through the process of deframing those that didn't work and setting new higher frames. In this way, he awakened and empowered his own inner executive states of mind.

Six months later I asked him about the level of his personal mastery.

"I feel like a new man. It's not that everything goes my way, but I have a general sense of power and control over my own brain and my own states. If I get into a negative mood, I know how to shift my state and how to put myself in a much more resourceful state. It's great. I don't put things off as I used to. I act from my executive mind to make the goals that I've set come true. It's amazing."

The Secrets of Mastery

As Robert learned and used the *Secrets of Mastery* concerning his mind, emotions, actions, behavior, body, and life, so can you. These secrets are just awaiting your discovery and application. *If you want to learn and master them, you can.*

This does not mean that such mastery will come easily or quickly. I will not mislead you about that. *If* accessing your own personal genius came that easily or quickly, people everywhere would be living up to their potentials, being at their best, and living high quality lives, effectively communicating, enjoying relationships, etc.

Such is not the case.

Instead, everywhere we turn we see people *not* at their best and *not* living up to their highest potential. We see people sabotaging their own best interests. People ruining their health, their peace of mind, their relationships, and being deceived by a wide variety of deceptive schemes. We find people depressed, suicidal, hateful, full of revenge, and suffering from all kinds of psychological and psychosomatic problems.

It does not have to be that way. A better way beckons. We all can become much more masterful at running our own brains, controlling our own states, and engineering our own successful futures. *Sanity* (good adjustment to the constraints of reality) is possible. So is personal excellence or genius. And that's why I wrote this book.

Two Things
Now regarding the secrets of mastery in other fields, from physics to mathematics, from computer science to human relationships, from linguistics to literature, from education to professional athletics—to become truly masterful you have to *have* two things and you have to *do* two things:

- First, you have to have a high quality model and develop a masterful *understanding* of that model.
- Second, you have to exercise the personal discipline to practice using that model until you become fully competent in using it.

Regarding the secrets of *personal* mastery, i.e. mastery over yourself, your states, thoughts, beliefs, emotions, behaviors, etc., this book presents both. First, you will learn about and become competent in a high quality model for running your own brain (i.e. the Meta-States Model). As you do this, this book will provide you with many practical exercises for developing your personal mastery. So if you truly want to achieve such mastery over yourself, you will here find a basic road map that will help with navigating that territory.

To facilitate your exploration and discovery in this realm of personal excellence, I have organized this work around a few basic principles. When you learn *the art of applying these principles*, you will have everything you need to access personal excellence.

To make the process fun and as simple as possible, I have designed each chapter to build upon the former. In this way, as you encounter each new *secret of mastery* you will find it as simply the next step in the process. It will emerge naturally out of the previous steps. When you complete the process, you will have an understanding and skill development of a complex domain, yet it will seem totally natural and easy.

Also, along the way, I'll introduce lots of new words and terminology—again with simple definitions and explanations.

"New words? But why?"

Primarily because it's part of the heart of *mastery in any field*. Whether it's the special language and terminology of baseball or soccer, mathematics or music, computers or ecology, politics or economics, to master any field you need *a precise language*. The everyday language that serves for watching TV sitcoms won't do. There are some things we simply *cannot say*, and therefore cannot conceptualize, without a specialized language.

At the end of every chapter I'll highlight the new words that serve as the basis for *personal excellence*. Then, with this precise terminology, you will have a road map that can take you places for mastering your own mind that others lack. In fact, while I have not designed it as one of the secrets of mastery, *being able to language mental mastery* comprises a crucial facet in mastering this realm. If you can't speak it, how can you get there? If you don't have the language of it, how can you coach yourself or anyone else to get there?

Secret #1
The road to mastery begins as we appreciate thoughts as neuro-linguistic programs.
Consider the very nature of what we call *"thoughts."* What are these things? What do your "thoughts" do for you? Are they all alike?

The first secret of personal mastery hardly seems like a *secret* at all. It's so easy to understand. Yet, it serves as *the basis* for all of the latter secrets. Every subsequent *secret* builds upon this first one. For this reason, we have to guard against its simplicity for deceiving us. The more challenging secrets that follow build upon this first secret and necessitate a full appreciation of it. The first secret?

> *The foundation for mastering your personal power lies in your thoughts. What you think determines what you feel, how you perceive, your internal reality, in a word, your states. They also give you your initial road maps for navigating life.*

When we "think," we do far more than just merely entertain ideas in our head. "Thinking" actually activates pathways in our brain and nervous system. Doing so sets into motion a vast array of neuro-transmitters and signals that become "emotions," behaviors, and patterns of interactions with our environment. Thinking, as you will soon discover, also occurs at many different levels: perceptual, representational, and conceptual. Practically this means that we do not *merely* think, but we *think-feel* in a dynamic way that involves our body. Our thinking does *not* occur apart from our feeling, nor our feeling apart from our thinking. Our mind-body system works holistically. Thoughts affect physiology; physiology affects thoughts. Even our breathing effects our thinking. This holistic functioning organizes us as neuro-linguistic creatures.

Neuro-linguistic creatures?

Yes, our very *neurology* which includes our body, physiology, and entire physical being creates our mental and linguistic processing of the world. As we use symbols and various linguistic systems, we create the strategies that activate and program our neurology and bodies to operate in certain ways. That's why we react to *symbols* so profoundly and experience "semantic reactions." Just a word or label can rattle us from top to bottom. "Jerk." "Failure."

Unlike lower animals, we do not come fully programmed with a set of "instincts" for what to do or how to behave. We have to learn such. Rather, we come equipped with a set of neurological processes that provide us with the flexibility and freedom to generate our own self-programming. We learn. We learn how to do things. We learn how to behave. We learn how to be who we are. We learn about our learning.

[*Neurology*: "neuro" referring to neurons, our nervous system, our neuro-physiological processes describes *the embodiment* of our thoughts. We think with our *body-brain*. We are not *dis*embodied beings at all. We take our bodies with us everywhere we go!]

John said, "I don't know what's wrong with me. I can't get myself motivated. Nothing seems very important. It all seems so futile."

Jill, wanting to encourage him, said, "But think about the great job you've got!"

"Yes, but it's not really what I want to do and it's not even very important. I could so easily be replaced."

When I heard this conversation, I knew a great deal of John's mental strategy for "depression." In entertaining *thoughts* of meaninglessness and futility, he was embedding those thoughts inside a higher frame of "discounting."

"Wow, John, you sure are skilled and powerful at depressing and discounting encouragements!" I said. "And I bet you aren't even aware of how effective you are at using such depressive thoughts to depress yourself in this way?"

He didn't. Yet he was willing to look at his thoughts in order to discover the structure of his depressing so he could stop it. That was his motivation. He was sick and tired of being depressed. When he did look at his thoughts, he used his executive levels of mind (his higher thoughts) to transform everything. As he changed the way he spoke to himself, he discovered more meaningful activities in his life. He also discovered his executive self and that empowered him to take charge of his life. What was the leverage point for John? The leverage point involved taking charge of his *thoughts*. He found the old programming, discounted the discounting, and then replaced it, and practiced a new kind of thinking.

Secret #2

Mastery comes from discovering the higher states as your "executive operations."

*We humans never just think—we also **think about** our thinking, and then we think about that thinking. Our thoughts-and-feelings forever and inevitably **reflect back onto** themselves to become more and more layered. Therefore the secret of personal mastery lies in discovering our higher thoughts-and-feelings and choosing those that serve us well.*

While our thoughts-and-feelings are vitally and crucially important to our everyday experiences and our ability to access our very best states, our *meta-thoughts* play an even more important role.

The term *"meta"* refers to something *above* or *beyond* something else so that it refers or relates back to a previous item. When we meta-communicate, we communicate *about* our communications.

In making a *meta-move* in our thoughts, we *conceptually* step back from our thoughts and feelings and then think and feel about our first thought-feelings. When we do this, we react to our reactions. We become aware of the pictures in our mind and the things we say to ourselves *about* those images.

We will never discover *the secrets of truly taking charge of our lives* in order to achieve mental, emotional, verbal, and behavioral mastery without discovering **the executive operations** of our higher mind. To take charge of our lives and to achieve *personal mastery*, we need to fully discover and awaken our higher executive operations.

Executive operations?

Life mastery?

Higher mind?

Yes, indeed. We have *executive functions* in our "mind." This arises from a very simple mechanism that any child can tell you about. Yet this mechanism expresses a profound mystery in our lives that even the greatest philosopher cannot explain fully.

Teasing Out the Layers and Levels of Mind

Consider what you already know about your mental capacities, that you have an internal power in your mind-body by which you *gather and process information*. In this, your brain operates like a computer—*it detects patterns and organizes (or sorts) that data into "information" structures* (like "beliefs," "values," etc.). Yet unlike a computer, our brains do not come with a full set of software programs. That's what we do. That's what cultures provide—the software packages of the mind. Our brains are by no means fully developed at birth. The brain does not mature or activate all of its processing capacities until we experience the hormone bath during the early preadolescent years.

In the beginning, our brain operates more like a self-programming computer. As infants, we can, at best, only *represent* things (literally, "present" things "again"). We track and record the sights, sounds, sensations, smells, and tastes that we encounter in the world by means of our sense receptors (eyes, ears, tongue, skin, etc.), hence we use the "sensory systems" (visual, auditory, kinesthetic, olfactory, gustatory) for our basic representations. Soon we begin to develop the ability to hold our representations constant. In child developmental psychology, we call this *constancy of representation*. At that stage, we can *hold* a representation *constant* so it doesn't "go away" when the object goes away.

You can easily recognize when a little child lacks this skill. When you put a newspaper over your face so that the child cannot see you—*you* no longer live in the child's world. Poof! You're gone. When you pull down the newspaper and suddenly appear in the child's visual awareness—*poof!* You suddenly appear out of nowhere. It's magical. And it's a lot of fun when you do this with a baby.

But that stage of mind does not last. When the child develops *constancy of representation*, the game ends. If you attempt to play peek-aboo with an older child or your spouse, you'll discover that they will not experience the same level of thrill. Gone is that innocent mind that didn't know. Now the child *knows* you are there. The baby no longer receives the cognitive shock that so jarred its awareness earlier. Now the child's brain can not only *represent* your presence, but can also *hold that representation constant* even when you are no longer present.

Young parents sometimes become painfully (and stressfully) aware of this when they first leave the child with a baby sitter in order to get away for a night alone. When the child cannot *represent* the parents and their presence—fearful terror strikes. The conceptual idea, "It's okay; momma will be back," does not soothe or comfort. The child cannot understand that level of concept yet. The child *literally* lives in a world where "out of sight" means "out of mind."

Mind as Representer—Conceptualizer

So we begin with *mere perception*. We see what we see. We hear what we hear. We feel what we feel. But nothing stays. Think of that as the first level of mind, or consciousness. It is the consciousness of a small infant and that of most animals.

The second level begins with the development of the incredible power of *representational constancy*. This allows us to move on through several developmental stages as identified by psychologist Piaget: concrete thinking stage, pre-operational, formal operational or conceptual stage, etc. As we do, our mental-emotional capacities develop into a new and higher level ability, namely, the ability to *format and program*. At the *Representational Level*, we are able to construct, remember, and create an internal world. We remember things seen and experienced. We imagine things that could be. Dogs and cats "think" in this way. They *know* us, remember where we put the food dish, and can even engage in some very simple *constructing*.

Representationally, thinking creates information. And this happens not only externally as we can externalize our internal sights, sounds, smells, and sensations, it also happens literally. As we "think," our "thinking" *in-forms* us. It *forms* us on the *inside*—molding and making us according to the structure and organization of the data—our style of thinking *forms* and *formats* our sense of the world. This describes how ideas and information "program" us. It highlights the significance of data, and that data are not neutral. So unlike computers, *we* play a central and key role in our own *programming*. This endows us with the near-magical power of operating as our own self-programmers.

Unlike a computer that can operate only *from* the software that someone has installed, *we* have much more flexibility. We can actually *program* our own functioning. Because we can construct and keep an internal world, we can also carry it around with us. We do this with thoughts and words, and with pictures in our mind. This allows us to move beyond the world of signs that govern the communication systems which animals use. In communicating, animals use a piece of a behavior (a growl, bark, snarl, showing of teeth, etc.) as a message *about* a message. They give a *signal* or sign.

But we can use full-fledged *symbols.* We can use totally arbitrary and meaningless things *to stand for* and represent other things. We can put together such marks as "dog" and "cat" to symbolize our pets and communicate much more efficiently than miming out a dog or cat in the air with our fingers or making barking or purring sounds. This allows us to create even higher levels of consciousness—*concepts and conceptual realities* such as "animals," "sentient life," "time," "relationships," "authority," "self," "purpose," etc.

This *conceptual level* of thinking moves us to our *higher levels of mind.* Here *mind* sets frames-of-references and establishes higher level mental "entities" including our beliefs, values, understandings, memories, imaginations, choices, etc. Here we build up all kinds of higher level constructions: philosophies, theologies, principles, paradigms, etc.

John did that with his work. Originally he viewed it as his passion for music. From that point of view, working in the retail store as an assistant manager didn't measure up. Then when John thought about spending all his time doing that, having little to no time for his music, and thinking of this as going on for years (another concept), he then thought, "I feel trapped."

Once we move up to these higher levels, *"mind" influences "mind."* After all, you can *think* about your thinking. You can experience *feelings* about your feelings. You can make *choices* about your choices. You can develop *understandings* about your understandings. This takes us to a **new level of development**. We have moved beyond mere "mind" as a representer and mapper of the world—we have now moved to a higher mind, a *meta*-mind. As we do, we begin to discover an infinite regress of "mind" that keeps creating ever higher levels of mind. As it does, each higher level of "mind" governs or dominates the previous levels.

When you ask anybody about an experience (and it really doesn't matter what, something about work, home, recreation, anything), they will give you their thoughts-and-feelings *about* that immediate object. But they will not stop there. As soon as they speak about feeling bored or upset or angry or joyful or satisfied or whatever— they will then have "a second thought." They will then utter some more thoughts-and-feelings *about* those first thoughts-and-feelings.

Figure 1:1

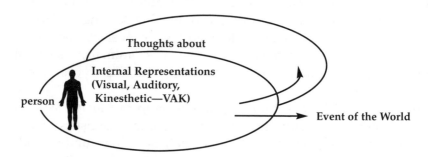

Some of the higher animals can also go beyond mere *representation* and can move to a *meta*-level *above* such so as to create primitive kinds of "ideas," "understandings," even "beliefs." Yet eventually at some level, every animal stops "abstracting." But not us humans. We never stop. Whatever idea we experience or emotion, choice, understanding, thought, belief, etc., we can then generate yet another thought or feeling *about* that one. We develop awareness about our bodies, minds, feelings, etc.

What power of mind or soul creates his infinite process? Philosophers of mind call it *self-reflexive consciousness*. This refers to the power we have of *reflecting back on* our previous mental-emotional experiences. In this lies our **executive power and operation.** In this mechanism we have our *ultimate power to take charge of our life—of our mind, emotions, language use, behaviors, choices, relationships, etc.*

What does this mean for you?

- It means that your current *thoughts* do not have to run your brain.
- It means that your *emotions* do not have to lord it over your experiences.
- It means that your *experiences* do not have to dominate your choices.
- It means that you—as a living, breathing, symbol-using semantic class of life—can develop these executive powers and commission them as your guiding and self-organizing frames of mind.

This gives all of us the ability to engage in a wide range of *self-programming options.* It means we can *actually operate from our highest executive states of mind-and-emotion* and assume control over our life.

Interested?

TAKING CHARGE—of Life, Mind, and Destiny

Is there anyone who does not want to *take charge of his or her life?* We all do, do we not? Yes, of course we do.

Do you know anybody who really does *not* want to feel in charge of his or her life? I don't. After two decades working as a psychotherapist, I cannot remember a single depressive who didn't want to have more control and power over his or her life. Actually, it was each person's sense of *not* being in control, that he or she was *out of control* and powerless that triggered the depression and sense of helplessness.

We all want to *take charge* of our lives. We have not been made to passively float along, just taking whatever happens to us with a spirit of resignation and feeling hopeless. We have inside of us a drive for taking charge of our lives and destiny.

If we come equipped with this *internal drive* for taking charge, for discovering our own passions and interests, for growing and developing, for learning and discovering, for mastering and attaining excellence, and even for genius, then *how well do we succeed* in fulfilling this drive? If it lies in our nature to embrace challenges and sally forth to opportunities, and invent goals and objectives, then *how well* do we succeed?

That sad truth is that many people live without a strong and vibrant sense of their own *inner executive*. Many just stumble along through life, taking whatever "life throws at them," and feel out-of-control in taking charge of their thoughts, feelings, and responses. In terms of what they really want to do, experience, achieve, and feel—they seem to not know that they have within them all kinds of *executive powers*. Nor do they seem aware of the processes for how to activate these powers. Consequently, without an awakened inner executive, they do not experience anything close to mental mastery and so lack the high level executive solutions.

Taking Charge Necessitates Mental Mastery

Let's begin with a *Thought Experiment*. I want you to choose two memories that we will later compare. First, think about a time when you felt *out-of-control*. Then, think of another time when you felt *in-control*. As you do this thought experiment, make sure that you do **not** base your in-control memory on something that was happening *to* you. Instead, base it upon your own inner strength to *choose your response and to stay in control* regardless of what was happening in the external environment.

1) *Think for a moment about two instances in your life.*
   First think about a time when you felt out of control and unable to govern your own destiny. Recall that experience, and for just a moment— for the purpose of this learning—step into it again to identify the structure and form of that experience.

2) *Now shake that state off.*
   Throw it off from yourself as you reject it and refuse it any place in your way of being in the world. Breathe vigorously. Shift your posture to access a pleasant and relaxed state.

3) *Now recall a time when you felt in control of your life, your thinking, your responses—when you felt able to govern the direction of your life.*
   Be there fully in that memory and enjoy the feelings fully. Absorb them.

Good.

4) Now detail the differences.
Having completed that experiment, let's explore the differences between these two experiences.

- How do the two experiences differ?
- How do the *qualities and distinctions* in the various sensory systems differ?
- What characterized the *out-of-control* experience in terms of your thoughts and emotions?
- Were the pictures in one closer/further; clear/fuzzy; black-and-white/in color, etc.? (Visual)
- Check also with the *qualities and distinctions* that you might find regarding your internal sounds. (Auditory)
- Check your body in terms of your breathing, posture, eye focus, internal dialogue, etc. (Kinesthetic)
- What characterized the *in-control* experience mentally and emotionally?
- How did your languaging differ in each experience?
- Did you say different things? Did you use a different tone of voice?
- How did your behavior differ?

The Secret of Mental Mastery
Minding Your Mind to "Make it Mind"

Did you find *the secret?* Did you discover that the secret lies in your own sense of *mental mastery?* Did you not find that, above and beyond everything else, even above the things that happen to you, that *your attitude, your choice of attitude, your thinking, and your conceptual mind* played the most significant role?

Discovering *the powerful influence* that *mind* plays in our lives highlights what we mean by **mental mastery.** This describes the ability to *control* our mind—*how* we think, *what* we think about, *how* we interpret things, the meanings we give to events, etc. This generates the ability to "run our own brain" as we say in NLP (Neuro-Linguistic Programming). This power endows us with the power to effectively manage our emotions and behaviors. This also means that we can set and operate from our highest states of mind—the meta-mind that we program ourselves.

We now have *the first two secrets for personal mastery:*

#1. Our thought-feelings operate as neuro-linguistic programs.
#2. By our thought-feelings, we create higher levels of mind.

Secret #1 identifies the neuro-linguistic mechanism involved in how we make our internal maps of the world. We do so by perceiving, representing, and conceptualizing. As we do, we do not have "thoughts" apart from feelings, but a holistic experience *"thought-feelings."* By these we engage in self-programming.

Secret #2 identifies the *reflexive* nature of our thought-feelings. We never just think. Instead, we think about our thinking, and then think about that thinking, etc.

I have called these "secrets." Yet describing these principles as *secrets* does not imply that this is a new truth in human history. They are not new at all. Dr Albert Ellis founded Rational Emotive Therapy (RET) in the 1960s on the very premise that *our minds* control and govern our emotions and subsequently, our behaviors.

> "Human thinking and emoting are not radically different processes; but at points significantly overlap. Emotions almost always stem directly from ideas, thoughts, attitudes, beliefs … and can usually be radically changed by modifying the thinking processes that keep creating them."

Nor was he the first to say that. Much further back in history, Marcus Aurelius, Emperor of Rome and a philosopher in the second century AD put it succinctly:

> "If you are pained by an external thing, it is not this thing that disturbs you—but your judgment about it." (*The Meditations*, A.D. 121–180)

More recently David Burns formulated these ideas as the basic principles of Cognitive Therapy.

> "The first principle of Cognitive Therapy is that all your moods are created by your cognitions or thoughts. A cognition refers to the way you look at things, your perceptions,

mental attitudes and beliefs. It includes the way you interpret things, what you say about something or someone to
yourself. You feel the way you do right now because of the
thoughts you are thinking at this moment." (pp. 11–12)

And even before the first century, an ancient Hebrew philosopher
put it poetically when he wrote, "As a man thinketh (appraises) in
his heart, so he is." (Proverbs 23:7).

Mental mastery (and thereafter the ability to access our personal
genius) comes from our understanding and willingness to "run
our own brains." It comes when we decide that we will *take charge
of our own brain and that we will intentionally run it with elegance, precision, and purpose.* We cannot take charge of our own lives until we
learn that and do that.

This marks out for us the path to excellence. To experience *mental
mastery* and to create *solutions of excellence* we have to learn and
practice the principles, skills, and processes involved in assuming
ownership of our own mind. Doing this builds the very mental,
cognitive, and emotional skills whereby we can face reality and
build road maps that will lead us to desired experiences. Such creates a tremendously satisfying sense of *self-efficacy*.

Working Definitions in this Book

Since the heart of the strategy for personal excellence involves
thinking, we need to clarify the kind of *thinking* this involves.
Obviously, this does not mean a mere mental understanding in the
"head" apart from the ability to apply it. Nor is *thinking* detached
from emoting, valuing, believing, etc.

Here *"Mind"* stands for *a holistic and systemic description of the entire
mind-and-body system.* As an interactive *system,* how we think
directly affects how we feel and a great many other nervous system processes involving neuro-transmitters, our bio-chemistry,
our autonomic nervous system, basic physiology, etc. Therefore, as
neuro-linguistic beings, we need to shift our understanding to realize that our mind-body system work together as a coordinated
system.

Neuro- refers to our *nervous system* and all of the processes neuro-logically that arise from the information processing of "mind." Today the burgeoning field of *the Neuro-Sciences* studies and researches how *neurology* (our central and autonomic nervous systems, endocrine system, immune system, fight/flight general arousal system, neurons, neuro-transmitters, cells, body, brain, hemispheres, etc.) come together to create our sense of conscious awareness, "mind," etc.

Similarly, **linguistic** refers to a wide range of symbol systems or languages, both propositional language as in words, sentences, terms, etc. and non-propositional (poetry, music, proverbs, story, narrative, etc.), as well as musical, mathematical, geometric, etc.

So Who Is Really In Charge?
The Part of Me That Feels Apart
When was the last time you said or did something about which you later commented, *"I* don't know why *I* did that. I didn't intend to do that. It just popped out."

Or perhaps you had one of those "bad hair" days when everything seemed to go wrong? Dozens of things frustrated your plans and you just did not seem to think, feel, or act resourceful at all? Afterwards you commented, "I just don't know what's going on with me or what's gotten into me. I don't seem to be myself today."

Consider the significance of such scenarios. When they occur, and especially when they occur with any degree of regularity, we have to ask, *"Who's in charge anyway?"*

- How can we speak about having such different parts?
- How can we learn to take more charge of ourselves?
- How can we learn the art of running our own brain?
- How can we develop skill at self-management of our emotions, moods, states, and attitudes?
- What causes our mind and emotions to go into such recursive loops?

It's My Brain and I Can Fry It If I Want To

In the 1990s, a series of television commercials in the USA aired that featured a frying egg on a hot concrete surface. The commentator's voice had asked, "What is a brain on drugs like?" The answer came in the words, "This is your brain on drugs."

In that line of thought, what is it like when we just let our brains run on and on without giving them any direction—without *taking charge of our mind?* After all, it certainly seems like lots of people simply do *not* "run their own brain." Many people seem to just let the brain "run" randomly and chaotically without any giving it any specific purpose or direction. Indeed, this may actually describe what most of us do. Instead of running our own brains, we let our brains run us!

Actually, *just letting the brain run ...* fittingly describes what happens when people "go on automatic." When that happens, you never know what a brain may do or where it may go. Now letting a brain run does imply a certain level of awareness. When this happens, we do have an awareness *of* something. But it does not imply *self-reflective* consciousness, i.e. conscious awareness of our own awareness.

Infants, small children, and animals all demonstrate *basic level consciousness* that have some higher level functions. They represent information. They recall things. They imagine possibilities and make predictions about the future. They experience a *primary level of consciousness.* Their brains "run." They "run" in the sense that they do what brains do best—they *"process information"* and create internal representations. These brains on automatic pilot tend to take the earliest learnings and use them as their *default settings.*

Summary

- *The Art of Personal Mastery* refers to how we can use the NLP and Meta-States Models to take charge of our own neuro-linguistic and neuro-semantic powers.
- When we learn to *detect and recognize our own higher level or executive states,* we have the ability also to make informed choices about our own internal programming.

- The first Secret of Personal Mastery: **Mastery emerges when we appreciate our thoughts as neuro-linguistic programs.** *The power to take effective action lies in "thought." What you think determines what you feel, how you perceive, your internal reality, and your initial road maps for navigating life.*
- The Second Secret of Personal Mastery is this: **Mastery comes from discovering our higher states as our executive operations.** *We humans never just think—we think about our thinking, and then think about that thinking. Our thoughts-and-feelings forever and inevitably reflect back onto itself to become more and more layered. Therefore the secret of personal mastery lies in discovering our higher thoughts-and-feelings and choosing those that serve us well.*

Special Terms

Neurology: "Neuro" referring to neurons, our nervous system, our neuro-physiological processes describes *the embodiment* of our thoughts. We think with our *body-brain*.

Meta: This term refers to something *above* or *beyond* something else so that it refers or relates back to a previous item.

Executive operations: The higher levels of the mind that allow us to *think* about our thinking, *make decisions* about our feelings, *feel* about our thoughts, etc.

Representations: We *think* by *presenting* to ourselves *again* (re-present) images, sounds, words, ideas, etc.

Sensory Systems: The *language* of the mind. We *think* in pictures (visually), sounds (auditorially), sensations or feelings (kinesthetically), tastes (gustatory), smells (olfactory), words (linguistically), and other higher level symbols (mathematics, music, etc.).

Self-reflexive consciousness: The power to *reflect back on* our previous mental-emotional experiences. This creates our executive powers and operations.

Neuro-Linguistic Beings: A description of humans which highlights the interactive and systemic nature between neurology and linguistics. Neurology alone does *not* rule or govern our lives. Biology and neuro-chemistry, the rush of hormones, and the effect of psycho-active drugs upon us certainly play a role, but comprise only part of the picture. Our interpretations, understandings, beliefs, appraisals, and ideas govern *how* we think-and-feel about our drives, "instincts," urges, and feelings.

The Next Secret
of
Personal Mastery

Secret #3

Our reflexive consciousness enables us to always layer yet another level upon our model of the world.

This gives us the ability to always step outside of our frames-of-reference and go right to the top—to our highest executive states. We do not have to be stuck or limited any more than we want to be. We can always outframe. This gives us the ability to truly Take Charge of our mind, emotions, reality, and destiny.

Chapter 2

Discovering Your Inner Executive

"May I Speak to the Executive In Charge?"

"Every time you make a choice, you are turning the central part of you, the part of you that chooses, into something a little different from what it was before and taking your life as a whole, with all your innumerable choices, all your life long you are slowly turning into a heavenly creature or into a hellish creature, either into a creature that's in harmony with God and with other creatures and with itself—or else into one that is in a state of war and hatred with God."
(C.S. Lewis)

You *have an inner executive.* May I introduce you to that **higher frame of mind** residing within? If you're game, then you will find this chapter designed to assist you in this very discovery. Think of it as the rare and unprecedented opportunity to experience a thorough and complete introduction to the *executive within.* This inner executive governs your states of mind and emotions, your perceptions, beliefs, values, purposes, mission, identity, skills, motivation, and destiny.

Though you may not know that you even have an *inner executive,* or may have only a vague sense of it, you certainly have one. We all do. But we do not all recognize it, develop it, appreciate and honor it, or know how to take orders from it. We may even get into fights with it! Many folks do. In fact, that inner executive preeminently makes you a human being.

So on to the first order of business.

Meet the Boss

Before we do the introductions, let me first encourage you to relax your mind for just a moment by thinking about anything that you experience as a pleasure and a delight. You might want to recall a time at a beach playing in the warm ocean waves or feeling the sand between your toes as you walk along the beach, or sit on a blanket with a loved one watching a glorious sunset. Or you could send your brain to one of a thousand other delights—in the past or in the future.

Take a moment to do this and as you do this, just experience fully the sights, sounds, sensations, smells, tastes, words, and any other aspect of the experience. Do so until it seems like you have stepped into this experience again …

Did you like that?

If you follow those simple instructions in that "thought experiment," then you just *ran your brain* as you intentionally accessed some specific information. Now step back and think about the mystery of that. How successfully did you do that procedure? How well did your brain respond to your request to fully *step into the experience again?*

In the way that our brains process and represent information, they work somewhat like a computer. You key in the right signals or commands—and the computer's programs activate. In a similar way, we have a kind of *internal movie screen* onto which we can ask our brain to reproduce information. To discover this, notice what happens *on that screen* when you read the following …

- The Statue of Liberty
- Big Ben in London
- A bowl of strawberries
  —covered with whipped cream …
  —that you bring up to your mouth …
- George Washington
- The Washington Monument
- A Nuclear Bomb Explosion
- Float like a butterfly, sting like a bee
- The Great Pyramid of Egypt
- The sinking of the Titanic.

Most brains respond very quickly as they shoot scenes of sights, sounds, smells, and sensations across *the mental theater* that we experience internally. Most people, in fact, until they have practiced *noticing* the visual (pictures), auditory (sounds), kinesthetic (sensation), do not even pay much attention to this—they "just know" what you mean by those words. It operates, as we say, "intuitively."

Yet when you begin to *notice* the sights, sounds, and sensations— it develops not only your inner cognitive and creative powers, it also moves you to a *meta-level of awareness.*

["Meta," remember, refers to something "above," or "about" something else, hence a higher level—an awareness of awareness.]

If, at this point, you don't have a lot of *awareness* about the internal sights, sounds, or sensations, do you experience some thoughts "in the back of your mind" *about* that? Many people do. They hear judgment thoughts, "What's wrong with me that I don't visualize?" Others hear thoughts of curiosity. "What does it mean that I don't hear particular tones of voices very well in my head?"

Step right up now and shake hands with some *mid-level manager in your mind*. That's right. You have just experienced a higher frame of mind—a part of your mind by which you direct your immediate awareness. True, you haven't yet reached your highest Inner Executive yet, but you have gone up a level. You have flushed an internal manager out of the executive closet. And with this, the adventure has begun.

Thinking About That Thinking

Now I would like you to notice, and fully appreciate, how you have the incredible ability to "jump logical levels in a single bound!" Because with the *Thought Experiment* that you just completed, I invited you to *think* of something pleasant. So *you* then engaged in thought ... and if your brain cooperated with you, it brought up and reproduced for you some pleasant thoughts. So somehow *you* directed *your* brain to do something, and it did so.

At first you might not have noticed all of the qualities and properties of those pleasant thoughts—the actual sights, sounds, sensations, smells, etc. that comprised the pleasant experience. Yet just as soon as *you* became aware of these facets of your thoughts, *you* (using a particular power of "mind" called reflexivity) got your brain to do that. Pretty nifty, wouldn't you say?

- Did you see your pleasant thoughts in color or black-and-white?
- Did you have a big or small picture? Life-size, smaller than life-size, or bigger?
- How close or far did you see it?
- Did you hear the sounds coming from one spot or in a panoramic fashion?
- Well, how would it feel—in terms of its pleasure, if you turned up the colors and made them brighter?
- What if you stepped so much into the picture and sounds that you could feel the sun shining on your skin and the sand between your toes?
- What if you heard the ocean waves louder and yet louder?
- What other qualities would you like to shift so as to make the experience more real, more compelling, more pleasurable?

Figure 2:1

First Level Representational Reality

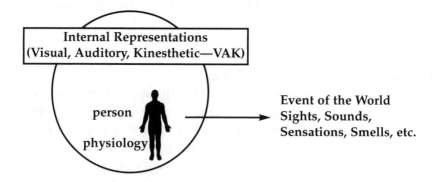

Going Higher

As you respond to these requests and suggestions, you exercise your own ability to "run your own brain" as you direct its operations. With each move you "step back," so to speak, from your *thinking-and-feeling* and observe the products and reactions of your consciousness. Doing this self-reflexive shifting involves *going meta,* or taking a meta-position, to your own consciousness. This introduces you to higher and higher Managers in your mind— mental executives that we will be putting to work for us.

Each time you do this, you *move to a higher* perceptual position. First, you merely observe something in the world. Then you *observe* your own observing, then you observe your observing of the observation. With each move, you attain (conceptually) a higher logical level as each level operates *about* the lower level. At each level, you reflect back onto your previous thinking or experiencing.

Figure 2:2

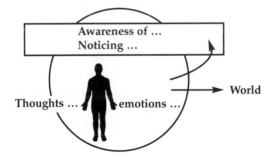

So What?

This represents something *so important* in terms of our experience, personality, identity, skills, frames of references, success or failure, pleasure or misery, etc. that you may find what follows difficult to believe. It may, at first, appear *too incredible, too fantastic.*

So just for the moment, I will ask that you only track with the following for the purpose of *understanding* it. After you have a good grasp of this model of our multiple-level mind functioning, then feel free to evaluate and critique it. In fact, I hope that you will. But if you critique it too soon (i.e. before a comprehensive understanding of the Model), your critique will probably be premature, and it may also make it difficult to fully comprehend the full significance of this abstracting, representing, and jumping logical levels process. Also if you bring *critiquing, criticizing, finding fault,* etc. to bear upon your thoughts-and-feelings and experiences here— consider what kind of a meta-state structure you will be building for your mind. Do you really want to do that? How will that serve you?

One more thing. In the following paragraph, I have layered many complex concepts one upon the other. Be patient. An explanation follows that will simplify it.

> With each reflection back that you make onto the working or products of your consciousness (i.e. how and what you think-feel), you set another higher frame of reference which, in turn, establishes your internal mental contexts— your executive states. Doing this, creates the meanings that you find and experience in life—which, in turn, runs the way you feel, think, perceive, and experience the world. Each level layers consciousness upon consciousness (i.e. thoughts about thoughts, feelings about feelings, etc.). This layering means that the learnings and responses (i.e. output) at one level of awareness then becomes the input at the next level up. This endows the whole process of consciousness (self-reflexive consciousness) with a systemic nature. This makes each layer or frame a context for "mind" itself. Mind then functions as a self-fulfilling prophecy or an attractor for the system.

Teasing Apart the Layers of Your "Mind"

To make the complexity of consciousness easier to understand and appreciate, let me now tease out from that paragraph the parts that will assist us in comprehending how all of this works.

We first begin with *consciousness* at the primary level thinking, representing, and abstracting as it attempts to comprehend the world that it faces. It does so in "thoughts," "emotions," somatic (body) responses, etc. As it does so, it attempts to *build a model of the world.* We generate such *internalized models* or maps of the world in order to more effectively relate to it. At the experiential level (i.e. how we experience the world), we *sense* internally in our mind that we *see, hear, feel, smell,* etc. the world. We call these *representational modes of awareness* our "sensory systems" of representation.

We use the "sense receptors" in our body and nervous system (i.e. our eyes, ears, skin, etc.) to first *sense* the world. This *perceptual mapping* of the world occurs as an interaction between our sense receptors (eyes, ears, skin, etc.) and the energy manifestations "out there." Then, we somehow *reproduce* the same inside our heads. We do not do this literally or actually, only cognitively or conceptually. In other words, *it seems to us* that we can close our eyes and *see* our childhood home, the color of our living room, a loved one's face, Donald Duck, etc. Actually, when we open up the skull and look inside the brain—we don't find any internal movie theater or pictures at all. At that level, we find only three pounds of grey matter comprising billions of neurons of various sizes and shapes, neuro-pathways, neuro-transmitters, the exchange of icons at the cellular level, etc.

Our *representational map of* the world exists only at the *phenomenal level.* This means that it only *seems like* ("phenomenon" or appearance) we see, hear, feel, smell, taste, etc. the world. Yet *that level of reality* seems quite sufficient and powerful as it gives us the tools for navigating the external world. It's a model. It's an internal map that organizes, structures, and forms a reflection of the external world.

Next, we *think* about that map. We make another representational map about our representational map. We experience thoughts-and-feelings about our previous thoughts-and-feelings. When we do, this *conceptually frames,* or sets a mental context, for our previous thoughts.

Figure 2:3

Perceptual mapping	*Representational mapping*	*Conceptual mapping*
of what exists — what lies out there in the world	of what we recall inside our heads— *how* we code and present on our mental screen	of what we think about our representations

| I see two people talking on a park bench on a Saturday afternoon. | I remember the two people at the park—I see my memory of the couple as a movie as I was talking, holding hands, walking. | I believe that couples have to take time for talking and enjoying each other ... |

Neurological Processing	*Mental "Thinking"*	*Levels of Concepts*
Created by our senses and sense receptors. Not controlled or generated consciously, but by nervous system structures outside of conscious awareness.	Conscious awareness about our world—sensory based images, sounds, sensations that dance around as a movie in our head, which we can manipulate consciously	Ideas upon ideas that we create about other ideas ... conceptual, an internal mapping that we learn from people, books and experiences

For example, imagine taking a hike into the mountains and transversing a deep ravine. Your representational mapping enables you to *represent* such sights, sounds, and sensations. But after *representation* come other thoughts—thoughts that set the frame. So *how* do you think about transversing a deep ravine? What do you think

34

about doing so? What do you focus on? The danger? The excitement? The adventure? What emotions arise as you think about the danger, the excitement, the adventure, the comradeship? If you think about the experience as scary, dangerous, and unpleasant, you will set these thoughts as *the frame*. If you think about the experience as exciting, fun, adventurous, etc., you will set those thoughts as *the frame—your mental context.*

Suppose you then think one of the following:

> "I don't like taking such risks. I'm not a risk taker. I'm more of a city slicker than outdoors person."

> "I like doing this. I have such great fun doing it. I'm the kind of person who likes pushing the limits."

With these thoughts, you move up to another level of consciousness and *set a frame for how you identify yourself.* This creates an executive decision. It creates a *mental context* for how you will think about danger and risk. Layering thoughts upon thoughts, emotions upon emotions in this way formats *the meanings* that we find and experience in the world. For one person, mountain climbing becomes highly meaningful, full of significance, and a very pleasurable experience. For another person, it holds nothing of value and means nothing positive. It evokes feelings of distress, fear, unpleasantness, etc.

In this way, *we create* (or construct) *our meanings* from the experiences we have as we move through life. These *meanings* do not exist "out there" in the world. We give birth to them as we *attribute various significances* to things. This reveals our nature as **human meaning makers**. We associate thoughts and feelings to things, then we link thoughts and feelings to those states. The *meaning* does not exist as "real," "right," "wrong," "good," or "bad." It merely exists as *our interpretation* and construction about such. It arises as a function of how we have *mapped out* the world. It arises, and we experience it, as our Model of the World. And as such it governs our experiences and emotions.

This explains how it's possible to get some really crazy, irrational, stupid, dysfunctional, toxic, and even hurtful ideas in our head and then build our lives around them. *The meanings* we attribute to something do not have to be logical or sane in order for our minds to "take" them. In this way, brains function as do stomachs. *They process whatever you feed them.* Put junk food, garbage, or poison in your mouth and your stomach doesn't know any better than to just process it. Although, come to think of it, stomachs can vomit. They can reject spoiled or distasteful food. But how does the brain vomit out sick and toxic ideas?

If the brain just processes whatever you feed it, then *we* have to take charge of the *quality control* process over the ideas, meanings, beliefs, values, decisions, understandings, and concepts that we feed it. We have to check things out. We have to reality test things. We have to invent and install an Executive Program for Quality Control—which we will be doing later on.

Experience itself does not "make" us formulate the world in a par-ticular way. It only provides the opportunity. Experiences, as our interactive relationship with something or someone, do not inher-ently *mean* anything. We *learn* to give events various meanings. Other people teach us (consciously or unconsciously) to *attribute* a certain meaning to an experience. Our culture provides us with lots of ready-made meanings and frames for meaning-making. This provides insights about the wide range of different meanings, understandings, interpretations, opinions, etc. that can exist between people.

Once we have *set a frame of reference*, that mental context inevitably operates as our "reality structure," Model of the World, or an inner executive. Once we have attributed significance, value, and impor-tance to something, that meaning **programs** our brain to run our perceptions, emotions, behaviors, talk, etc.

"You better not climb up there. That's dangerous. You could fall and hurt yourself!"

"Look at him climb! What skill and courage. He's a natural. Hey, look to your right—above your head, I think you could reach that ledge and then ..."

In this way our maps, and maps of maps, and maps of those maps, etc. become our internal referencing system by which we "make sense" of things. They become our internal managers and executives. And as executives in a business set the policies and enforce the rules, so our inner executives control our very *perceptions*. They program what we can and will see, even what are allowed to perceive. This sets up a self-reinforcing process. Thereafter we tend to "magically" find more and more support for our beliefs, opinions, interpretations, and understandings—our Executive Level thoughts. Anything outside of our personal paradigm of understanding, meaning, and values tends to get discounted and filtered out. We don't see it! It doesn't "make sense."

Say Hello To Your High Level Executives

What do you think or feel when your business slows down or when you experience criticism or rejection at work? Where does your brain take you? Which emotional state or experience do you go to? What do your mental maps and Models of the World tell you?

— Discouragement	— Wonder and Curiosity
— Depression	— Exploration
— Frustration	— Acceptance
— Anger	— Learning
— Fear	— Sensory Awareness
— Regret	— Patience
— Guilt	— Creativity

To the event, you make some first response. In identifying that first response, we discover our *perceptual and representational mapping* about the event. Having made that response, what do you think or feel *about* that? What do you think or feel about feeling discouraged? What do you think or feel about feeling angry?

Whatever you answer in response to that second level—what do you think or feel about that?

In this way, we can coax our higher level executive states of mind to come out of the closet and show themselves. So say hello to your higher executive states.

I have just introduced to you a systemic model of mind. What mechanism runs and governs this mind model? It involves *consciousness reflecting back onto itself* to thereby create layer upon layer of mental frames of reference. When you understand *that*, then you understand how people can become so complicated, so difficult to deal with, and so locked into closed mental systems. This model equally explains how others can experience *us* as weird, strange, wrong, closed-minded, etc. This explains why they don't "get" us; why we seem a mystery to them. We operate from a different map. This meta-level model of mind also provides an explanatory model of "personality," of what it means to get "stuck" in one's own maps of the world, and what we can do to become more effective and empowered.

With this model, we can sort and separate *the complexity* that we find in ourselves and others. It provides a way to track down (or "up") our maps and meta-maps that generate our way of relating to the world. What may seem as "irrational," "unreasonable," "senseless," and "crazy" responses (in ourselves or others), actually makes perfect sense. Think about it. When we know the frames, contexts, meaning structures, and reality strategies—we have access to understanding why and how a person thinks and responds as he or she does. Would you like to understand others better? Yourself?

This model opens up to our awareness the domain of *choice*. Knowing the *structure* of our maps and meta-maps *empowers us to remap* whenever we find a patterning that doesn't serve us well. We don't have to remain stuck at all. We can go right to the higher levels frames—**the inner executives**—and get things changed at the top. We can issue forth from that level a new policy, new model, new meaning.

Figure 2:4 offers a schematic diagram of how we build the meta-levels, forever layering upon thought, more thought, thereby constructing our frames-of-references or mental contexts within which we then "live and breathe and have our being."

Figure 2:4

Meta-Levels of Self-Reflexive Thought

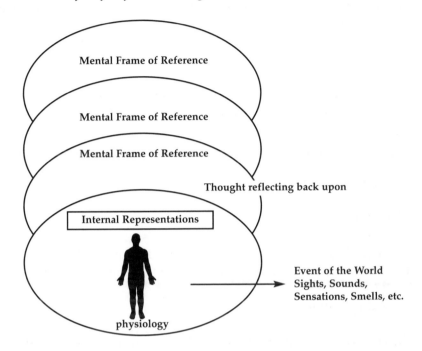

I asked Jim if he liked the program he was running about his work.

"Of course not!"

"Are you sure? Maybe you ought to keep making yourself frustrated, upset, discontented, depressed … maybe it's good for you."

"Are you kidding? I'm here because I can't stand this any longer."

"Jim, are you willing to do anything it takes to change your frames and frames-of-reference?"

"Yes."

"Anything?"

'Well, yes."

"Good. Then I want you to step back, in your mind, and notice your old program so you can catch it and refuse to allow it to run. Notice your tone of voice, as you tell yourself how you'll never go anywhere at your work, and that you're wasting your time. Does this put you in a resourceful state?

"No."

"Even if you can't change your situation immediately, Jim, do you know that this only makes things worse?"

"Yes."

"So it does not enhance your life?"

"No, it does not."

"So you don't need to run your brain this way? Talking this way to yourself and saying these things will not empower you?"

"No, they will not."

"If you weren't thinking this way, how would you want to think? Do you know of any other things you could be thinking that would put you in the direction of your personal visions?"

"Well, I suppose I could be thinking that this is just temporary, or that it's only a stepping stone to a career in music, and I could begin to make plans about the next steps."

"And that would help?"

"Yes, then I wouldn't feel trapped in a dead-end job and I could be looking forward to moving in the right direction."

The Highest Executive Level

We began with the simple information processing of the brain that generates *a state of mind, emotion, or body*. At this primary level, we experience *embodied thinking-feeling*. This describes how thinking-and-emoting *within* a human nervous system and body does not occur dualistically, but holistically or as a system of interactive parts. It also describes a dynamic, ever-changing, and non-static experience. A neuro-linguistic state refers to an energy field, one that powerfully affects our entire mind-body system.

Then we described *a Meta-State*—a state-*about*-a-state. This refers to having *a thought about a thought or an emotion about an emotion.* Hence:

— Fascinated about being creative
— Wondering about a new company vision
— Curious about questioning an old procedure
— Afraid about feeling afraid
— Angry at feeling embarrassed
— Joyful about learning
— Fearful about failing
— Uptight about confronting

Yet, as you have noticed, it does not stop there. As you can layer one set of thoughts-and-emotions upon another set, so you can continue *the layering process.* You can become pessimistic about forecasting a new line of products, and then afraid-of-being-pessimistic because it might become a self-fulfilling prophecy, but discouraged because you don't have the courage to make yourself think more optimistically, and then wondering what's wrong with you! Talk about a *muddle* (a meta-muddle) of consciousness that turns in on itself!

All of this illustrates that *all "states" or "frames" of mind do **not** work on the same level.* We have regular, or *primary,* states of mind and emotion. We also have higher level frames of mind that involve more complexity and layers. When we, our employees, business associates, or friends and loved ones, get into *high level states of mind,* we access a "place" or "attitude" that has more influence, more power, and more extensiveness than just a regular, everyday frame of mind. They *govern* experience. That's why *the attitudes* we built and carry around with us are so important and powerful.

With *Meta-States* we describes these higher frames of mind and states-about-states as meta-level states, or *Executive States.* And, precisely because they operate at a higher logical level, this explains precisely what makes them more complex, stable, and extensive. Consequently, to work with, communicate with, and relate to these states require higher level understandings than we typically access and use.

In the process of learning how to effectively speak and relate to our own (or another's) *executive states of mind-and-emotion*—we go right to **"the boss."** We go right to the boss who runs the show with regard to our emotions, behaviors, reference system, and paradigm or model of the world. Wouldn't that be valuable? Yes, of course. Doing so would cut through all of the lower-level states and frames-of-references. It would empower us to communicate directly to *the governing influence* in our own thinking, valuing, and believing or another person's. As a result of that, we could then:

- speed up communications
- facilitate higher quality communications and relations
- recognize the governing influences in a person's life
- provide insights about why a person thinks and feels as he or she does
- set new influential frames
- work effectively with negative states.

As our highest frames-of-references, we typically do not experience our *executive states* consciously. They typically operate outside of our awareness as simply our frames or mental contexts. Yet they influence and govern our thinking, perceiving, understanding, reasoning, etc.

Of course, using the term *executive* for these highest states, does not make them right, accurate, or even useful. Not at all! In fact, when we or another person suffer various forms of self-limitations, limited thinking, and sabotaging strategies, it usually means that we have some inaccurate, un-enhancing, and destructive *executive state* in charge! Like the Peter Principle in business, sometimes we may keep on promoting various states or frames-of-reference to levels of incompetency. When we do that, we empower them only to operate in more destructive ways.

This model of first-level mind along with the *levels and layering of thought-upon-thought* in our meta-states, simply describes how we set frames-of-references, and then embed that frame within larger frames. Tracking thought in this way gives us a structural format for what we more commonly call "personality," beliefs, values, etc. This model also gives us two other things: first a way to recognize the structure of our levels as well as the levels in others. With that understanding, we can then, secondly, use Meta-State procedures for effectively managing, governing, and influencing our higher states of mind as well as influence those of others.

Have you ever ("tried hard")^{Level3} to (make yourself)^{Level2} (go to sleep)^{Level1}?" If you have, then you know what happens when you *ineffectively* manage one level (facilitating sleep) by another level (order, commanding—"trying hard"). This more typically introduces *paradox* into the mind-body system. Then, the more you enact that process, the more you make the matter worse! The *attempted solution* only increases the problem.

When we bring one level to interact with another level, we set in motion all kinds of dynamics. Will it makes things better or worse? Will it intensify the primary state or reduce its energy? Will it neutralize the first order experience or create some distortion of it? Will it generate paradox, humor, trance, or dissociation? The Meta-States Model identifies many *interfaces* that can occur in the process of bringing one state to bear upon another (more than 16 to date). Frequently, an entirely new gestalt emerges when we set one state as a frame of reference for another state. Sometimes the effect of one state upon another state amplifies it. Sometimes it reduces it, nullifies it, or softens it. At other times it creates paradox, interruption, amnesia, etc. (See Appendix C)

The Third Secret for Personal Mastery
Having come this far in the process of *discovering our inner executive powers*, we can now articulate the next secret.

Secret #3

Our reflexive consciousness enables us to always layer yet another level upon our model of the world.
This gives us the ability to always step outside of our frames-of-reference and go right to the top—to our highest executive states. We do not have to be stuck or limited any more than we choose to be. We can

> *always outframe. This gives us the ability to truly take charge of our mind, emotions, reality, and destiny.*

Your New Emergent Executive State

In a system of interactive forces, a new and strange and yet wonderful phenomenon occurs—*emergence*. Out of the interactive forces and energies within a system, *new properties and realities emerge*. The *gestalt* of the new confirmations reveals that the new emergent properties contain more than the sum of the parts. This brings us to a another and new kind of *state*—**a gestalt state**. When we have one state of mind-emotion setting a frame for another state, often an entirely new kind and quality of a state emerges.

Courage offers a good illustration of this. The state of courage describes much more than just a primary state. To have courage, in fact, we begin with the primary state of fear and apprehension. Without a primary state of a sense of danger, threat, fear, etc., we cannot get to courage. We don't call it "courage" to just "go for it" when things seem inviting and when nothing dangerous looms on the horizon. We call it *courage* when dangers beckon and threatening possibilities would urge us to take counsel of our fears, but we do not. Instead, we face our fears and boldly proceed. *Courage* emerges when an overwhelming passion or an ability to see past peripheral threats moves us to face the fear, move toward the danger, and not let such put us off.

Not only do new emergent states arise from this kind of self-reflexive consciousness, so does a higher sense of one's own self.

Normally, humans tend to *identify* (or over-identify) with temporary and peripheral facets of life—roles, jobs, relationships, status, looks, wealth, geographical origin, etc. Typically also, as a species we also tend to far too easily *identify* with various facets of our person—our thoughts, emotions, choices, body, etc. For Korzybski, *identification* inevitably leads to *unsanity* because it confuses map and territory. We "are" not our bodies, thoughts, emotions, any more than we "are" our roles, status, etc. "Unsanity" in this sense refers to a poor adjustment to reality. We see this in ineffective behaviors at work and self-sabotaging actions.

As we become *aware of our awareness* ("conscious of abstracting"), we begin to recognize our *self* as a thinking-and-feeling being, and then of that *self* as an observer of our thinking-and-feeling, etc. This enables us to *dis-identify* with any and all of our powers, processes, experiences, and temporary roles. We recognize, more accurately, that sometimes we play out this or that role, that sometimes we focus more or less on this or that expression, etc. But we do not fall into the confusion of thinking that our *abstractions* (mental maps) about our *self "is"* (i.e. exists as) that map. We exist as so much more than our ideas or conceptualizations about ourselves.

Ultimately, we exist as an ever-transcending *self* who with every jump up to another meta-position creates another lower level self (or frame of reference). People have called this aspect of our species—"spirit," "soul," "higher self," "inmost being," etc. By it, we certainly do experience a sense of *transcendence*. In this sense, it does seem to describe what we mean by the term "spiritual."

Here then lies your *Executive Self*—that "you" which ultimately chooses, decides, takes charge, and thinks in higher and higher logical levels.

C.S. Lewis, author, linguistic, theologian and professor of classic literature wrote this about our executive state,

> "Every time you make a choice, you are turning the central part of you, the part that chooses, into something a little different from what it was before and taking all your life as a whole, with all your innumerable choices, all your life long you are slowly turning into a heavenly creature or into a hellish creature, either into a creature that's in harmony with God and with other creatures and with itself—or else into one that is in a state of war and hatred with God."

Using Your Inner Executive For Enhancing Your Life
Since the practical use of a model sets a powerful model apart, let's explore some of the everyday values that result from using this model. Precisely what can we do with this model? How can we use it to improve the quality of our states and life?

1) *We can streamline our communications to make them more elegant and powerful.*
In business, to *really* cut to the chase, to get through all of the front-line people (secretaries, receptionists) and through the middle-men (managers, supervisors, etc.), a person needs to go to the person who has *the final say,* and to the person who actually *brokers the power.* We need to go directly to the CEO. Whether we *can* do that in a given corporation is always the big question.

This same principle holds true when we want to communicate and relate to the most influential factors in our own lives, or in the lives of others. We have to get to our own, or the other person's, executive frame-of-reference. We have to access the *executive state* of consciousness, to the highest and governing beliefs, values, understandings, and paradigms.

But do we know how to do that?

How can we do that? *How* can we do that without getting bogged down in a lot of psychological theory and jargon? *How* can we do that quickly, efficiently, and directly?

Utilizing the principles and patterns in the Meta-States Model, we begin by reminding ourselves that the higher frames always govern. This enables us to step back and think about the structure of an experience or state. This, in turn, saves us from getting lost in content. Doing this enables us to begin flushing out higher level frames-of-reference—the governing conceptual states of beliefs and understandings.

Recognition of levels. In business, government, medicine, school, family, the human nervous system, and in fact, in most things—*things operate on various **levels**.*

- We have levels of hierarchies that organize and structure.
- We have levels of expertise and skills.
- We have levels of responsibility.
- We have levels of values and understandings.
- We have levels of functioning.

Levels describe a *structural and organizational fact* about life in general. It is really no surprise then that we also experience "thought," "emotion," "attitude," etc. on various levels. We have not only "thoughts," we have meta-thoughts. The nature of consciousness operates so that just as soon as we "think" something, we then *think* something *about* that thought.

- Did you just "think" that thought about thinking? Did you represent it?
- Can you now think something about having that thought?
- And now that you did that, what do you think about that?
- And as you're thinking all of those thoughts, are you not wondering where this is going?

We cannot but entertain thoughts-about-thoughts and "thoughts in the back of our mind" given the nature of our *self-reflexive consciousness*. It's just part of how the human brain-body system works. Count on it. As we reflexively *think* about our thinking (meta-thinking), we create higher and higher *levels* of states and frames-of-references. We create *executive states* of awareness that then set the frame for our experiences.

- Undoubtedly you have had *thoughts* "in the back of your mind" *while* you communicated with someone that you never actually expressed, but which actually operated as your governing frame-of-reference?
- Have you ever wished that you were privy to some thought "in the back of someone's mind" that would have then allowed you to more fully and accurately understand them or something else?
- How much misunderstanding, confusion, and dis-information arise in human communications and negotiations because we *stay at just the primary level* and never access the person's *Executive States?*

Just as we want to get the *highest quality information* within a business, we have to get past the receptionist, and move up the line to those who are "in the know" or who make the decisions, so with relating to ourselves and others. We have to go higher. We have to access higher levels states of mind. If we don't, we may never really understand what's going on, why we (or others) do what we do, how to make quality decisions, etc.

This *Top-Down Approach* to consciousness and human personality saves us a lot of time and trouble going through every defense, excuse, surface issues, symptoms, etc. Business executives have learned well in recent years how to protect themselves from outside influences, especially sales people and regular customers. They use receptionists, voice mail systems, answering machines, etc. So going through "the chain of command" from the bottom up typically takes a lot of time and energy.

So imagine the power and delight of getting through by starting at the top, or at least pretty close to the top when you want to communicate with your own inner executives or those of someone else. Wouldn't the Top-Down Approach really give you a sense of control over the situation and not become a victim of "the system"?

2) *Take charge of your higher states so you can get yourself to do the things you want to do and cut out the frames that sabotage your success, happiness, and productivity.*
Consider the very idea of *managing our own self.* This concept presupposes that somehow, in some way, we can step aside from ourselves, and identify the process by which we can exercise more control over our thinking, emoting, valuing, believing, perceiving, etc. In this vein, the very terminology of "self-control" or "self-discipline" highlights a meta-level state. Inasmuch as these phrases describe the process of *controlling* oneself *by oneself,* they refer to yet another higher level of one self. That implies levels of "self" as well (more about that later).

To take charge of ourselves, we have to build up a strong sense of ourselves, develop a strong ego-strength, access and build empowering resource states such as confidence, self-esteem, resilience, assertiveness, sensory awareness, etc. Adding a core relaxed state to this set of resources further enables us to then meta-state other experiences with a clear and calm mind-set. Building such meta-states and then using them as our basic frames-of-reference for moving through the world obviously elicits a powerful sense of personal mastery.

Such self-management would then cultivate the ability to live and operate from personal resourcefulness. So the ability to intentionally access our best resourceful states and operate from empowering as our everyday frames-of-references. Higher levels not only set the frame for how we think and feel, but they also establish the higher states which we can access.

3) Figure out people more accurately to eliminate unnecessary conflicts.

If the higher levels of thought-and-emotion set our frames-of-reference and operate as executive states, then recognizing and knowing such will increase our understanding of both ourselves and others. Imagine that. Suppose you could fairly quickly detect that higher level states and frames of others. That would enable you to more accurately and understandingly *figure out people*. Then, knowing what makes them tick, what drives their thinking, emoting, speaking, behaving, and relating, you would be much more "intuitive" in how you would work with them and communicate with them. This would add true elegance and grace to your style. And that then, in turn, would cut out so much of the unnecessary conflict, argument, stress, headaches, and misunderstandings that get in our way.

Understanding human "nature" or "personality" using Meta-States, we recognize from the start that our everyday experiences (i.e. thinking, feeling, valuing, etc.) have all been constructed. Everybody we meet has used their thoughts-feelings to create layers of thoughts-and-emotions on thoughts-and-emotions. This makes everything *human* and *changeable*. It prevents us from needing to de-humanize, demonize, or judge those experiences that seem weird or perverse or unfathomable. We can then move into the other's space knowing that it's just different and also that it makes sense.

"Makes sense? Are you kidding?"

No, I'm not. It all makes sense. It was constructed out of thoughts-and-emotions about something which then got layered into higher and higher concepts and ideas. Yes, many of the ideas may be very toxic and destructive. But ultimately, *it's all ideas*. None of it is externally real. This has proven extremely useful as a model for working with what psychiatry has labeled "Personality Disorders." Knowing that *we* are the ones who can, and often do, *disorder* our states and meta-states, we know that there is indeed a structure even to pathology. This now provides us a way to tease out the structure of "personality" itself, whether our own or someone else's. This understanding also allows us to "read people," including ourselves, with more accuracy and understanding. This provides a more thorough understanding of "human nature" and further empowers us in gaining *rapport with different personality types* effectively.

Of course, after understanding, empathy, and acceptance, the same meta-level model puts into our hands a whole array of processes for working with the meta-levels and layers. For anyone working with other multi-layered human beings, we first need the skill of jumping logical levels faster than the client or customer. After all, we now know that the person who sets the highest frame will indeed *govern* the resulting experiences and interactions. So we use this *meta-function* to continually step aside and away from the communications to recognize when someone has jumped outside the frame. Linguistically, we then simply meta-comment about their meta-comment.

By way of comparison, suppose that you as an employee, a manager, a customer, or even a CEO does not know the higher levels of a company—its mission and purpose, its structure and operational processes, its policies and constraints, etc. To not know the higher structures would all but prevent you from any complete understanding of the company, how it works, or those who work at its various levels. In other words, *structure* gives us both a higher level of understanding of things as well as the ability to take more effective action.

4) To work with "personality" problems, hone right in on the leverage points that govern communicating and relating.
When you understand structure and can detect the meta-levels of states, frames, and operational programs, you will know how to work with "personality" problems—whether your own or another's. Understand the levels of the systemic nature of consciousness endows us with the ability to quickly and intuitively identify and communicate with *the governing influence* (or states) that controls subjectivity.

In the field of systems thinking, we know that every system of interactive parts has leverage points. Peter Senge (*1994*) has described this extensively in *The Fifth Discipline*. This refers to those places in the system where a small nudge in a certain direction will result in significant changes in the whole system. We also have leverage points in our mind-emotions-body systems. Since our minds-emotions-bodies exist as *a system*, and since this cycling system spirals into numerous levels, having a model to track such provides us the systemic knowledge about where and when to intervene in a system.

Thinking systemically about a person, a company, a family, etc. enables us to create transformation in the shortest time possible. After all, in a system, the higher levels always modulate and govern the lower levels. Thinking systemically moves us out of the linear thinking of Stimulus—Response.

Such high-level thinking also enables us to more elegantly and intelligently frame, reframe, de-frame, and out-frame in our communications. This allows us to facilitate the best states in others so that they can operate from their best. This allows us to model examples of expertise and excellence wherever we find it in our careers. As we recognize the layeredness of consciousness, we can identify the higher levels that drive the excellence.

From the Penthouse View

When you fully understand your own inner executive and those of others, and have learned the meta-level principles or secrets, you will feel empowered to do things that you once assumed belonged to a small group of experts and geniuses. You will develop the ability to distinguish between levels of communication (sensory based and evaluative based) as you converse with people. You will be able to recognize the various levels of states (primary states and meta-states) so that you immediately recognize *at what level* they speak.

You will discover the key secrets which govern your inner executive and the internal policies that have been set. At that point, you will arrive at the choice point. Then you will easily decide, "Do I want that particular program running the show?" If not, you can fire it. This gives you the ability to change any and every old response pattern that doesn't serve you.

This empowers you to clean up the mental-emotional muddles that keep you confused and incongruent. By going right to your inner executive, you will develop an empowering clarity of purpose and vision for your life. You will cultivate the higher wisdom of awareness that has traditionally been reserved for "the enlightened." Now you will experience a form of enlightenment itself. In this way, you will learn to operate from higher mental levels than you ever dreamed possible.

Empowering your inner executive enables you to transform your fire-breathing dragons into friendly and energetic dragons for fun and profit . This also gives you the ability to transform your "personality" from the top-down as you establish new policies for your identity, self-esteem, sanity, relationships, etc. You can even re-invent yourself and your life as you learn how to go straight to the Boss in the first place. And, of course, dong this empowers you to nourish and develop the genius within you.

What Else Can You Do By Empowering Your Inner Executive?

- *You can get unstuck from your feeling stuck state.* If you have ever used all of your highest expert communication techniques and still not gotten to the real *source* of an issue with someone, then this model provides additional insights about what to do then.
- *You can turn confusion into understanding, enlightenment, and even wisdom.* Have you ever wondered *why* in the world, or *how,* a person could think or feel as he or she does?
- *You can deal effectively and powerfully with anyone who gives you an "attitude."* Has someone ever "copped an attitude" with you that didn't seem to make sense at all, and the person seemed stubbornly stuck in that attitude?
- *You can recognize and play with the source of neuro-linguistic "magic."* Have you ever experienced a state-of-the-art skill or technique which typically worked like magic seem amazingly ineffective at other times? Now you can recognize this and

play with it. You can outframe. You can jump logical levels faster than your client.

Summary

- *You have an Inner Executive.* You have a part of yourself that *emerges* over time and through your experience of consciousness. It *emerges* because you have a very special and unique kind of consciousness—*self-reflexive consciousness.*
- As a symbol user, you can move up to a higher level of awareness—conceptually, and think about your thinking. This meta-move puts you in a whole new place and generates a higher sense of your very self.
- *Reflexivity* can operate as both a curse and a blessing. If you don't handle it aright, you can create all kinds of dragon states and living hells in your life, "personality," and even in your body. Always check the quality of your reflexive thinking. "Is this feeling serving me well? Is this thought enhancing my life?"
- Now that you've said hello to your inner executive, it's time for *fully developing your executive powers.* Doing that means building up an inner executive that can run the show with effectiveness, grace, and congruency.
- Secret #3 for developing personal mastery is this: **Our Reflexive Consciousness Enables us to always Layer yet another Level upon our Model of the World.** This gives us the ability to always set outside of our frames-of-reference and go right to the top—to our highest executive states. We do not have to be stuck or limited any more than we want to be. We can always outframe. This gives us the ability to truly Take Charge of our mind, emotions, reality, and destiny.

Specialized Terminology:

Phenomenal: appearance.

Concept/Conceptual: Relating to ideas about things.

Frame: A reference that we use that provides a context for our thinking, emoting, choosing, acting, etc.

Reframe: When we change our frame-of-reference and use another.

Outframe: The process of stepping outside of our frames, conceptually (stepping outside of the box), and establishing an entirely new frame. Putting ideas, beliefs, feelings, etc. within a higher frame.

Unsanity: Picked up and used by Korzybski by a psychologist, P.S. Graven, it refers to a place between *insane* and *sane*, between a complete break with external reality and a good healthy adjustment. Unsane means that our maps for navigating the world kind of work, but not very well. They tend to leave us feeling anxious, nervous, and incomplete.

Three More Secrets
of
Personal Mastery

Secret #4

A strong sense of vitality and mastery emerges from owner-ship of our basic neuro-linguistic powers.

A physical and mental sense of vitality, of being alive, and of learned optimism comes from owning, accepting, appreciating, and immersing ourselves in our basic powers of mind (thinking, evaluating, believing, valuing, understanding), emotion (caring, valuing, somatizing), speech (speaking, languaging, symbolizing, narrating), and behavior (acting, relating, incorporating, expressing).

Secret #5

Mastery emerges from our power to detect and to set higher level frames.

Our neuro-linguistic and neuro-semantic powers blossom even more when we move to a higher level and use our thinking, feeling, speaking, and behaving to set a frame of reference.

Secret #6

Whoever sets the frame governs all of the subsequent experiences as determined by that frame.

The ultimate power over human experience, states, perception, thought, emotion, skill, etc. derives from the higher level frames. To understand the meaning and the dynamics within any thought or feeling state, we have to detect the governing frame.

Chapter 3

Developing Your Executive Powers

The Inner "Power" Trip

While the executive has come out of the closet,
he or she doesn't seem all that powerful
so it's time to "power up" the executive states.

Joel didn't feel very powerful. He felt that his wife, Brenda, was always "making" him angry with her demands and dissatisfactions. He also felt that his boss "made" him feel inadequate and inferior. Then there were his parents who, in spite of his 33 years, still "made" him feel like a little kid. And so it went.

After listening to Joel's story, I commented, "Joel, it seems like everybody knows how to run your emotions—Brenda, your boss, your parents, even strangers on the street can 'cause' you to have feelings—everybody, of course, but you.

"Yeah, I guess so." He commented in a not-quite knowing what I was leading to tone.

"Wouldn't it be great if you were let in on the secret that they all know about your emotions and how to make you feel things?"

"What do you mean?"

"Well, all of these people can 'make' you feel angry, inadequate, upset, guilty, etc. Wouldn't you like to know how to push your own keyboard?"

He did. And so I focused on accessing his inner executive powers so that he could learn the art of "powering up."

Powering Up

Are you ready to **power up?** Are you ready to get your inner executive to power up as well?

On the road to *personal mastery,* we began with the first secret about using *the tool of thinking itself.* Mastery begins with your ability to appreciate your thoughts as "neuro-linguistic programs." The power of *thought* itself serves as the foundational component in our mental-emotional mapping of reality.

The second great secret follows immediately from the first. The *stuff* of *thinking-feeling* that we experience at the primary levels generates all of the higher functions of consciousness also. Nothing new is added to the mix. Our higher states and executive operations arise from the power of *reflexivity.* When our thoughts-and-feelings *reflect back* onto prior thoughts-and-feelings, they become more and more layered, and we *move up into "meta" levels of consciousness.* To attain personal mastery we have to discover these higher level structures and learn to manage them to our welfare.

The third secret grows from the first two. As we can reflexively notice, detect, and manage our awarenesses from higher levels, we can always layer yet another level upon things. We can always step outside of our frames and outframe.

So what? This means that we do not have to remain stuck or limited in our thinking or feeling. We need not feel stuck with any particular way of viewing things, belief system, or meaning construct. We can renew our mind by making *new* what and how we think.

Imagine the potentials of these powers. As you discover and explore the possibilities in these first secrets of human consciousness and our higher mental powers, you can begin to develop and use *the power of your self-reflexive consciousness* to re-program the very structure of your life. Of course, if you do not consciously take charge of these systemic processes which create both your meta-states and executive states, the processes will continue to work anyway. But they will be outside of your awareness and thereby control you in ways that you might not understand or desire.

What significance does all of this have on our everyday lives?

It applies to everything!

After all, everything important in making our human experiences rich and fulfilling emerge from this: *meaning*, emotion, motivation, skill, expertise, happiness, relationships, freedom, individuation, connection, transcendence, etc. All of these spring from our higher states of mind. Having established the foundational secrets, we now need only to mark out precisely how to set these kinds of frames in our executive states.

As we engage in this process, let's aim first to develop our first level *powers* of mind. Why? Because out of these will emerge the more profound and extensive higher level *powers*. After all, beyond the primary level, *it is beliefs all the way up* and these belief levels are made out of the same *stuff* as the thoughts of the primary level.

Imagine wasting such powers. Wouldn't that be a shame? Yet many (perhaps most) people end up doing precisely that. In the end, they squander **their executive powers** on minutiae, or they totally abdicate such powers. Or they let those powers create demon states that make everyday life a nightmare. Sometimes we micro-manage our lower mental levels, and thereby waste time, energy, and creativity. Joel did. He gave his powers away to everybody and then complained that they were misusing them on him! To avoid these traps, we need to learn *the Art of Developing our Executive Powers*.

The State of "State"
First, let's talk about *states*. *States* refer to the holistic, dynamic, and systemic experience that arises from "mind," "emotion," and "body," and which together merge to create something more than the sum of the parts. Sometimes we label these states which emerge as our "moods," "attitude," or "disposition" even "personality." States are dynamic, always moving, changing, and transforming and this is especially true at the lower levels.

States are also holistic. By *state* we refer to the sum total of mind-body, mind-emotion-within-the-body-as-a-whole in an environment. So even though we sometimes pull the facets and components of a state apart and talk about our "thoughts," or our "emotions," or our "body," it's just *talk*. These do *not* actually or literally operate apart from each other.

This means that in speaking about *states*, we use this as a shorthand for a **neuro-linguistic state**, the fully-fledged experience comprising our state of mind, state of body, and state of emotion. From this we experience an overall attitude or mood that's made up of all of these elements.

In recent decades, the Cognitive Psychologies and Sciences have recognized *the holistic nature* of "thoughts" and "emotions." So while we may sometimes speak about these two "things" as if separate elements, we can do so only in speech and linguistics. In actuality, they function as part of the same *thought-emotion system*. In fact, they do not radically differ. Those who speak of "thoughts" and "emotions" as two radically different kinds of experiences speak from the eighteenth and nineteenth centuries and from the dualism of old "faculty" psychology. Today's neuro-sciences recognize the holistic and interactive nature of "mind" and "emotion."

This means that within "thought" we have "emotion." Within anger, you can count on finding *angry thoughts*. Try to experience anger without entertaining any angry thoughts. Within fear, you'll always discover thoughts of danger, threat, and apprehension. Within joy—pleasant thoughts of delight and fun. Within love— thoughts of attraction, delight, and extension. And so it goes. As we think—so we feel.

Now states themselves can seem quite magical. Once "in a state," the state itself can seem to have a life of its own. When this happens the state operates in a self-protective, self-fulfilling, and self-organizing way. The neuro-sciences refer to this as a mood-set, a predispositional set of an attitude, *state dependency*, etc. **State dependence** means that all of our psychic functions (thinking, feeling, valuing, believing, remembering, speaking, acting, relating, perceiving, etc.) *operate from* and *in accordance* with the state. More about this in a bit.

The Roads to State

Given that we have states of "mind," "emotion," and "body," we can also utilize these expressions to identify what I like to describe as the *two royal roads to state*—mind and body. In NLP, we speak about these two roads as *Internal Representations* (Mind) and *Physiology* (Body). From this we get the phrase "neuro-linguistic" which combines the facets of our nervous systems and neurology with our linguistic processing that occurs within the brain and nervous system.

After all, our "thoughts" and our internal "sense" that we create by our mentally coding of things occurs via the functioning of our nervous system and brain. Think about that.

What does the nervous system do? Korzybski said that it "abstracts." It pulls information from the world "out there" and creates abstractions using the particular nature and qualities of the human body. In this way, it creates internal representations or maps of the world. This shows up as neurological and linguistic summarizing, condensing, and concluding.

An example. In the sub-microscopic world there is "a dance of electrons" in perpetual motion that makes up everything in the universe. But we do not see such. We do not hear, feel, smell, or taste such. This understanding, in fact, had to be discovered using extra-neural devices—machines that could extend what our eyes, ears, skin, etc. could detect in the world. Our nervous system operates at a macro-level. It translates the *energies* into more gross forms. When we look at a still fan with three blades, we *see* three blades and probably hear, feel, smell and taste nothing. When we switch the fan on, we may for a while continue to *see* three blades, *feel* the wind, and *hear* the buzz. Eventually, we will stop seeing three blades and instead see a disk. The blades will appear as a disk. There is no disk there, we see a disk. Our eyes cannot see fast enough to pick up the distinctions between the blades. And if the blades move even faster as the blades of a prop plane, the disk and blades will entirely vanish. We will then see nothing.

Our nervous system with its end-receptors (i.e. eyes, ears, skin, mouth, etc.) picks up information and creates "abstracts" from the world. It takes in "information" from the energy manifestations "out there" and translates them into nervous system "abstracts." We then experience such as representations and "thoughts," which evoke somatic feeling states and other higher level abstractions.

In this lies the basis for all of our personal "powers," our powers of mind-emotion, speech and behavior.

Primary State Powers and "Power Zone"

What are the fundamental powers that we experience at *the primary level?* What powers at the first level can we later utilize at meta-levels for frame-setting, mind-managing, emotional tracking, etc.? These primary level *powers* describe our fundamental *power zone.* Within this zone we all have four powers, or responses, that nobody can take away from us. And although over the life span of the typical person, these powers will naturally evolve along with our maturing, we still have to cultivate and develop these powers.

We can separate these four powers into two categories: two private powers and two public powers. The private powers speak predominantly about our own internal world of subjective experience where we map our Model of the World (our mental paradigm), and then use it to navigate the territory out there. The two public powers, derived from the private powers, describe *how* we go about the process of adapting, adjusting, coping, and mastering the territory.

We can quickly and succinctly summarize the two private powers as our *thoughts-and-feelings.* In thinking-and-emoting we collect up all of our **cognizing**—i.e. thinking, information processing, valuing, believing, making decisions, understanding, etc. and all of our **somatizing**—i.e. emoting, emotionalizing, feeling, registering knowledge in our body in terms of how we move, breathe, gesture, etc.

A few years ago I had a rare and unprecedented opportunity to work with a group of boys, coaching them in "anger control." These boys, 14 to 18 years of age, lived in a special home and had all been court ordered there due to crimes of violence or drug abuse. Quite a group! "Nobody can *make* me angry!" I began each session. "That's the beginning of the Anger Control Creed. 'My anger is mine. I create it. I create it by how I use my thoughts and my body.'"

Of course, at first that was a come-on.

"Nobody can make you angry?" one or more of them would ask or call out.

"That's right. Go ahead and try in vain to *make* me angry. Call me anything you can think of."

I even had some takers at first. After the outburst of obscene language, I would hold my wrist as if taking my pulse, get quiet for a moment and then comment, "No, still not angry. Guess you weren't man enough to '*make*' me angry. Anybody else?"

Of course, it was all to get their attention and drive home the central point about our executive powers. I chose that approach because even before I began, I knew that talking about "responsibility" would neither capture their attention, appeal to their imagination, nor win their allegiance. So I re-languaged "responsibility." I called it **response power.** And that led me to talk about our **Power Zone**. I would say,

"Each of us have *four* very central and inescapable *powers* by which we can *respond* to the world. Two of these human powers operate very privately (thinking and emoting) and two operate as our public contributions to the world (speaking and behaving). Here lies our ability to cope and master the challenges that we face. Herein also lies the essence of our *response-ability.*"

Figure 3:1

Power Zone

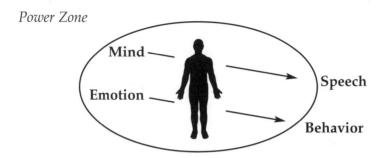

- To what extent have you fully owned and accepted your *powers*?
- To what degree have you cultivated and developed these powers?
- How much of your powers do you give away to others?

The Human Power Zone

The *power* of thinking-emoting (which comes with and reflects ego-strength and personality development) means that we have the *ability* to make mental-and-emotional *responses* along with awareness of this power. For this very reason, nobody can *"make"* us think-feel in a particular way unless we allow it.

Certainly people can *invite* us to feel upset. Yet in order to do that, they have to communicate or act in such a way to which *we then think* upsetting thoughts, and so *feel upset.* Certainly, people have the ability to provide incredibly powerful stimuli that invites, urges, provokes, incites, and elicits upsetting thinking-and-emoting response from us. Yet ultimately, *each of us responds with the corresponding thoughts-and-feelings.* Ultimately, such thinking-and-emoting belongs to *us.* We create them in our nervous system-and-brain *in response* to the stimulus.

Wouldn't this make an incredible difference at work and at home? Suppose everybody at your work assumed their own personal *power* and distinguished between *the stimulus of others* and *their own response*? Wouldn't that change the dynamics in the office? We wouldn't feel so disempowered. This would put an end to such statements (and the states out of which they come) as:

— "My boss makes me so angry that I can't stand it."

— "I know that he uses that tone of voice with me in the board meeting just to put me down and make me feel degraded. I just hate the way he controls me."

— "I had to retaliate as I did, she made me feel worthless."

This kind of talk sounds as if the recipients have no power, no choice, and no response-ability. It sounds like the old *Stimulus— Response Psychology Model.* When this *stimulus* occurs, you have to *respond* in this way. Push the button, and the robot activates. Ring the bell, and the dog salivates.

Such language of *reactivity* suggests that someone is living in a simple Stimulus—Response world. At least, they live in that kind of deterministic world *in their mind*. As long as they *believe* that others control their responses, that higher level conceptual frame will govern their everyday states. As long as they let that idea form and formulate their semantic world, it will generate this kind of victimization talk and emotions. The language of reactivity also indicates that the individuals have also either abdicated their response-power or never developed it in the first place.

By way of contrast to this way of thinking-and-feeling stands the state that we call *proactivity.* In proactivity, we recognize and own our *powers.* As we do so, we then think-and-feel response-*able.* Access the breathing, posture, and other physiology that also correlates to proactivity.

"My responses of thought and emotion result from the way *I think and emote.* Nobody 'makes' me think in a certain way, my thoughts arise from how I choose to think. Nobody 'makes' me feel in certain ways, my emotions arise from my thinking and valuing. I will not play the victim and give all my power away to others."

This leads us to state expressively *the fourth secret of personal mastery.*

Secret #4

A strong sense of vitality and mastery emerges from owner-ship of our basic neuro-linguistic powers.

A physical and mental sense of vitality, of being alive, and of learned optimism comes from owning, accepting, appreciating, and immers-ing ourselves in our basic powers of **mind** *(thinking, evaluating, believing, valuing, understanding),* **emotion** *(caring, valuing, som-atizing),* **speech** *(speaking, languaging, symbolizing, narrating), and* **behavior** *(acting, relating, incorporating, expressing).*

Owning Your Power Zone

With Joel, I asked him to step into an awareness of his four pow-ers and experience them as his. "Now just enjoy the deep knowl-edge that when you think and feel and speak and behave—they are your expressions, your responses, and your powers ..."

"Now Joel, say, you know I don't even know when you and Brenda first met. When was that? And where?

"Why, we met in Chicago when we were both in college."

"And I suppose that you now are so egotistical as to think that you just created that thought, don't you? But, then again, maybe I *made* you think that thought!?"

"Of course, it's my thought.'

"But Joel, maybe I haven't told you about a special power I have. I have the power to force you to have thoughts! Did you know that? And just now, I did that to you. I made you think about when you first met Brenda in Chicago."

"No you didn't. You asked a question and I told you where we met."

"See! I told you. I triggered you to think those thoughts. That makes me the controller of your mind. I *forced* you to think about Brenda and Chicago. I *made* you think those thoughts. You only think they are your thoughts."

"Are you nuts?"

Figure 3:2

THE WORLD OF REACTIVITY Reactivity	THE WORLD OF PROACTIVITY Proactivity
The **Stimulus-Response** World	The **Choice** World
Live/Act/Respond *as if* Stimuli, Events, People, etc. **make** you respond as you do (mentally, emotionally, verbally, behaviorally etc.)	Live/Act/Respond *as if* one always has a Choice about **how to respond**. Recognize that Responses operate as functions of **thinking** that occur between **S-R**. Humans have **Consciousness**

↓   ↓

VICTIMIZATION!   **EMPOWERMENT!**
Disempowerment   **In Charge of One's own Life**

Language Patterns

"You" statements	"I" statements
"You make me feel ..."	"I think, feel, choice ..."
Excuses/Blaming	Owns responsibility
Transferring of Responsibility	Holds Self Responsible

Neurological Patterns

Defensive! Reactive!	Defense*less*
Passive/Aggressive behaviors	Assertive behaviors
Unresourceful States	Resourceful States
Shallow breathing	Full and Deep Breathing
Poor Posture	Straight and Healthy Posture
Tense muscles	Relaxed Muscles Ready for Action
Tense eyes that strain and glare	Soft and relaxed eyes that can Attend

Phenomenological Experience

Passively suffers emotions, moods states, drives, etc.	Intentionally chooses and manages emotions and states
Mood-drive/Condition-driven	*Consciousness driven*
External orientation	Internal orientation
Deterministic/Fated	Freedom/Choice

Quality Representational Power

At the primary level, our ability to *think-and-feel* and to *create internal representations* gives us a most critically valuable capacity. We have the *power* to choose and manipulate our *representations*. We can control what we represent and the way we represent things. We can send new and more useful messages. We can cue our mind-and-body with sensory-based and languaged representations. This means we can play a key role in the construction and organization of our internal world. This provides the basis for "running our own brain."

- What messages do you send to your brain-and-body?
- What images, sounds, internal dialogue, sensations, etc., do you punch into your bio-computer?
- What is the quality and quantity of your signals?
- Do they serve you well?

Let these questions access your higher mind and assist you in taking a proactive stance toward your own internal world of thoughts-and-emotions. Let them coach you into fully accessing and running your higher levels of mind, and of developing more awareness of these powers.

Culturally, we have hardly noticed the relationship between *the quality* of our mental representations and *the quality* of our lives. Yet *how* we represent experiences and ideas greatly determines the quality of our internal world and our subsequent life. When we have poor quality of representations in our mind, this shows up in the way we talk, act, and relate. Check the quality and nature of how you encode your ideas, understandings, beliefs, decisions, values, etc. Do they carry great or little power? When we weakly represent things using little pictures, tiny sounds, distant feelings, etc., we dis-empower ourselves. The poor quality of our internal movies prevents us from getting much juice or pizzazz. Conversely, when we make our internal world dramatic by creating big, bright, close, three-dimensional, life-like, and intense pictures, sounds, and feelings, we experience more dramatic feelings.

Increasing the Vitality

As a Thought Experiment exercise, create an internal movie on the theater of your mind about some outcome that you would like to really experience (i.e. a new car, a promotion to a new office, a vacation to the Bahamas, etc.). Stop, in your mind, for just a moment and do this ...

After you have completed the thought experience, examine the *quality* of your pictures, soundtrack, and sensations. Gauge them on a *Dramatic Scale* from 0 (meaning not dramatic or sensational at all) to 10 (signifying Senso-rama Land!). How close to a 10 do you have?

If you do not yet have a 10, then turn all of the facets of the images, sounds, and sensations up. Make your picture of that outcome that you really desire as if on a ten foot by ten foot screen. Now double that. Make your sound track panoramic and loud enough to vibrate the walls. Now step into that movie so that you feel as if you are there ...

This *Juicing Up Your States* technique highlights what we mean by representational power and lies at the heart of the NLP Model. This means that our internal sense of ourselves, others, the world, etc. flows from our very nature as information encoders. Thus, the more dramatic, powerful, and compelling we make our internal Model of the World, the more it will send commands throughout our entire body to actualize it. For most people, no one has ever taught them how to do this. Some people may even have to go against old childhood taboos and constraints to run their own brain in this way. The good news is that no Mind Police will arrest you for making your internal world more compelling, vigorous, intense, and dramatic. So go ahead and just feel free to crank it up anytime you need more juice. And, as you will soon discover, this technique offers an incredibly powerful tool for self-managed motivation.

Linguistic and Behavioral Powers

As thinking-and-emoting describes our two private powers (thought and emotion), *speaking and acting* describe our two public powers. From the way we think and feel, we move out into the world to interact by speaking and acting. This gives us our ability to affect the world and others, to cope and master the environment, and to make a difference.

Yet not only does the way we talk and act spring from the internal communications of our thinking-and-feeling, but the way we talk and act (including tone, pitch, speed, volume) also influences our thoughts and emotions. Sometimes as we hear ourselves speaking to others, we discover new and surprising things about ourselves. Sometimes our over-hearing of ourselves in communication with others reinforces or modulates our internal self-talk.

We primarily use our public powers of speaking and acting in order to influence, affect, and communicate with others or to adapt or master some aspect of our world. Our *linguistic powers* give us the ability to affect the thinking-emoting of others. *How* we package our thoughts and use language forms, patterns, processes, devices, etc. greatly impacts the quality of our influence.

Our *behavioral and action powers* speak about how we physically and behaviorally respond to the world. Here we have the power to structure our activities, time, relationships, learning, etc. Here we procrastinate and waste time in confusion, indecision, self-contradiction, etc. Here we take effective action as we use our skills and aptitudes.

Within our *behavioral powers,* we have the ability to create the kind of environments and situations that increase our other powers. We *behaviorally* can take effective action in eating right, exercising in a balanced way, taking care of our bodies, getting plenty of rest, etc. *Behaviorally* we can take effective action in keeping our minds and spirits invigorated by getting our daily dose of invigorating thoughts, significant conversations with loved ones, and making plans for moving toward our hopes and dreams.

Via our *behavioral powers,* we can "act" ourselves into new ways of thinking-and-feeling. Using **the "As If" frame of reference,** we can use our nervous system and body to run the neuro-pathways of actions and external responses—*as if* we felt confident, courageous, worthwhile, excited, cheerful, pleasant, etc. We can consciously breathe fully and deeply even if we feel anxious or fearful or angry. As we do so, we alter our external behavior and set in motion forces and energies in the mind-body system that will assist us into feeling more confident, relaxed, and calm. William James spoke about this when he said that when you don't feel confident, begin to act as if you did. Doing so eventually affects and activates feelings of confidence. This offers yet another pragmatic way to take charge of experiences. We can even set *non-verbal frames-of-references* by the way we act. Without saying anything, think, "Confidence" and then move, gesture, walk, etc. and let your face, movements, breathing flesh out the idea of "confidence." What happens?

Linguistically, we can language ourselves and others with the kinds of words and ideas that validate ourselves and others, vividly portray our purpose and sense of destiny, that keeps our values and beliefs alive and vigorous, and that creates an enriched social environment. We can use our *linguistic powers* to support people, confirm their values, explore their understandings, learn from their different opinions, identify new resources, and build ever enriched maps.

We have used the various facets of our power zone to build a higher frame and create less stress in the work environment. In *Instant Relaxation (1999)* we use representational powers to activate our full power zone in order to access and amplify states of relaxation for stress reduction and stress management.

Frame Power

Given this access to these four incredible powers in our primary states, what happens when we move to higher levels of mind? What *powers* do we have in those higher executive and Meta-States?

First and foremost, as we make a move to a meta-position, we retain all of these basic powers of *thinking-emoting, speaking, and acting*. These powers do not cease as we move to higher levels. Indeed, we continue to *use* these very powers in the process of *going meta* as we bring higher level thoughts-and-emotions to bear upon our primary or previous thoughts-and-emotions. And yet, as we do so, our thinking-and-feeling becomes more developed as it takes on more conceptual qualities.

71

This means that *the power to set a frame of reference* does not differ from the *power* to create a representation of an idea, and to hold it before the mind. *Frames*, in fact, grow and take form by simply *repeating* a thought, idea, picture, word, etc. This *habituation* of the thought empowers it to become our default choice of what and how to think. This identifies the Fifth Secret of Personal Mastery.

Secret #5

Mastery emerges from our power to detect and to set higher level frames.
Our neuro-linguistic and neuro-semantic powers blossom even more when we move to a higher level and use our thinking, feeling, speaking, and behaving to set a frame of reference.

Whether we create a "thought" at a primary level or at any meta-level, that representation (whether a picture, sound, sensation, word, phrase, metaphor, etc.) involves *symbolism*. We can use it to "stand for" another referent. This allows us to use any and all of the sensory systems as languages of the mind to perform this higher level function, namely, of setting a higher frame-of-reference.

What *frames* have you set in life? What thoughts-and-feelings have you applied or brought to bear upon work, people, yourself, or any other thought, experience, or idea?

Early in life Bill set a frame (by his *thinking* and *feeling)* that his worth was completely conditional upon how well he performed. So throughout life, every mistake, inadequacy, and fallible expression provoked him to think of himself with contempt and disgust. This created both high motivation for him as a salesman as well as frequently put him in an emotional roller-coaster. Over the years, however, every failure made this frame a program of self-contempt. And when it reached that level of influence, it came to govern his everyday states and experiences making any effort harder and harder. Toxic higher level frames have a way of doing that.

This *power* (or ability) to *set a frame of reference* arises from our power of thought. Whenever we bring any thought or emotion, any language or behavior and let it *reflect back onto* a previous experience or product of consciousness, it sets a frame. It takes a meta-relationship to the previous state. And when that happens, the new thought *moves upwards to become a higher mental level.* Then, our subsequent responses have the potential of creating a new internal context of meaning.

Actually, this represents a pretty frightening power. And we all have used this very power to build frames of references long before we knew what we were doing or its implications. As a semantic class of life we cannot but set frames, because this describes *how* we create our mental maps.

1) First we have an experience.

2) Then out of the context of that experience, we build rudimentary maps about what it "is," what it means, what it says about us, our future, others, etc.

3) Then as we keep repeating and habituating our ideas and understandings, it becomes our frame of reference.

Suppose we fail at some task. *Experience.* What then do you make of that experience? Does it mean that you "are a failure"? Does it indicate that you simply "don't have enough experience to master it yet"?

The *experience* exists at the primary level—the meaning that we assign to it exists at a meta-level. How we generalize from that to create additional meaning moves us to a meta-position. This creates *our frame of reference.* As a *frame*, it provides a format for all similar (and even dissimilar) experiences. As it does, it filters other experiences through the perception of that frame.

This explains why this operates as *frame power.*

Frames, Meta-States, Canopies of Consciousness

The frames we set become the very mental atmosphere that we breathe and within which we live. It becomes our *conceptual reality*—the concepts that we then use as our reference point for other experiences. It becomes our *perceptual filter* for understanding, making sense of, and attributing meaning to, other experiences.

Frames also perpetuate themselves. Once we have *set a frame*, that frame will *govern* our thinking, perceiving, believing, valuing, emoting, responding, speaking, languaging, acting, relating, etc. It *governs* our subsequent experiences, in part, by keeping out anything that doesn't fit its paradigm. We commonly call this dynamic "a self-fulfillment prophecy."

This explains some of the cultural beliefs, myths, and propaganda about the early programming of a child. You've heard the cultural story that asserts that only in the early years of childhood can a person set a new direction or frame:

"A child's personality is set by the age of seven."
"You can't teach an old dog new tricks."
"There's no use talking with him, he's set in his ways."

Yet what we have here actually has little to nothing to do with age, childhood, the ability to learn, change, or grow. What we have here simply involves *the power of frames.* This means that we do *not* here have any innate, inherent, or developmental stage issue. Nor does it mean that somehow only the earliest frames set a direction and highly determined consequent experience. We rather have a case of a person having *set of frame*, or bought into *a frame*, and never called it into question. Its power, in fact, lies in how we do **not** question it, but just assume it.

Frames function as our *reality structures.* So unquestioned frames operates as our *assumptive map* about what's real. This means that the statement about personality being set by seven years of age does not represent the lack of ability to change, but rather a case where one does not *believe* one can change. Accordingly, each and every subsequent experience simply gets ordered, organized, and filtered *in terms of the previous frame of reference.*

Figure 3:3

The Self-Organizing Nature of a Frame of Reference

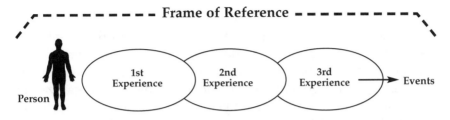

Framing Power Resulting in Executive States

How do we identify our frames? Or our frames-of-frames? To identify any given meta-level state *about* any primary state, simply inquire about *what* you think or feel about that experience.

Key Questions—Going Meta:
  • How do you typically think or feel when you get criticized?
  • When you go through a disappointment, what thoughts and emotions do you typically then experience *about* that?
  • When you succeed at something you thought would be hard, what do you think or feel *about* that?

Such questions invite us to move up a level. When we answer such questions, we create a mental-emotional state *about* the previous state. To move up another level, keep asking the meaning question.

  • And what does it mean when you feel defensive about criticism?
  • What does it mean when you feel angry about a disappointment?
  • What significance does surprise about easy success have for you?

Moving up the levels of thoughts-and-feelings *about* previous states has no hard and fast structure. It all depends upon the internal structuring and patterning of consciousness that we have learned as well as the accidents of the moment. One person may predominantly favor *emotional* meta-states *about* primary states. Another person may more typically go into *conceptual* states about states. Yet another may access *identity states*, or *capacity* states, *spiritual* states, *action* states, *decision* states, etc. Yet each and everyone of these higher level frames consists of *a belief* or a conceptual reality.

Ultimately, we all move up to those **belief frames** that create our sense of person, identity, and destiny. When we do, we reach our *executive states.* At that level, the states or frames exert considerable influence as they govern all of the lower frames and organize our lower levels around them. And yet ... *who* decides upon our identity and destiny? We do. *We* at a higher level. This *transcendent* sense of self that never stops at any one level, but always resides in "the back of our mind" or "above the highest frame" operates as our ultimate *executive state.*

Here we always have choice. Here we always have the ability to step back, or up, from anything we think or feel, anything we believe, or any concept we create and think about that thought.

Joel's frame of reference was one that assumed that others were the source of his emotions, especially his negative ones. He took experiences of reacting to what others said and did and used it as his reference point. Eventually, he began to believe in this frame. That's when it turned toxic. That's when he gave up his personal powers to that frame. When he assumed that frame, he presupposed the frame of dis-ownership. This led to passivity and reactivity.

Outframing Power
The Technique of Just Stepping Aside
Now, *if* indeed we don't have a case of some genetic or innate problem of age, but more actually a case of *a governing frame of reference*, we need only to step *outside* of that frame. To step *outside* of a frame of reference frees us from its influence and power. Then we can think *about* it. Doing this provides us *a space* from which we can think, perceive, remember, create, imagine, etc. in new and different ways *not controlled* by the meta-level structure.

We call this higher power **outframing.** *Outframing* refers to the process of stepping completely outside of a frame of reference and setting up an entirely new frame. In NLP and Neuro-Semantics, we frequently speak about *the "As If" frame* (pretending something and acting "as if"). Doing so works a very special kind of "magic." We step outside "just pretending" to *not have to* think, feel, invent, respond, etc. using the formulations and organizations of the old frame. "Just for the fun of it" we play around with new, different, and even impossible frames. This move to an awareness of our frames then makes outframing possible. In this case, we outframe with the idea of *new possibilities.*

We can outframe in a great many other ways. We can *outframe* to run a Quality Control on our thinking and feeling. This enables us to check the *"ecology"* of the frame. Do this by simply asking about the "ecology," or long-term health and balance of the experience.

> When I step back from this way of thinking, feeling, responding, living, etc., I ask myself just how well has it served me? Has it enhanced my life or created unpleasant limitations?

We can outframe using the perceptive of objectivity.

> As I look at this problem from a larger perspective of time and space, how much of a problem would I consider this ten years from now?

> What would this situation look like from a visitor from Mars? How problematic would it seem to a truly objective point of view?

Anytime that we *step outside of a frame,* and then go above it to question it, explore it, test it in some way (ecology frame, reality testing frame, etc.), or bring some other value or resource to bear upon it—we have *outframed* it. When we do that, we evoke one of our highest executive states—that part of our mind and person that can make life decisions and set new directions. This explains the power of the NLP linguistic model known as "Sleight of Mouth" Patterns which Bob Bodenhamer and I (1997) reformulated using meta-levels as *the Mind-Lines Model.*

With this we now have the Sixth Secret for Personal Mastery, a very special and important secret, one I first discovered in the writings of Gregory Bateson.

Secret #6
Whoever sets the frame governs all of the subsequent experiences as determined by that frame.
The ultimate power over human experience, states, perception, thought, emotion, skill, etc. derives from the higher level frames. To understand the meaning and the dynamics within any thought or feeling state, we have to detect the governing frame.

Executive Development Exercises
The set of skills that enable us to effectively manage our states describe some of the highest executive functions. This includes inducing, accessing, and anchoring states. It includes amplifying and altering states. The following summarizes central state management skills. The more you give yourself to using them, adopting them into your own repertoire of skills, and practicing them— *the more you will develop true expertise with them.* Practice using them to "run your own brain" and to make your mind *mind.*

1) State Awareness
We cannot manage what we lack awareness of. This makes the first step for state management *raising our awareness* about our states. You can do this in numerous ways. You could track your states daily by journaling them. Journaling would enable you to pay more attention to your states, to naming them, and to noticing their components of physiology and internal representations, etc.

If you use a bubble to stand for a state, specify the *states* that you begin a day with, the *states* that you shift to over a day's time, and the *states* that you end a day on. Most people will typically go through 8 to 40 *states* in a day. Notice also the cues that trigger the states.

- What do I call this state?
- How much intensity do I experience in this state?
- How much mixture or purity would I estimate this state?
- What internal representations really drive this state?
- How resourceful or unresourceful would I gauge this state?

Techniques:
- Track your states via Bubble Journaling
- Name them as you experience them.
- Note your physiology that corresponds to a state.
- Evaluate them for ecology: enhancing or limiting?
- Identify the cues that trigger them.
- Develop three questions to ask yourself daily:

1) What did I learn about myself today?
2) What shall I continue working on?
3) How am I moving closer toward my vision?

2) State Interruption

There are times we cannot do much about a given state of consciousness. Except to **interrupt** it. After interrupting it, we can
then do numerous other things to slow it down. Neuro-linguistic
states can develop a life of their own to such an extent that once
we get into the state, it can become so strong and so powerful that
it seems nearly impossible to stop it.

If you have ever driven in the Rocky Mountains, you will have
noticed *"Runaway Truck Lanes."* These sideroads, made out of
gravel and sand, provide a way to stop a hundred-thousand
pound truck after its brakes have given out as it races down a
mountain out of control. These lanes have six to twelve inches of
gravel, parallel to the highway, and frequently go up a hill.

- How do you *slow down* one of your runaway states?
- How well does your conscious braking system work?
- What things can you do to make it hard for a state to contin-
  ue functioning?

State Interrupts comprise anything that can enable you to stop a
state. The most effective of these not surprisingly involve interrupting the physical components of the state:

- Standing on your head
- Using the "T" signal (Time-Out)
- Shifting to talking in a sexy tonality
- Picking your nose (a gross-out pattern interrupt)

- Zooming in to a Stop sign
- Hearing "STOP" shouted in your head, etc.
- Looking up in the sky, pointing, and asking, "Is that Halley's comet?"
- Shout a bold or outrageous *"No!"* to the ideas that feed the state.

In each of these, the aim and design of the Pattern Interrupt is simply to jar consciousness so that it cannot continue in its current direction. To discover the natural things that can interrupt your states, simply pay attention to the everyday interruptions that jar you. Do you ever get interrupted to such an extent that you have difficulty returning to where you were before?

3) State Deframing

By offering something very different (or weird) to think, do, hear, see, etc., we can interrupt a state. *Interrupt patterns* essentially deframe states. We can also deframe by altering or transforming the components of state—internal representation and physiology.

If you have a 3-D color movie of something that "cranks your case," turn it into a black-and-white snapshot. Sit back in the theater of your mind and just watch it. Push the picture back a block in distance. Hear your internal critical voice in Elvis' tonality. Hear Donald Duck quack out the words. Doing such things tends to *deframe* the structure of the experience that gives us so much trouble.

Run a *contrastive analysis* between your unresourceful state and some similar state that you experience resourcefully (stress/relaxation; insecurity/confidence; off-balanced/centered, etc.). Doing this provides information about what facets of the experience you can shift to deframe it.

4) State Accessing

As we can catch a state, interrupt or deframe it, we can also send other internal representations to our brain in order to construct a more enhancing state. We *access states* by either:

(1) *Using Memory* to recall a time when we experienced a referent state.

(2) *Using Imagination* to creatively imagine what such a state would look, sound and feel like if we did experience it.

The first process enables us to use our history to re-induce ourselves into a state. The second process empowers us to use the "As If" frame of reference to invent new possibilities. This allows us to populate our mind with all kinds of wild and wonderful images, sounds, sensations, and words that will make our internal world more dramatic, powerful, and compelling.

We can improve our powers of state accessing by learning to use our senses more consciously and intentionally. To do that, spend a little time every day to make mental "snap-shots" of sights, sounds, sensations, etc. Move into an uptime state and use your sensory awareness to enrich your inner world of mind. For instance, the next time you shower, fully experience it. Hear the water, see the steam rise, feel the hot water on your back, arms, legs; smell the lathering soap, allow yourself to feel the zest and delight of the experience.

We can do the same with eating a meal, giving or receiving a hug, talking with a loved one, watching a sunset, walking barefoot in the rain, taking a drive over a mountain, listening to beautiful music, hearing various voice tones and qualities on TV, etc. Snapshot the experiences and code them into your memory. Later you can build all kinds of new experiences out of these pieces.

This process involves intentionally using our *representation power.* Then we can punch in the kind of signals so that our brain-body system will respond in the most resourceful ways. After all, we always have a choice about *what* to represent. We can let thoughts come and go in the stream of consciousness, and we can decide to set our mind on things that build resourcefulness, can we not?

We can also use our physiology to access resourceful states. We can put our body into the posture, movement, and breathing of confidence, love, joy, peace, etc. We can practice "the eyes of appreciation," "the sounds of congruency," "the gesturing of wonder," etc.

6) State Amplification

As mentioned earlier, we can not only access representations in our mind, but we can **amplify** them so that we really crank up or intensify our states.

Suppose you wanted to access a state of gentleness and tenderness. For myself, I need only to think about holding a newborn baby in my arms. Such thoughts put me into state. I fly into a state of tenderness. To amplify this—I need only to hear a baby's gurgling sounds, smell baby powder, feel its soft skin, and bring it closer.

What sensory modality and what qualities of that system have the greatest impact upon you? Our *driving representational distinctions* ("submodalities") provide us with a way to amplify our states through the ceiling. Doing this can make our inner realities more dramatic and powerful.

7) State Utilization

With the ability to become aware, interrupt, deframe, access, and amplify states, we can learn to use them in the times and places that make them truly useful for us. Where would you like to think-and-feel with self-confidence, resilience, forgiveness, assertiveness, etc.? Future pace yourself with the resourceful state and build up the connections. By thinking of a context and then accessing the state fully and completely, we begin to train our nervous system to respond.

8) Meta-Stating

Since linguistics and other higher level symbols primarily drive our executive states, we can build and glue higher states via empowering words to access and bring that resource to bear upon a primary state that we want to interrupt. Doing this constructs a state-*upon*-state structure. To design such, simply begin exploring, "What resourceful thought, emotion, belief, etc. could I bring to this state that would temper and qualify it so that I would have more control and personal mastery?"

Summary

- By detecting and becoming aware of our *powers of representation* and *conception*, we can learn to effectively run our own brain.
- Appreciating the meta-level moves and jumps that our minds inevitably and inescapably do now gives us the ability to use this transcendent power so that we further develop our higher executive states.
- Secret #4. **A strong sense of vitality and mastery emerges from ownership of our basic neuro-linguistic powers.**

  *A physical and mental sense of vitality, of being alive, and of learned optimism comes from owning, accepting, appreciating, and immersing ourselves in our basic powers of **mind** (thinking, evaluating, believing, valuing, understanding), **emotion** (caring, valuing, somatizing), **speech** (speaking, languaging, symbolizing, narrating), and **behavior** (acting, relating, incorporating, expressing).*

- Secret #5. **Mastery emerges from our power to detect and to set higher level frames.**

  Our neuro-linguistic and neuro-semantic powers blossom even more when we move to a higher level and use our thinking, feeling, speaking, and behaving to set a frame of reference.

- Secret #6. **Whoever sets the frame governs all of the subsequent experiences as determined by that frame.**

  The ultimate power over human experience, states, perception, thought, emotion, skill, etc., derives from the higher level frames under which it operates. To understand the meaning and the dynamics within any thought or feeling state, we have to detect the governing frame.

- We need only to decide to empower our meta-levels of thought-and-feeling (our meta-states) by making sure they serve us well, and then validating, enhancing, highlighting, adding new resources, etc.
- Developing our inner executive means making more explicit, articulate, and defined our *powers* of mind-and-emotion, our languages of the mind, our *response-able* powers. This then strengthens these innate *powers* and enables us to become more and more *conscious* of them.
- It's never too late to set higher and more enhancing frames of references that will make us more resourceful at any age or income level.

The Response-Ability To/For Distinction

Internally:

Responsibility FOR speaks about one's ownership, acknowledgment, and development of one's *power zone.* This describes the domain and phenomenon that we label *Accountability.* It pretty much ends at our nose.

Externally:

Responsibility TO speaks about the giving and receiving of our public powers (speaking and behaving) that we experience with others. This describes the domain that we typically label *Relationships.* We can generate numerous *kinds* of relationships: dependent, independent, inter-dependent, co-dependent.

Figure 3:4

What we Give To and Receive From Each Other

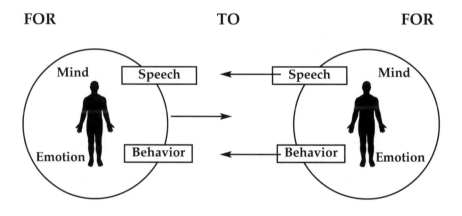

Specialized Terms:

Neuro-linguistic state: The total experience comprising our state of mind, state of body, and state of emotion, described commonly as an attitude or mood.

"As If" Frame: Imagining something and pretending it to be true and then operating from that perspective.

The Seventh Secret
of
Personal Mastery

Secret #7

Installing new executive or Meta-State frames is as simple as linking ideas, thoughts, feelings, etc. together in an "about-ness" relationship.

When mind reflects on something so that it thinks about something in terms of something else, it creates meta-relationships, logical levels, and higher frames. It is as easy as that—as profound as that.

Chapter 4

Commissioning Your Executive

Making Your Higher Mind an Active Boss

*"Your Inner Executive Won't Do You
Any Good Locked Up in the Basement!"*

First we *detect*. The pathway to **personal mastery** (empowering inner executive states) begins with the aim to *detect* the higher levels of mind. We first set out to simply identify the inner executive levels of mind that run the show. We set out to *flush out* the higher frames under which we have lived.

We've noted that our *self-reflexive consciousness* creates these higher states and frames. So, as we get acquainted with our higher levels and the thoughts we entertain *about* our thoughts, we become intimately aware of the very nature of human consciousness that makes it so unique and magical—*self-reflexivity.*

We're Up to Something Big

Reflexivity speaks of a never-ending process. In an infinite regress, we can always think something about whatever we just thought. We can always *make a meta-jump* as we rise above our previous thoughts and emotions. What makes this so unique or magical? This gives us the human power whereby we can *step aside* from ourselves (conceptually) and take stock of things. We do not do this literally, we do it conceptually. We do it at a higher level of mind. And, when we do, something *magical* happens. *Transcendence.* We *transcend* ourselves. We experience states, thoughts, feelings, and experiences that we call *"transcendental"* because they differ *so much* from our "regular" thinking and feeling.

The *meta-jump* to a higher frame-of-reference seems and feels like a *stepping aside* from ourselves. It feels like we have risen to a higher level of consciousness. And, so we have.

Engaging in this kind of *meta-thinking* leads us to higher levels of mind. It leads us to a whole list of functions that occur at *higher* (or meta-levels), hence, the *meta-operations* that provide some of the most **empowering options:**

- meta-feelings (feelings about feelings)
- meta-levels of awareness (higher and broader perspectives)
- meta-communicating (talking about our talk)
- meta-commenting (reflecting on our language use)
- meta-reality structures (our frames-of-reference)
- Meta-States
- and all other meta-level phenomena: what we call "beliefs," "values," "decisions," "self," etc.

These "transcendent" experiences and powers of consciousness move us up into those realms that philosophy and religion have occupied. These address the *existential* questions about life. In this way, our "thinking" constructs not only our primary level *representational maps* of the territory, but also our meta-frames of reference, our maps of maps, and our meta-maps of those maps, etc.

From Detection To Development

After the ability to *detect* your higher frames and states comes the stage for *developing your inner executive* (the subject of the last chapter). *Developing* means **activating** the powers of our "person" (or "personality") which supports our mind-emotion consciousness. This includes the components of "thoughts" (the sensory representational systems of sights, sounds, and sensations, and our symbolic system of words and language).

Developing inner mastery over our executive *states of mind* starts with identifying and detecting our powers of thinking-emoting, speaking, and behaving. Using these core processes allows us to set the frames or mental structures that will bring out our best. When we do this, we *set* the meta-frames that we can then commission to operate as the fabric of our "reality" structure, or matrix. Obviously, knowing how to **set** such frames (what we typically call beliefs, values, decisions, understandings, paradigms, etc.) facilitates personal excellence. It enables us to choose and install the kind of beliefs, values, decisions, etc. that will support our higher states, wisdom, and intelligence.

On to Installation

To fully **take charge** of our higher frames-of-reference, we have to not only *detect and develop*, but also *install and implement*. So we now turn to the subject of **implementation** and **installation**. Let's do so by asking the following questions:

- *How* do we get to these higher level frames—these executive Meta-States installed so that they become truly operational?
- *What processes* will enable us to *install* our inner executive so that it takes charge and uses its frame-setting powers and meta-level decisions?
- *What* cautions do we need to attend to in installing higher frames?
- *Do* I have permission to think differently or to install new programs for being?

Asking these questions acknowledges that we can default on our *inner executive*. We can simply fail to utilize these higher levels of mind in an empowering way. We can also default by letting various childhood frames of reference, understandings, decisions, values, beliefs, etc. run our brain and states. Whenever we regress, we fall back to less mature and more primitive frames. In doing so, we essentially default to limiting beliefs, self-sabotaging ideas, immature conceptual structures, and out-of-date decisions. By way of contrast, **executive development** involves programming ourselves for ongoing growth and learning so that we continually keep updating our highest frames of mind in alignment with our gifts and talents.

In this chapter we describe the following facets of *installation* of Meta-State structures.

1) A One Minute Induction
2) A general pattern for building and installing empowering meta-level structures, frames, executive states, etc.

3) A generative pattern for building an ongoing meta-level format so that you have an inner structure always updating and empowering your frames.

One Minute Induction

We can create a meta-level linkage any time we experience a strong and intense thought-and-emotion (state) and then *bring* that state *to* any other thought, feeling, idea, or experience. This structure arises from simply developing a *feeling* state **about** another state. That alone creates a meta-level linkage.

- You could *feel joy and delight* **about** *learning*.
- You could *feel respect* **about** *expressing your frustration and anger* about something.
- You could *feel calmness and relaxation* **about** a *worry or fear*.
- You could become *respectful and empathetic* in *confronting* an employee or peer.
- You could feel playful about making cold calls on the phone.

This process simply involves *relating* the first experience (or state) *to* the second. When we do that, the first state becomes a higher level *frame of reference* for the second. The first operates in a position of *aboutness* to the second. Our *joy* is *about* the learning.

This significantly differs from merely connecting up two states. Calm *and* anger will dissolve both. Nervous *and* calmly mindful dilutes both states making each of them weaker. NLP describes this merging of two divergent states, the *"Collapsing Anchors."* We do this by accessing two energized mind-body states, set up a trigger or anchor for each of the states, and then "fire off" (or stimulate) both triggers simultaneously. Typically, in collapsing anchors, the two divergent experiences become diluted as the different sets of physiologies interfere and interrupt each other. We essentially cue the nervous system to go into two very divergent states at the same time. More often than not, this initially creates confusion and disorientation because the mind-body cannot feel both tense and relaxed at the same time. As a result, it disperses mental-emotional and neurological energy.

Similarly, this process might remind some readers of yet another NLP pattern called *Chaining States*. Sometimes in the process of moving from one undesired state to a much more desired state, as from depression to happiness, we cannot make the shift in one step. The difference between depression and happiness is too big a jump. Instead, we first veer into a less negative state like frustration, then into a more neutral state (just observing our state), then into a somewhat positive state (interest or curiosity), then into a more positive state, joyful. We do this by simply connecting the two extreme states by a series of ever evolving states that more slowly nudge us in the positive direction.

The process works by accessing the states and anchoring them. We do not *collapse* the states into each other, but *chain* them together so they form an orientation. Later, when we elicit one anchor and state, we elicit the next anchor and state. They have become chained together. This sets up a direction and veers our neurological energy so that it moves along a continuum from negative to neutral to positive.

By way of contrast, in meta-stating we have a very different kind of relationship. We set up the situation so that one state takes *a meta-position* to another. One state stands as the frame for another state. We can do this in both negative and positive ways.

Suppose we start with fear about public speaking *and* then add to that anger that we have to give the speech. This sets two negative emotions as the frame for public speaking. On a more positive note, we could feel calm *and* mindful about public speaking. We could feel embarrassed and shame in hearing a criticism of our work, or we could feel calm and curious about that criticism.

This process described contains a different kind of structure from simply adding one state to another. It does not move out horizontally, "This *plus* That." Instead, it moves up vertically to a higher logical level. It sets one state in *a higher relationship* to another. To do this, we make a meta-move to elicit and apply a resource state **about** something else so that the resource then functions as *the frame of reference*. This specifies the most basic meta-stating process.

To use this process consciously and intentionally and design better experiences—to design engineer resourcefulness and higher states of excellence, we can now specify the process in the following steps.

A One Minute Meta-Stating Pattern

1) Access a state of mind-body fully and completely. Perhaps you would like to bring *Calmness, Confidence, Courage, Commitment, Kindness, Acceptance, etc. to another state.* Name your magic and then fully describe what it looks, sounds, feels, smells, and tastes like. Speak the words that govern the state. What do you have to say to yourself in order to access this state? What memory would assist you? What imagination?

2) Amplify and anchor the state so that it becomes intense and energetic. Increase the internal drama of the state, turn up the distinctive mind-body features that make the state more intense. Then anchor it by simply *connecting* or *associating* some other trigger, a sight, sound, or touch to the state.

3) Analyze the "ecology" (balance and integrity of the entire system) of relating that state to other states and experiences. Would it serve you well? Would it enhance the entire working of the system? Would it enable you to operate with integrity, congruence, and honor?

4) Apply it to another state or experience. With the first state fully *in mind,* think-and-feel *about* the second state *in terms* of the first one. This applies one state to another. It allows us to bring it to bear upon the second. What does calm anger feel like to you? How would gentle courage show itself as you call on that customer?

5) Appropriate it to your future as you imagine having and experiencing this way of thinking-and-feeling and the actions and speech that will emerge from the state in various contexts of your life and out into your immediate future (one to five years from now). This both future paces the new construction and begins to install it.

Outframing Self with Acceptance

When I met Richard, he wanted to have more acceptance about himself. "So you'd like more *self-acceptance*?" I asked him.

"Yes, indeed. I don't accept myself very well. I tend to be very critical and judgmental."

"So you can really give yourself a bad time? You've got that skill really well developed?"

"Yeah, I've got that one mastered!"

"And I bet that really enables you to succeed at work, achieving the things you want to achieve and enabling others to feel comfortable in your presence."

"Not at all. It makes everything harder. I constantly worry about what people think of me and fear that customers won't like me. I just don't like living this way."

"Good. So you're ready to utter an emphatic and definitive 'No' to that old frame of mind about self-judgment?"

"Yes, I am."

"So, Richard, is there anything that you just nicely **accept** with a sense of *welcoming it with open arms*? Have you ever just accepted and welcomed and enjoyed something simple like a sunset, or walking through the grass in the summertime in your bare feet, or the purring of a kitten?"

"Sure."

"Then just for a moment, go back to one of those specific times when you knew the experience of acceptance—and, in your mind, just step back into that experience so that you see what you saw then … noticing whether it was in color or not, and the closeness of your pictures … and hear what you heard then … noticing the quality and nature of the sounds … and also the words that you said to yourself, if any, during that time so that even now you can *fully and completely feel that acceptance* …

"You can do that?" I asked.

"Sure."

"And you can notice the breathing of acceptance ... the posture of it, the face and eyes of acceptance ... the full presence of yourself when you *feel accepting*...?"

"Uh huh. I can."

"And if you had this even more ... just allowing the feelings of acceptance to increase and grow in just the way you would like it ... now ... and you *feel this* completely when you think about yourself ... notice just how that would change things making you more resourceful ... because you can *accept* that, can you not? And I wonder what it is like now to fully experience that sense of acceptance if you felt this completely about yourself as a human being ... Isn't that nice? And wouldn't that be a marvellous way to move through the world ... tomorrow ... at work ... with friends? But then again, you might not want to *feel this resourceful* ... oh, you do?"

The Seventh Secret for Personal Mastery

With these powers of mind, we can now articulate the next governing principle that reveals the secrets for truly taking charge of your mind and life.

Secret #7

Installing new executive or meta-state frames is as simple as linking ideas, thoughts, feelings, etc. together in an "about-ness" relationship.

When mind reflects on something so that it thinks about something in terms of something else, it creates meta-relationships, logical levels, and higher frames. It is as easy as that—as profound as that.

Your First Executive Decision

The first executive state development that I did with Joel involved accessing his *willingness* to imagine new possibilities about his personal powers.

"Would you be interested in discovering how to expand your own sense of personal power? Would you like to de-commission all of your own buttons that give power to others to play your keyboard?

"Yes, I would. That would be great!"

"So you'd like that?" I asked again, prodding him a bit.

"Yes. Of course."

"Are you really open to this idea?"

"Are you kidding? Of course I am."

"How much *willingness* do you feel right now about that?"

"A lot."

"Like a 7 on a scale of 10?"

"More like 9."

"Great. So if you felt all of that *willingness* about owning and re-owning your personal powers so fully and completely that you give that power away to others very carefully, to people who you trust ... what would that be like for you?"

Designing and Installing Empowering Executive States

Actually, none of this represents anything new, different, or strange in terms of human experiences. From childhood, all of us have been building and installing higher mental levels. Doing so simply describes the operations of human consciousness. All of us have set up multiple frames of mind which then govern our every-day primary states. This process does not describe an esoteric strange process that only gurus or geniuses use. We all do it. And, we all do it all of the time.

- Whenever we bring any significant thought-or-emotion to bear on any other state, we generate a Meta-State.
- *Whenever* we *let* the thoughts-and-emotions of others, of our culture, of mass media, of a friend or counselor to bear upon our thinking-emoting, we create a higher level frame.
- *Whenever* we think about something *in terms of* some other idea, we set a higher executive frame of mind. It's all built

out of the same stuff—*thoughts-and-emotions*. It's built from how we *think and emote*.

This development of our executive states operates according to the *"Bear in Mind"* principle.

- *Bearing in mind* that I expect you to mind yourself at the restaurant tonight ...
- *Bearing in mind* that if you don't finish this job on time, your job will be on the line ...
- I hope you *bear in mind* that 'Quality is Job 1' around here.

If you open your ears, I think you will be surprised at how often in a day's time you will hear or read this phrase: "bearing this in mind," "that has no bearing on what I'm saying."

We cannot help but to *bring* some thoughts and feelings to *bear upon* and *set the frame* for other thoughts and feelings. This simply describes how we can use our thoughts and feelings in relation to other states of consciousness. Nor is this way of talking strange. Once you begin to detect meta-levels and meta-states, you will discover them all around you. You will hear people conversationally meta-stating all of the time.

- *With that in mind* I now want you to really apply yourself to this job ...
- *Above and beyond* those things, just remember to keep the bottom-line in mind as you negotiate with him next week, okay?
- Now *realizing the power of this model,* you can begin to use it in your everyday life, can you not?

The power for doing this, and the process for doing it, simply lies within the very process of how our human minds work. In fact, we cannot *not* meta-state ourselves or others. Yet we can do something new and creative, namely, we can use this process consciously. We can intentionally make sure that we apply high level values and criteria in line with our visions so that we set frames that we will find empowering, enhancing, and ecological as we generate our higher levels.

Meta-Stating Consciously

The following process offers a more extensive meta-stating pattern and yet general enough to apply to all of the higher states. This pattern puts into your hands a process by which you can build up *executive states* that will serve you in positive and empowering ways. As you learn to *meta-state* yourself in this way, you will find yourself able to design specific executive states for yourself. This will give you the ability to custom-make executive states and make them most appropriate for yourself. With this process then you can engage in a kind of "human design engineering" (Alfred Korzybski).

1) Identify a Positive and Empowering Executive State that you would like to Experience

Would you like courage, proactivity, self-esteem, forgiveness, presence of mind, or seeing opportunities? What higher level executive state would you like?

Take a moment to step back from yourself. As you now move to a meta-position of just witnessing and observing yourself, consider what resourceful meta-states you would like to have as part of your "model of the world," as part of your repertoire for moving through the world. As you do, keep asking yourself:

- "What state-upon-a-state (thought-and-feelings *about* thoughts-and-feelings) do I want to have as a resource?"

Make a list of states, moods, emotions, attitudes, dispositions, etc. that you would like to have as part of your personal "programming." Continue to enrich and expand this list as you talk with people, read biographies of people who have made a difference in the world, go to the movies, interact with exceptional people, etc. What other higher level states of mind-and-emotion would you like?

After you have made your list, identify the primary states from the meta-level states. This will have to do primarily with the layered-ness and complexity of the higher levels and the fact that they reference other internal thoughts-and-feelings. Primary states, by way of contrast, have a simplicity and typically reference things "out there" that we can detect with our empirical senses.
[See Appendix B for a list of distinctions between these kinds of states.]

2) Quality Design the Executive State
Because a poorly designed meta-level state or frame will work against us, and to our detriment, we need to aim specifically to format the meta-level executive state so that it meets the conditions of being well-formed.

Well-formed conditions in outcome designing simply refers to those qualities that make for smart goal-setting. On the surface, "setting goals" sounds like an easy and simple thing to do. It is not. If it were so easy most people would not have so much difficulty with goal-setting and goal fulfillment. The process of moving from present state to some desired state necessitates clarity of both states, the resources to bridge from one to the other, and a supporting structure that enables one to negotiate the steps and stages, the challenges and traps along the way.

The NLP Well-Formed Outcomes pattern specifies several key factors that play an enabling and contributing role. Together these enable us to identify what we want so that we can then organize our responses and take definite and positive steps to translating our desires and hopes into reality. This also provides an informed way to work with someone to facilitate their process of attaining a desired objective.

Key Criteria That Make an Outcome Well-formed
1) *State it in the positive.* Specifically describe what you *want*. Avoid writing goals that describe what you do **not** want. "I do *not* want to be judgmental." Negation ("not") as a command typically first *evokes* the very thing it then seeks to negate. "Don't think about Elvis Presley." "Don't think about using your wisdom to live life more graciously." "I don't want to be like dad."

Rather, describe what you do want. "If you weren't like your dad, how would you be acting, thinking, relating, etc.?" "If you didn't have this problem occurring, what would you have occurring?" If we had a video-recording of your goal, what would we see and hear?

Describing what you do *not* want may give your brain information about what to avoid but will not provide any specific details about what to go after.

2) **State what lies within your area of control or response.** A statement like, "I want others to like me" does not describe anything that you can *actually do.* Instead, it puts your goal at the disposal of others. As a result, *that* goal will **disempower you.** State things that you can **initiate** and **maintain**, things within your ability to respond in your power zone. What specific actions could you take this week to either reduce your difficulty or to eliminate it altogether? What one thing could you do today that would move you in that direction?

3) **Contextualize.** Define and emphasize the specific environment, context, and situation needed to reach your goal. Don't write, "I want to lose weight." State specifically how much weight to lose (i.e. 10 pounds within two months). This gives your brain information about what to do. Identify the place, environment, relationship, time, space, etc. for this new way of thinking-feeling, behaving, talking, and so on. Finally, "Where don't you want this behavior?"

4) **State in the outcome sensory-based words.** Describe specifically and precisely what someone would see, hear, and feel. Whenever you use an abstract or vague word, specify the behaviors that someone could video-tape. Rather than, "I want to become charismatic in relating to people," write, "I want to smile, warmly greet people with a handshake and use their name ..." In asking for see-hear-feel language, over and over, it eventually re-trains us to think in terms of behavioral evidences. This makes our goals more real and less abstract or vague.

5) **State the outcome in bite-size steps and stages.** Chunk the outcomes down to the size that becomes do-able. Otherwise the goal could feel overwhelming. Not, "I will write a book." but "I will write two pages every day." Not, "I will lose 50 pounds," but "I will eat 10 fewer bites per meal."

6) **Load up your description with the personal resources that will specify how to engage in the goal process.** What resources will you need in order to make your dream a reality? More confidence in your ability to speak in public? Then write that as a sub-goal. As you think about living out this new objective in the next few weeks, what other resources do you need? What about assertiveness, resilience, confidence, the ability to look up information and check out things for yourself, reality testing, relaxation, etc.?

7) **Check for ecology.** Does this goal fit in with all of your other goals, values, and overall functioning? Do any "parts" of yourself object to this desired outcome? Go inside and check to see if this goal is acceptable to all the parts of yourself.

8) **Specify evidence for fulfillment.** How will you know, in addition to the previous criteria, when you have reached your goal? Make sure you have specific and precise evidence for this.

Using these criteria, either with yourself or with others, provides us with a way to quality-check our objectives. This enables us to form our desired outcomes so that we code and map them in a well-formed way about the future we want to create. Smart goal-setting will take us where we desire to go.

Figure 4:1

Well Formedness in Desired Outcomes	• State in the positive • State what you can do • Contextualize • State in sensory-based words • State in bite-size steps and stages • Load up with resources • Check for ecology • Specify evidence for fulfillment

Figure 4:2

Questions

- Does this state have *enough vividness* for you to elicit it?
- As you describe it, does it provide *enough process information* so that you know *what to do?*
- Do these feel like *small enough pieces* so that you can take each step?
- Do you have *clarity* about the *steps and stages* of the process?
- Can you specify *the evidence* that you have accessed the Meta-State?
- What words will you say to yourself?

Un-Energized Thoughts

While "thoughts" play the most crucial role in our *states of consciousness,* we know that not every "thought" will induce a state. This realization has numerous implications. Apparently, we can "think" in such ways that the "thinking" does not evoke and activate a mind-body state. What explains this? How does this work?

Earlier I noted that we induce or *elicit* a state in ourselves and others by means of the two royal roads to state—internal representations (mind) and physiology (body). Yet mere representation and even mere physiology must reach a certain amplitude in order to create the holistic result of a "state." This means that state *induction* doesn't happen automatically apart from regard to *the quality* and *intensity* of the thought.

We can "think" in certain ways that fail to generate the corresponding state. If we think in un-energized ways, dissociatedly, analytically, doubtfully, etc., we will not go into state. Those *kinds of thoughts* do not have enough "juice" or energy, to induce state. Or, to think about this in terms of frames—setting a frame of dissociation, mere analysis, doubt, etc. over our thought reduces its power and prevents it from inducing much of a state.

What kind of thoughts will induce, access, and/or create a full-fledged neuro-linguistic state? Thoughts that have energy and power. Intense thoughts with enough amplitude will move us. Thoughts that we have energized and empowered. Having specified this in terms of a well-formed and strongly desired outcome, we can think about the well-formed pattern which also enables us to energize our thinking. So, beginning with the content of your thoughts, use the following processes to energize it.

- *Make it vivid!* Make sure that you have a set of rich representations with plenty of graphic details.
- *Give it enough completeness* so that when you think about it, you begin to feel compelled.
- *Value it.* Give it significant meaning so that you feel it as relevant and important.
- *Desire it.* Make sure that you turn up your passion for this outcome. Fan your passions and wants for it so that you have many reasons for desiring it.
- *Language it.* State this outcome using the kind of words and language forms that give it a strong, coherent form that you find compelling.
- *Repeat it.* Use the power of repetition to "run those neuro-pathways" until your mind quickly and automatically goes to this outcome. Do so until it habituates as a "program" in your very neurology.
- *Act on it.* Do something about this outcome or thought so that you begin to connect it to your physiology and neurology. The actions, gestures, responses, and behaviors that you use to flesh it out will make it more real and present for you.

3) Sequence the overall experiential state together. Glue the Executive States together using your most compelling linguistics. Once you have all of the parts and pieces of thoughts, emotions, awarenesses, concepts, etc. then create some empowering and compelling linguistics to glue the meta-states together for yourself. Meta-level states of consciousness involve languaged constructions that order our world of meaning.

Words and languaged expressions (poetry, proverbs, stories, narratives, etc.) *glue* things together. Nor do the words (as mental constructions) have to represent anything real, rational, or even accurate. The nervous system and neuro-circuits of human processing and experiencing are not so constrained. We do not have an innate Quality Control program for our thinking or emoting. This, by the way, explains why and how we can get delusional, deceptive, erroneous, irrational, crazy, and have really weird things installed in our minds-bodies and *feel them as "real."* Indeed, at the level of neurology, they are real. They exist and operate as "real" maps that govern our thoughts, feelings, somatic responses, etc. But as maps, they do not accurately or usefully reflect the territory—and so lack *"reality"* at that level.

This explains the power of a language model like the Meta-Model (Bandler and Grinder, 1975; Hall, 1998) for reality testing language as well as language elegance. When we *question the lack of specificity or fluffiness* of words, we elicit in ourselves or another more precision and clarity of thought. And clarity of thought gives us the power to make things happen.

To do this, think about it as the process of *Video-Thinking.* Begin with the words that a person offers and *track immediately* from those terms without adding any of your understandings, memories, or references to *an imaginary mental screen.* Pretend that you will turn the words into a mental motion picture. Whenever you have an unspecific term (i.e. reject, hurt, they, men, etc.), simply ask for clarification. "How did he *reject* your idea?" "How did they feel *hurt?*" "What men specifically?" This *indexes* the referents. It enables us to make a clearer picture of what the person is describing.

In NLP, we call these kinds of questions *"challenges for well-formedness."* By inquiring about a person's language use, we transform confusing and ill-formed statements into more clear and precise descriptions. [Appendix E provides a brief overview of the Meta-Model.]

Utilizing this understanding about how we use language in the first place to create our mental maps enables us to construct maps for higher level experiences like resilience, proactivity, self-esteem, etc. We can now also use statements that tie together ideas about cause-effect, meaning, identity, etc. to sequence "thinking" at these higher levels. Doing this empowers us to tell our brain where to go (conceptually), what to think, and what frames to build.

Simply use language in these elegant ways until you find *just* the right words for yourself—words that *compel* you. How will you know that you have the right words? When they pull on your neurology and induce you into the desired state.

Such languaged sequences partake of the nature of what we call "hypnotic language." Here the hypnotic languaging patterns offer a great resource in your linguistic constructions. When you have the words, *write out a Executive State Induction.*

- What words put this meta-state together for you?
- How else can you express this meta-level structure of state-on-state that will make this even more entrancing, compelling, and attractive?

4) Check and eliminate incongruencies in Your Meta-Level Frames

Identifying and designing a meta-level frame of reference may create conflict, antagonism, and/or tension between other frames (beliefs, values, decisions, understandings, etc.).

We can check for incongruencies by utilizing two *technologies of balance*—running an ecology check on the new frame and by future pacing it. Both of these processes enable us to discover and flush out any internal conflicts. We *run an ecology check* by moving to a meta-position and asking within:

- Does any part of me object to this frame of reference?
- Do I sense any internal objection to using this new orientation?

- Does this new frame make for health, balance, and well-being in the long run?"

We *future pace* the new frame by imagining ourselves moving out into tomorrow and next week and next year with the new frame and notice how it affects the other facets of our lives.

We can also check for internal objections to a newly designed executive state construction by noticing any responses of acceptance and/or rejection, congruency and incongruency that we have in response to it. First identify something that you fully and completely *accept*. As you think about it and imagine it fully, just notice the internal kinesthetic signals of *acceptance*. Next, identify something that you reject. Consider something about which you have no question or hesitancy in rejecting. Once you do, again, just notice the internal kinesthetic signals of *rejection*.

Now that you have identified and brought into awareness your kinesthetic signals that cue you about acceptance and rejection, fully imagine the executive state that you have designed. Step into it completely. Notice if you sense any *rejection* about it.

Repeat this same process with regard to the experiences of *congruency and incongruency*. Then once you have brought into awareness your kinesthetic cues for each, step back into the experience of your designed engineered Executive State to check for how well it fits into the rest of your values and beliefs.

If you find some incongruency, you can eliminate it by *outframing* it with an integrating higher frame or by reframing its positive intention. We reframe the objection as we consider internal objections as providing highly useful feedback about our overall programming. By then building the insights of the objection into the Executive State, we can positively validate the objection and temper the new frame.

Suppose, for example, that in building up the meta-state of being "un-insultable," a part of you thinks that this *means* that you will just ignore people and become hard-headed and stubborn, and that you'll lose the ability to listen fully. That's a significant objection. And it's positive intention stands out pretty clearly. It wants to make sure that you connect with people and pay attention and not miss significant feedback. So build those thoughts-and-feelings as states and resources into the executive frame of being "un-insultable." Bring *thoughtful, considerate,* and *understanding* to bear upon the primary state of receiving an insult ... so that along with *non-personalizing, strong sense of self, self-esteem,* etc., the quality of being Un-Insultable doesn't lose its human touch.

5) Sequence the pieces and parts in order to rehearse the process.
Complexity arises in the executive states due to how we layer one thought-feeling upon another. As a consequence, to install these meta-level states, we need to sequence the primary states so that they build up the strategy. This will create the format for the higher level state. Upon doing that, we then need to only rehearse the pieces individually and together until they form an efficient sequence.

For example, I may first sequence my *acceptance* of my fear, and then my *excitement* about a *dream* until that generates a sense of *boldness* in spite of the fear, and then move to accessing *a reality oriented state* of taking small but definitive steps to making the goal real, and then feel a strong sense of *"Yes!"* to this decision.

This need to rehearse identifies another difference between primary states and meta-states. Because consciousness becomes layered with levels of linguistics and needs to have just the right sequencing, typically we need to *abundantly rehearse* the executive state that we want to coalesce into a seamless unit. Frequently, you may want to access your creative part, or your dream part, and give it the task of creating, inventing, and dreaming a dream of this new process.

- When you access this executive state, what comes first? Then next? And after that?
- How many times do you need to repeat this so that it becomes automatic?

6) Step into the executive meta-level state in order to experience it fully.
This experiential step allows us to expand our consciousness so that we take a moment to notice precisely how the executive state

will now drive our lower primary states in new and different ways. As you step into the newly constructed state, imagine using this way of thinking-and-feeling as you move through life day by day, with business associates, personal relationships, etc.

- As you experience this executive state, how does it transform things?
- How does it *set the frame* for your life and response?
- What other effects will result from this resource?
- How will this work out ten years from now?

7) Future pace the executive state.

What specific environments would you like to imagine yourself moving into with this new way of being? Fully imagine this state vividly as you *step into* those future contexts with this new way of thinking and feeling. Feel the transformation as you watch the new responses that it elicits in others. Do this with intensity knowing that this furthers the *installation* process for the new executive state.

Where do you especially want to have this way of referencing, giving meaning, thinking, feeling, and responding? Where else?

8) Symbolize your Executive State.

Allow yourself to relax and access a light trance state so that your conscious mind can provide you with some symbol of your meta-state: a picture, word, sound, diagram, proverb, koan, riddle, etc.

- What picture or icon comes to mind about this whole meta-level structuring of consciousness?
- What metaphor or song or proverb could you use to summarize it?
- Where in your body would you want to store this icon inside of you?

A Meta-level Structure For Continual Improvement and Updating

Not long ago Edwards Deming popularized, in the business context, the whole idea of *quality control and development by means of continual improvement.* The simplicity of this idea empowered its profundity. It simply involved a commitment to continual (daily, weekly, monthly, yearly) *improvement* at the most minute levels—1% improvement, 2% improvement. If a person, business, or company attained a 1% improvement every month, this would amount to 12% every year.

A willingness to commit oneself to small, incremental improvements on a regular basis in terms of one's personality powers, ongoing development, new skill acquisition, etc. likewise has profound effects over the long run. Consider the meta-level structure of this:

A willingness to *commit* oneself to **ongoing improvement**.

To build this into your mind and personality as an executive state, a state *meta* to your everyday states, would provide for you a generative frame of reference for continual self-improvement and enhancement. As a meta-level pattern or frame, it provides an automatic process and inner structure for always updating and empowering your frames and meta-states.

How do we build and install this one? Begin the process by personalizing your own answers to the following questions.

> 1) *What* would you have to *believe* about yourself, personal growth and development, ongoing improvement, incremental increase, etc., in order to make the ideas more solid, real, and compelling in your life?
> 2) *What values* would you have to deem as critically important and highly significant to you as a person in order to support the enhancing beliefs of #1?
> 3) *What self-definitions* and identity reframes would you need to create in order to allow yourself to increasingly become the kind of person with this kind of executive program?
> 4) *How* could you best amplify and make more compelling these meta-level ideas?
> 5) *What process* of repetition, learning, and installation would best assist you in getting these beliefs, values, and self-definitions deeply incorporated into your very neurology?
> 6) *What process* would you prefer for making a commitment to this way of thinking-and-feeling about yourself and life?

7) *Describe* fully and completely, using your creative imagination, *the future You* who has this program and how it manifests itself on a day by day basis.

8) Do you have anything left that might stop you from fully visualizing yourself in the future?

Summary

- *Installing* Executive States enables us to "run our own brain" and manage our own states and meta-states in new and more profoundly powerful ways.
- We can intentionally use the two royal roads to state—the things we internally *represent* in our mind and *how* we use our body and neurology to build up higher level states.
- Meta-State *installation* does not involve anything more than the normal use of consciousness. We need only to self-reflexively **bring something to bear on something else.**
- With this "Bear in Mind" principle in mind, what do you *bear in mind* when you move through everyday life? What would you like to *bear in mind?*
- How much do you now *appreciate* your ability to *intentionally* install new frames for personal *effectiveness?* Did you hear all of the meta-levels in that question?
- **The Seventh Secret for personal mastery: installing new executive or Meta-State frames, is as simple as linking ideas, thoughts, feelings, etc. together in an "aboutness" relationship.** When your mind reflects on something so that it thinks about something in terms of something else, it creates meta-relationships, logical levels, and higher frames. It is as easy as that—as profound as that.

Chapter 5

Your Executive "Self"

Constructing A Self You Can Live With

We couldn't get very far without a self....
The Self appears to be one of the most important
contents of consciousness.
(Mihaly Csikszentmihalyi)

If you have read this far and have been *practicing the personal mastery principles*, then you know how to *Detect* higher levels of mind, how to *Develop* those executive functions so that they enhance your life, and how to *Design and Install* new executive, or meta-states, at will.

Right?

If not, stop. Go back. Read, learn, practice. You do want **Personal Mastery**, do you not? Good.

The Executive State called "Self"

While every state of mind-and-feeling sends you upward and enables you to build higher frames of mind, there's hardly a frame that operates more pervasively and powerfully than the frame we call "self." Every meta-state structure involves an executive level, and the higher you move up (conceptually), the higher the frame and therefore more powerful. Yet some *concepts* carry a lot more semantic weight. Nothing illustrates this more than the concepts we build about ourselves.

We all begin very early in developing our *"sense of self."* At first, we have only a *felt sense*. We have only a totally *kinesthetic sense* which is governed entirely by a few basic conditions: warmth, comfort, nourishment, touch. If we could put into words our consciousness, we are sorting for only these things. "Do I feel warm, comfortable, fed, and stroked?"

Self, first of all emerges simply from the fact of our existence and our life as a breathing, living, sentient (aware) being. At the primary level, this is *who and what we are.* Yet while that definition begins the game, it becomes entirely inadequate when *mind* starts jumping levels. Wouldn't you know it!

With mind *reflecting* on our life and experience, we begin *the existential search* for identity, selfhood, beingness (ontology), destiny, purpose, mission, spirituality, etc. We become *self*-conscious in the truest sense. We become aware of ourselves as a *Self.* And this gives birth to all kinds of *self*-concepts.

Will the Real Me Please Stand Up?

How many *selves* do you have? How many *selves* does your culture create? It all depends upon how many *concepts* you receive and create *about* yourself. Begin with the following list:

- Self-Confidence: confidence in yourself about your skills and abilities (what you can *do*).
- Self-Esteem: the value and worth that you give to your *idea* (concept) of yourself as a Person.
- Self-Efficacy: the power and effectiveness you acknowledge and feel regarding your ability to use your mind, reckon with reality, and cope effectively.
- Self-Image: the overall picture, image, or concept you hold about yourself.
- Social Self: your sense of yourself in relation to your social world, community, peers, race, etc.
- Career Self: your sense of self in terms of your job and what you do for a livelihood.
- Embodied Self: sense of self within our bodies, our "body image," feelings of like/dislike regarding shape, weight, size, etc.
- Spiritual Self: sense of self as a being with a "soul" or "spirit" that transcends the body, beliefs and ideas about beingness before and/or after embodiment.
- Musical Self

- Mechanical Self
- Mathematical Self
- Financial Self
- Recreational Self
- Sexual Self: gender, sexuality, etc.
- Racial Self

And the list goes on. We can have as many *selves* as we have *concepts* (ideas) *about* ourselves. And we have layers of Selves *in a self-reflexive system.* The following diagram sorts out *Self* as actor, doer, and experiencer at the primary level (Self[1]), then *Self* as our thoughts-and-feelings of *observing and witnessing* to ourselves (Self[2] in relation to Self[1]). Then *Self* as *deciding and directing* Selves[1 & 2] (Self[3]).

Now what do you think of all of that? Oops, that just called *Self[4]* into being! Now we have a *Self* as a theorizer of our other selves. And so it goes on. In using this terminology, Self[1], Self[2], Self[3], etc., I have used a shorthand version for saying, "*I* operating at level one, level two, level three, etc."

Figure 5:1

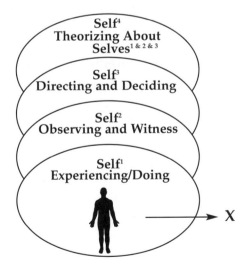

Me and My Multiple Selves

The ability to *reflect back* on previous thoughts-and-feelings endows us with a very powerful and unique ability—one that can make life gloriously delightful or a living hell. Every time we think or feel something *about* ourselves, every time we construct a concept about human beings, males/females, competency and skills, worth and personhood, race, work, intelligence, relationships, etc.—we build yet another meta-level executive frame of mind. We build yet another layer of complexity into our self-concepts and self-definition.

All of this starts out in such an innocent way. In the beginning of our self-definitions, we simply take *the responses* of caretakers and peers and construct a map about our *self*. In this way, the first messages of parents, other kids, and television *set the frame* for how we define ourselves. Pretty scary stuff, huh?

At that stage, our *self* understandings simply involved *representations* of what we were told, as well as *felt sensations* of being loved and nurtured and/or punished and rejected. Piaget and Erikson pioneered this field of child development and the mental (cognitive) and social stages that we experience. What messages did you hear?

"You are so precious and adorable!"
"Bad baby! Why can't you be a good baby?"
"What's wrong with you? You are such a bother!"

Then we get *conceptual*. We all do. We begin asking higher level questions that bring various "concepts" to bear upon our primary sense of self:

"What does this *mean* about me?"
"What *kind* of a person am I?"
"What *hope* do I have in life?"
"Do people like me or not, trust me or not?"
"What am I good at?"
"Do I have value?"
"What is my value and worth based upon?"

Self-Reflection on Your Executive Frames of "Self"

With this analysis of the higher frame of mind about "self," what kind of a *"self"* have you built? Do you like that construction? Does it serve you well? What *self* concepts have you layered upon your sense of self regarding your value and worth as a person (self-esteem), your confidence and competency about skills (self-confidence), your sense of competency and effectiveness in using your mind to cope (self-efficacy), your sense of acceptance by others (social self), etc.?

Even at the cellular level, our autonomic nervous system and immune system has to discern between *"me" and "not me."* Distinguishing the boundaries between self and other also describes several of the developmental stages that we negotiate as we break free from the dependency states and individualize. We do so in order to become an autonomous self, to become *ourselves.* As we become more independent, we individualize to discover our thoughts and emotions, our values and beliefs, our passions and commitments, our skills and way in life.

This then becomes the foundation for *inter-dependency.* With a strong sense of self, we can then *relate* to others and maintain our self-definition. Without a strong sense of *me* and *not me*, we could easily lose our self-constructions in relationship to someone with a strong and influential sense of self. We could "lose ourselves" in his or her presence. We could forget "who we are," what we like and dislike, what we value and dis-value.

At the other extreme we find people with such narrow and rigid boundaries that their mental-emotional world hardly allows for another *self* to exist. We describe this as narcissism from the Greek myth of Narcissus who fell in love with his reflection in a pool. A narcissistic mapping of self primarily refers to lacking room in one's mind for others, for the needs and values of others, etc. And that eliminates the basis for empathy and compassion.

Self boundaries extend and enclose as we *define* and *identify* with people, events, objects, and ideas. The word "cathexis" describes this. It refers to how we *open up our ego boundaries of self* (me, mine) to another person (my friend, my child, my mate), experience (I'm a skier, teacher, student, lover, parent), object (my car, my house, my clothes), and ideas (I'm a republican, democrat, Catholic, Buddhist, etc.). We *open up* (conceptually) to let these things become part of our *self-definition*.

> How do you define yourself? Who are you? What do you believe? What do you value? What do you do? Who are you connected to? What do you expect? What do you want? What have you been through? What groups do you belong to?

Typically, we use these kinds of things to *define* ourselves. At the beginning of modern psychology, William James (1890) defined Self in terms of identifications and *ownership*.

> "A man's Self is the sum-total of all that he can call his, not only his body, and his psychic powers, but his clothes and his house, his wife and children, his ancestors and friends, his reputation and works, his land and horse and yacht and bank account."

How much do the *things* you *own* define you? Are you a home owner or a renter? What about your ownership of other things in your life, from the car you drive, the music you prefer, to the things you collect or keep? It could be your retirement plan, stocks, beliefs, church, political party, clothes, just about anything.

As a symbolic-class of life, *we live on and for symbols*. We have to. We have no preprogrammed "instinctual" knowledge, so we develop and live through concepts. But this can become pathologically destructive if we misuse symbols.

How do we do that? By forgetting that they are but symbols—maps *about* the territory, and not "real" in an external way. Conversely, when we maintain *consciousness of mapping*, we can hold our mental mapping in a tentative and provisional way. To forget this is to confuse map and territory, and to then assume that our symbols are real. That's when we misuse them and begin treat our concepts with an absoluteness and "allness" that they cannot bear.

Since our self-definition determines the quality of our life, danger arises when we identify our *self* with our symbols. To do so is to become dependent on those symbols.

Identity and Identification

From our experience as a living, breathing being (a primary state) to all of our ideas (concepts) of *self* (a meta-state), we layer thoughts and feelings upon thoughts and feelings until we develop very complex self-definitions. We differentiate ourselves from others, develop ego boundaries, and then open those boundaries up to bring various things, people, ideas, etc. into our *self* world. We use experience, relationships, status, possessions, feelings, ownership, etc. to define ourselves.

Yet *how* we do this self-defining makes all the difference in the world.

Do we do it with awareness that we are *self*-constructors, that we invent our identities, that "identity" is not real externally, and that we can reinvent ourselves whenever we so choose? Or, do we think that "who we are" is fated by genes and culture? Do we think that our race determines us? Our gender? Our culture? Our experiences? Do we forget that *we developed our self-definitions?* Do we confuse our "self" with our mapping of self?

Alfred Korzybski (1933/1994) developed neuro-linguistic training in order to teach people to stop **identifying** map and territory. Map differs from territory. It provides us with only a symbolic representation of what actually exists. When we **confuse** map and territory, we confuse two very different levels—the primary level and all meta-levels. We then get disoriented. We attribute a false concreteness and reality to our *ideas and concepts!*

Korzybski called this **identification** and targeted it as the source and heart of ineffectiveness. He called it "unsanity." Playing off of "sanity" as "good adjustment" to what exists and "insanity" as a total break with reality, *unsanity* refers to a mixed state wherein we can get through life, but not without lots of stress and strain. The map that we follow will eventually guide us to our destination, or at least get us pretty close, yet it takes us over all kinds of unnecessary obstacles or through long and out-of-the-way detours, or leaves us full of nerves ("neurotic") in the process.

Identification does this. When we *identify* our "self" with anything—we jump to a totally unfeasible conclusion that we "are"

the "same" as the identification. This then *deletes* from our awareness everything that we "are," and typically creates all kinds of
limitations. Whatever you say you "are," you *are* so much more
than that. If we attach self to power, wealth, status, recognition,
achievement, or beauty, we create an ill-conceived ego that will
relentlessly pursue its identifications, often to the neglect of other
facets (health, relationships, etc.).

Csikszentmihalyi (1993) writes,

> "The problem is that the more the ego becomes identified
> with symbols outside the self the more vulnerable it
> becomes." (p. 79)

What ideas do you use as your central representations? How
much psychic energy do you invest into those ideas? Is your
investment of that energy appropriate to the symbol?

By way of contrast, differentiating enables us to create a much
more expansive and empowering self-map. This enables us to *dis-
identify* with things.

- — I think and have thoughts, but I am more than my
  thoughts.
- — I feel and emote (have emotions), but I'm more than the
  emotions that ebb and flow within me.
- — I speak and use language, but I'm more than the words
  I utter.
- — I act and respond, but I'm more than my behaviors.
- — I engage in specific tasks, job, activities, adventures, but
  I am more than what I do. No action or job totally
  defines who I am.
- — I experience life as a male or female, yet I am more than
  my gender.
- — I experience sexual thoughts and feelings, I engage in
  sexual activities, yet I am more than my sexuality.
- — I grew up in a certain location and within a certain coun-
  try, yet I am more than a member of that town, country,
  or nationality.

— I believe certain things about myself, people, the world, and yet I am more than whatever beliefs I hold at this moment.

Your Executive "Core" Self

We cannot do without this imaginary created entity which we call *"Self."* We will, and cannot avoid, creating a meta-level understanding of our self. Given that, we now ask: Is my self ill-conceived or well-conceived? What central organizing principle do I want to build my self around? Fame or fortune? Love or security? Achievement or relationships? To be loved or feared?

What kind of mental-and-emotional frames of reference (executive states) have you created for your sense of self? How well do these frames serve you? Do you need to revisit the *self-defining* that you've engaged in and update it so that you have a more enhancing way of mapping your Self?

Personal mastery begins as we realize that whatever we have mapped about ourselves, all of our ideas about *self* are just that— ideas, *mental maps*. It's a conceptual understanding that governs your everyday experiences. Now bring *acceptance, appreciation, and esteem* to bear upon your felt sense of yourself as a living, breathing human being. Take time to access and amplify each of these three most powerful resources:

Acceptance: acknowledgment and welcoming of what is without judgment or endorsement, just witnessing and bringing into your awareness that you exist and have powers of mind, emotion, speech, and behavior.

Appreciation: a gentle openness that finds simple delights and pleasure in existence, a warm welcoming that can magically find values in the simplest of things.

Esteem: the feeling of valuing something highly as important, significant, and worthwhile. The sense of awe and honor at the value and marvel of something to be held as precious.

Once you have fully accessed these resources, now *apply* them to your "sense of self" as a human being. Let acceptance first support and acknowledge your humanness. Say it out loud. "I accept myself fully and completely with all of my fallibilities." Feel the warming and welcoming feelings of accepting yourself as a *self*, as a human being.

Next, apply appreciation to your *self*. Nourish and validate with appreciation yourself with your powers and potentials. What can you appreciate about yourself? As you take the feelings of appreciation and engulf your sense of yourself with those ... let specific appreciations emerge in your awareness.

Finally, *esteem* self highly as having worth, value, and dignity in an unconditional way—as your birthright for being human. This separates and distinguishes your *Self* as a doer (your skills and competence, self-confidence) from a human being (yourself as a person).

You can now let this *highly valued, unconditional self-worth and dignity* operate as your Core Self—the you beyond the specific conditions and environments of your life. Then, with a dignity that cannot be taken away from you, an honor that exists as a human being, you can now executively decide *how* you want to run your thinking and emoting, *how* you want to speak and behave, the kind of person you want to become, the kind of experiences you want to enjoy, etc.

Constructing Self-Acceptance

"Is there anything that occurs which you could get frustrated or irritated about, but instead of going there, you just accept it as something that happens? However you pull it off, you just let it be without giving it much thought or emotion? It could be the weather—when its raining and you'd prefer a clear sky. Something like that.

"Yes, the weather. I pretty much just accept it."

"Good. So now feel what you feel when you experience what you call *acceptance*, and just experience it for a minute or so. Notice that it is not resignation, nor is it endorsement, or approval. You just think-and-feel, 'This is what exists today, and I accept it for what it is.' ... Do you have it?"

"Yes."

"That's great. Now as you do, get the breath of acceptance, the internal voice of this resource. Feel it in your muscles ... notice how it shows up on your face.... How much do you have this on a scale from 0 to 10?

"I feel it about an 8 or 9."

"Good. What would you need to do in your mind or with your body to increase it even a little more?... There you go. That's right ... and now as you *fully feel this resource*, I would like you to feel all of this about your *self* ... just feel this about your self ... and be with this feeling for a moment and just notice the transformations that begin to occur ... as you construct self-acceptance for yourself, and wouldn't this be a great state to take with you as you move through the world?

"And because your brain learns patterns so quickly, now pick something that evokes in you a strong feeling of appreciation, maybe a glorious sunset, holding a newborn baby, playing with a child or puppy, something small and simple and yet which evokes feelings of appreciation in you ... Do you appreciate anything simply and purely for itself?... Good. And let that feeling increase so that you begin to breathe the breath of appreciation, look out around you in this room with the eyes of appreciation, hear your internal voice with the sound qualities of appreciation, and let that increase fully ... There you go ... and now feel all of these tremendous feelings of appreciation about you ... about your self ... It may take a moment for the layering of these feelings about your concepts about yourself to fully take ... so just feel this appreciation about yourself as a person ...

"And yet one more time, let's move up the liking scale as we have done from acceptance where there was no liking to appreciation where there was a lot of liking to the ultimate place of total awe and honor and esteem for something of tremendous value. Does

121

anything in this world or beyond this world evoke in you a sense of ultimate esteem and wonder and awe and maybe even worship? Perhaps, once again, holding a newborn baby and sensing the miracle of life, perhaps the recognition of love … what do you most highly value and esteem? What brings out a sense of awesomeness in you? And when you have that fully … feel all of that awe and sense of dignity about yourself as a marvellous human being …"

Re-Inventing Your "Self"
With the foundational frames of self-acceptance, self-appreciation, and self-esteem, you now are ready to begin building, defining, inventing, and constructing a better concept of yourself.

- How do you want to conceptualize your *self* so that it provides an enhancing map for both *Being* and *Doing?*
- What qualities would you like to edit into your image of this more resourceful you?
- Develop your menu list of enhancing traits, qualities, ways of thinking and relating, etc.:

— Fallible	— Flexible
— Learning	— Growing
— Playful	— Loving and Caring
— Respectful	— Responsible
— Passionate	— Charming
— Disciplined	— Purposeful

Texturing Your Self
With every higher level state, emotion, thought, concept, or quality that you bring to bear upon your "sense of self," you set a frame and that frame will thereafter *texture* your self.

Imagine flexibility—having lots of options, the ability to adapt, alter your thinking, feeling, and way of responding. Amplify this resource and then bring it to bear upon your self. As you bathe yourself in this experience and let it set the frame for your perceiving of yourself … Begin to see the You that is ever-so flexible and adaptable.

I hope you see and appreciate and even stand in awe of the magic of outframing yourself with higher and higher frames. It puts into your hands a tremendously powerful way to reinvent yourself and begin to encode in your entire neuro-linguistic being—a new self-image that will thereafter self-organize all of your powers in its service. Imagine the possibilities!

Summary

- Your self-definition and identity frame operates as one of your most pervasive and powerful executive states. Make sure it serves you well.
- We map out our self-definitions from experiences, cultural and family beliefs and taboos, feedback from others, what we do, etc. Yet all of our higher level frames that create this "sense of self" are mental constructs—an imaginary entity that we have invented.
- As we stop identifying, we become free to build empowering executive frames. Whoever you think you are—you're not! You're so much more.
- Personal Mastery comes to those who refuse to sell themselves short to over-identifying with experiences, behaviors, feelings, thoughts, etc.

Two More Secrets
of
Personal Mastery

Secret #8

Mastery emerges when we align our *attentions* with our higher level *intentions*.

*Within every thought we think, we have both an attentional content or focus and an intentional design. If we do not **intentionally** take charge of our attentions from a higher level, our attentions will drive us and often run us ragged, but when we take an Intentional Stance from our meta-outcomes, personal genius becomes easy.*

Secret #9

Energy flows where attention goes as determined and governed by intention.

Our attentions at the primary level actually work in service of our higher level intentions and intentions-of-intentions. These intentions may, or may not, be conscious and explicit. Yet they govern experience. Now aligning our attentions to our higher intentions gives us the power to focus our energies of mind, body, emotion, and spirit so that we develop our personal genius.

Chapter 6

Setting Executive Policies

Establishing Operating Ideas

With a Mind that Can Make Meta-Moves—
Establish Policies to Enhance Your Life

"You will see it when you believe it."
(Wayne Dyer)

Policies—the "rules" we create which then allow us to run or manage things. We all have them. Companies have them. All too often, however, we hear about "the policy" of a business when we return with a problem or a complaint. Instead of getting help, we get a recital of "Company Policy." Nor do we have to look very far for policies. We have them in our homes, schools, hospitals, local government, etc. In fact, at all levels of functioning, we find policies. We can find explicit policies, as those written down in a book of procedures, as well as implicit policies.

> "So what's the policy around here about making a complaint?"
> "That's not your policy? Well, what is your policy?"
> "I thought the administration would care about customer perception. Hasn't that been established as a basic policy in this company?"
> "Okay, dad, what's your policy about driving the car?"

If *policies* seem to dominate in everyday life, do they similarly govern internal life? Do we also have mental policies? Do we have policies for what we will and will not believe? Do we have policies about how we run our own brains, use our intelligence, think, feel, reason, etc.?

You bet!

And as you might have guessed, these policies of our higher mind typically operate at various meta-levels and therefore out-of-consciousness.

- What *rules* do you have about yourself, life, happiness, effectiveness, commitment, play, relating to a loved one, learning, etc.?
- What *procedural guidelines* have you adopted in how to buy or sell, negotiate, ask for a raise, meet someone new, take a risk, bounce back from a set-back, or travel?

What policies have you set about handling criticism, coping with anger, springing back from a set-back, etc.? As we noted in the previous chapters about our executive states, when we set meta-level structures, those frames will *govern* our everyday experiences. We can count on those higher levels of mind becoming more determinative and governing more and more completely over time. This, in fact, describes one of the subtle and pervasive powers of meta-levels. Once our executive levels begin to *govern* our everyday experiences, we become accustomed to them. We then take them for granted. Eventually we assume them as just "the way things are." And so they become our "Reality" strategies and so encode the matrix of frames we live within.

Actually, in describing the meta-levels as directing and controlling everyday thoughts-and-feelings, the way we talk and act, the skills that we have access to, and our emotional states, etc., we also mean that they exert *an organizational influence* on our very experience of *life* and *personality*. This refers to how the higher levels magnetize and attract the events that correspond to them. A frame of *pessimism*, for example, works to give us *eyes for seeing pessimistic things*. According to self-organization theory, these frames become *the attractors* of a system. The executive system will attract and organize your focus, perception, and energy to fulfill itself as a frame. The judgment you sent out will be the judgment that returns.

If you have a *fear* frame of reference, this will endow you with the uncanny ability to find *fearful* things everywhere you turn. Then, your ability to think and feel *fearful* becomes so repetitive and so habitual that it establishes itself as one of your basic frames-of-reference, it then takes over and operates as an *attractor*. Thereafter, you will find all kinds of "proofs" that validate and reinforce that frame. Self-fulfilling prophecy!

The same thing happens with anger. If you establish an anger and injustice frame by thinking about and sorting for unfairness and injustices, and if you do so intensely and repetitively, then afterwards that frame will usher you into a whole world of unjust things. You will find yourself with the intuitively uncanny ability to discover all kinds of unfair things that violate your values. This will make you more and more anger prone. If you turn these energies toward healthy causes and balance it with some other traits (kindness, patience, wisdom, etc.), you might become an effective crusader. If you don't, you find yourself always in fights about your rights. You may find that you seem to draw injustice to you. Paradoxically, most people who suffer from the diagnosis of "a criminal mentality" have this kind of structure. They do not tolerate injustice well (to themselves!).

The same principle and psycho-dynamics apply just as much to the more pleasant and positive experiences. It happens with pleasure and happiness. If you establish a happy and friendly frame, and begin to move through the world looking for, thinking about, and anticipating delightful things, you will typically begin to discover precisely those qualities. Suddenly, as if by magic, you will find your world populated with lots of things to enjoy, and lots of pleasures to delight in. You will meet and enjoy people in a good hearted way everywhere you go. You will gain lots of experiences to celebrate as positive and hopeful.

It similarly happens to those who have a frame about *seeing business opportunities*. We sometimes call such individuals "lucky." And so they seem. They have only to take a drive through town, visit a restaurant, or make a call, and they seem to experience all kinds of opportunities knocking on their door. Yet at a higher level, they have layered consciousness in such a way that they have a *mind* for opportunities. This describes the mind of the entrepreneur.

These experiences describe the *organizing influence* of meta-levels. They illustrate the power of our neuro-linguistic structures for altering our perceptions as well as our conceptual world. Executive states at meta-levels operate as *self-organizing attractors.* Self-organization theory describes it in terms of systems, feed-back and feed-forward loops, etc. More commonly we talk "self-fulfilling prophecies." An old Jewish proverb expresses it in the succinct statement, "As a man thinks in his heart, so he is." The prophet of Nazareth put it, "Be it unto you according to your faith."

Part of what makes our executive or meta-states work this way involves how these inner executive states contain numerous *"policies"* and policy determining powers. *Policies* here refers to "the rules" that we live by, the values and criteria that set the standard for our decisions and actions, the beliefs and domains of understandings by which we operate, the choice points and default programs that govern decisions, and the basic presuppositions of life. The decisions we make and have made end up at high levels as operational energies.

No wonder our **inner executive** has so much power and say-so over our everyday life and emotions! Of course, this also explains why we need to detect our executive states and monitor them. If we don't monitor and evaluate and keep them updated, we may very well find ourselves living, feeling, relating, and reacting from out-moded executive policies that no longer serve us well.

All of this suggests several things. It suggests that we should become more conscious or mindful of our executive states and the policies incorporated in them. It suggests that we should develop the skills for updating and/or refining the policies that may have become outdated. It suggests that we would do well if we developed the necessary internal patterns for establishing ongoing executive states and policies that will enhance our lives in a generative way.

Identifying Your Own Executive Policies
We begin first with the process of detecting and identifying executive *policies*. This will involve *an exploration process* regarding our beliefs and values, our domains of understandings, decisions,

frames, paradigms, etc. All of these represent higher (or meta-level) mental phenomena. And within these lie our programmed and automatic *policies* about all kinds of things:

> — how to think
> — how to feel
> — how to act
> — how to talk
> — how to relate
> — how to use skills
> — how to negotiate
> — how to learn
> — how to function in the social arena
> — how to function in the work and career arena.

Generally, a *policy* refers to the prudence and/or the wisdom involved in the management of affairs. Derived from terms at the heart of *"politics"* and *"police,"* the idea of *policies* refers specifically to:

> "a definite course or method of action selected from among present and future decisions, a high-level overall plan embracing the general goals and acceptable procedures of a governing body."

For a company to operate efficiently, executives and managers have to establish polices regarding numerous things. The operation policies of a business specify how it will function, the rules that will govern its functioning, the general *modus operandi* of the business, etc. Without a policy, we don't know what to do. We play it by ear. We guess our way through.

In terms of human psychology or functioning, our executive states all involve various policies—guidelines, methods, procedures, action plans, permitted and tabooed protocols, etc. Such *policies* show up in language in the terms that we use to indicate our *modus operandi* (our style of operating). Linguists have a special term for these words—*modals*. This term leads yet another technical term, *Modal Operators*. These words that describe *our style of operating* include the following central modals that govern our lives:

- *Modal Operators* of *necessity:* need, must, have to
- *Modal Operators of option:* desire, choice, choose, opt for
- *Modal Operators of desire:* get to, desire, want to
- *Modal Operators of impossibility:* can't, not possible, out of the question
- *Modal Operators of possibility:* can, able to

Imagine a person with an executive state of necessity. They operate with a *have to* and *must* style in life. This sets a particular frame for those persons in terms of thinking, feeling, speaking, and behaving. As a result, we will find such persons referencing what they "have to," "need to," and "must" do. They will speak as if they have no choice. *Necessity* describes their motivation style and their basic attitude. It generally creates a sense of pressure. This leads to the person's *modus operandi* always involving needs and constraints.

Contrast that to the person who operates from the frame of possibility. This person will talk about what he or she *"gets to do," "can do," "might do," "what's possible,"* etc. Who would have ever thought that such a simple little *modal* would have such pervasive influence on mind-emotions, or personality? Yet, most of us can powerfully feel the effect of the shift from "I *have to* go to work," to "I *get to* go to work." "I *have to* finish that report," to "I *will* finish that report."

To identify the *policies* within a given executive state, simply step back, and as you adopt an observer position to yourself simply witness the behavioral parameters within which you operate. As you do this, listen for the language that describes, defines, and textures *how you operate* in a given area.

"I have to get this project done."
"I must get to that meeting."
"I can't stand the way he manages."

To flush out your own executive level policies, use the following sentence stems to evoke them. Write the sentence stem on a piece of blank paper and begin a free-flow of writing until you have half-a-dozen to a dozen completions for each one.

— When it comes to work, I have to …
— About exercising, I must …
— In getting along with people, I need to …
— About work, I get to …
— About learning, I choose to …
— About criticism, I can't …
— About negotiating, I must …
— About meeting new people, I can …

The resulting statements as beliefs and mind-sets may or may not serve you well. These may or may not be useful to you. Check them out. Are they? Would a different style of operation work better for you? What *must* you do? What do you *get* to do?

Setting Executive Policies

One of the highest executive states that we operate from involves what we commonly call *will* (as in "will power"). This refers to the *choices* we make as we move through the world and so describes *our volitional power* (power of choice) by which we make decisions.

This volitional power interacts with our *understandings and beliefs.* As we come to understand a domain, and develop *beliefs* about such, we inevitably **decide** what this means to us, how to respond, how to represent it, etc. Doing this sets various *policies* regarding actions, responses, criteria, etc.

By such *deciding*, we "turn our central self, the part that decides …" as C.S. Lewis put it in his vivid quotation. We "turn our central self" toward what to think, how to think, what to believe, how to respond, how to live our lives, what to value as important, etc. Consequently, *our decisions,* as a result, pervade our mental-emotional life and states.

To explore this subject, take anything (a situation at work, a topic in the daily newspaper, the conversation at the coffee shop, the gossip at the office, the concerns in Sunday's sermon, the e-mails you receive this evening, anything) and explore it in terms of your decisions. When you do this, this meta-stating will expand your mind.

- What have you *decided* about X?
- What have you *decided* to think or believe about X?
- What have you *decided* to feel and value about X?
- What have you *decided* to do about X?
- What have you *decided* to focus on?

Whatever you answer speaks about some of your personal *policies* that drive your states, meta-states, ongoing experiences, expectations, emotions, etc. More generally, we can ask the following questions to elicit other formative *executive policies* set in your meta-states:

- What have you *decided* about the purpose of life?
- What have you *decided* about love and relationships?
- What have you *decided* about how to relate to friends?
- What have you *decided* about the value and use of money?
- What have you *decided* about how to think about materialism?
- What have you *decided* about career and job?

Now go back and notice your answer to these and other questions that identify the very structure of your reality and your subjective experiences. As you do, ask yourself these questions about the things that have held you back and that can now propel you forward:

- What *limiting decisions* have you made in your life?
- What *limiting decisions* do you have that still runs things?
- What *limiting decisions* would you like to rid yourself of?
- What *empowering decisions* would you like to use instead?
- What *empowering decisions* have you thought about that would really make a difference in your life?
- What *empowering decisions* would you like to invent?

An Executive Policy to "Take Insult"

Because most of us have become highly skilled in *taking insult* from the words, tones, volumes, opinions, and criticisms of others, let's explore this from the point of view of our executive states. At the primary level of experience we experience *a stimulus*. Someone speaks to us in a tone of voice or a volume that we do not like or do not prefer. Generally this indicates that the speaker comes from a state of stress or displeasure. He or she may also use some cutting words.

- What do you think or feel about this?
- What state can you count on yourself accessing when you receive "criticism?"

"I don't like it."

Good. That expresses your primary state emotion. We have accessed an unpleasant or even a distressed state in reference to that stimulus. We really do not like it.

So given that you dislike it, what meaning do you give to it? What does it mean to you? You take it as a personal affront. You take it as a message of put down, insult, condescending, etc.

So what *state* do you access in regard to *feeling criticized?*

Obviously (or, maybe not so obviously), you **could** take an attitude of *interest*, curiosity, or compassion to that stimulus. Well, you could. Few do, but you have to admit, it's possible. You could have viewed it as a very fine example of someone in a very unresourceful state, and, thank God, you're not in that kind of nasty mood!

But probably not. Most of us have learned well to *refuse* to *accept* the criticism, to dislike it, hate it, and tell ourselves repeatedly that we "can't stand it," and that we just have to *defend* ourselves against it, explain "the truth" to the other person, set the other person straight, etc. As such, the *operational policies* governing our state probably involve such rules as:

"He does not have the right to talk that way to me!"

"She's doing that only to control me."

"Only a person trying to hurt me, put me down, embarrass me, control me, etc. would talk that way."

These are the higher meta-level frames (executive states) governing this experience. We really do think that the person is violating our most precious values and putting us down and feel that our "self-esteem" is somehow endangered. And, given that frame-of-reference, this activates numerous *high level policies* regarding what we now *have to do*. We have to defend ourselves, we have to get the obnoxious person to straighten up and apologize and take back those words, we have to talk to the person to understand him, we have to get away for our own peace of mind, etc.

To find our own operational policies, or those of another, we need only to explore how a person copes in the face of any given situation. What do they have to do when such and such happens? What can we expect of ourselves or another in the event of such and such? Then, once we have flushed out the policies, we can evaluate them in terms of accuracy, usefulness, practicality, and ecology. Doing so enables us to set new and better policies, policies more in accord with current reality.

"Willing" Executive Policies via Intending and Attending

We set the executive and meta-state *policies* that run our lives by a power that we commonly describe by the term *"will."* This refers to the process of *deciding, choosing, opting for, willing,* etc.

In a fascinating study on *Love and Will*, Rollo May (1968) analyzed the components that make up "will" and "will power" in terms of two primary elements, *attention and intention*. This analysis puts into our hands a way of distinguishing between levels which leads to a very practical way to actually utilize this "will power" phenomenon.

Separating out from "will" *attention and intention* highlights the *two-layered nature* of will (and consciousness at all levels for that matter). It opens our eyes to the fact that there exists, *behind* and *within* every thought, things which we *attend to* at the front of our mind and things which we *intend* at the back of our mind. At the primary level we experience *attentions*—the things "on our mind." This gives us our focus—our focus of attention. Above and beyond attention, however, at a higher level, we have *intentions*—the things in the back of our mind that we seek to accomplish. This comprises our motives, agendas, reasons, etc. This reveals *the two-layered nature* of the gestalt state of "will power."

Figure 6:1

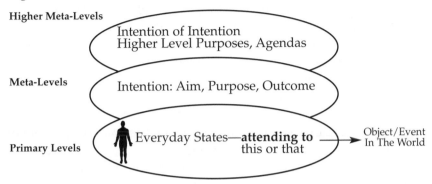

Higher Meta-Levels

Intention of Intention
Higher Level Purposes, Agendas

Meta-Levels

Intention: Aim, Purpose, Outcome

Primary Levels

Everyday States—**attending to** this or that

Object/Event
In The World

The Eighth Secret of Mastery

How can we use this understanding about the gestalt of "will?" It gives us the Eighth Secret of Personal Mastery which unpacks intention and attention and sequences them so that we can access our personal genius. This distinction further reveals the structure of excellence.

Secret #8

Mastery emerges when we align our *attentions* with our higher level *intentions*.

*Within every thought we think, we have both an attentional content or focus and an intentional design. If we do not **intentionally** take charge of our attentions from a higher level, our attentions will drive us and often run us ragged. Conversely, when we take an Intentional Stance from our meta-outcomes, personal genius becomes easy.*

In attention, we *represent* something. We have something "on our mind." Our focal attention processes something in the world and so fills up our inner mental screen with those contents. If we're at work in the office, we *think about* the report we have to write, the sale we need to make, the contacts we need to make, etc. These things dominate our *attentions. We attend to these things.*

Typically, our *attentions* seem to govern and dominate our mind. Ask yourself or anyone, "What's *on* your mind?" and the first things that we talk about are our *attentions*. We begin talking about all of the things that we have to do, all of the things "on our plate." At this level of mind, our *attentions* seem very volatile, shifting, impermanent, and elusive. Our attentions come and go. Our stream of consciousness rises and falls with the currents of the immediate environment. Things, people, and events "catch our attention." So we look. Here *mind* seems weak, fragile, ever-shifting, deficit in powerful focusing. At this level, the shiftings of mind operate as if we are moving through the world channel surfing. And, perhaps that's precisely what we're doing—jumping from one channel of awareness to another.

This describes how we all, typically, experience our primary level *attentions*. And, actually, this is good. There's nothing wrong or pathological about the ever-shifting nature of our stream of consciousness. Nor does this, in itself, mean that we suffer from *Attention Deficit Disorder.* Far too many doctors have over-used this diagnosis and far too many people have taken refuge in this psychiatric label. A great many of those who experience the disordering that has been labeled *"attention deficit,"* and who keep shifting their attention from this to that, then to another thing, actually suffer from a higher level disorder that I'll describe in a minute, *Intention Deficit Disordering.*

If we experience *attentions* at the primary level, we experience *intentions* at meta-levels. This means that *every thought also has an intentional drive or a teleological outcome.* The term *teleology* refers to our tendency to think about where things are going, the *end* results of our choices and actions (*tele*, "end," "final").

This means that behind our attentions we can find motivations, reasons, agendas, outcomes, etc. In "the back of our mind" we have some *intention* that describes what we seek to accomplish by our attentions. This analysis empowers us to step back and question our attentions. What thought lurks back there in the shadows of your mind *about* any given attention?

Intention operates at a higher logical level than *attention*. And because it does, it operates in a more stable and lasting way. Except for moments of intense indecision, we typically don't find our *intentions* shifting all over the place. When that does occur, we experience it as a painful sense of internal conflict and indecision over basic values, beliefs, understandings, etc. Do I want this or that? Why can't I have both? I kind of want this. But then again, I also want this other.

Of course, we seldom experience our *intentionally driven attentions* as separate. We experience them as a gestalt. The thoughts in the back of our mind combine with the thoughts in the front of our mind and this double-helix structure (like two snakes intertwining around each other) of "thought-emotion" seems as one thing—consciousness. And, our thought-feeling **states** move forward by these dynamics of our mind-emotion. In fact, these two psychic powers (intention and attention) govern the very direction and quality of our everyday experiences. *Attention* directs us to the primary level content that makes up the details and content on our mental screen while *intention* directs us to the meta-level frame of reference regarding our motivation, our wants, and our desired outcomes.

This analysis of the gestalt of "will" makes it clear that we have *one stream of consciousness with two dimensions in it*. We experience our attentions as *overt* and our intentions as *covert*. This explains why we think that our problem lies with the ever-shifting and volatile *attentions* that jump all over the place as "thought balls" pop in and out of the court of our mind. We're aware of our attentions, and much less aware of our intentions. We may not even know our intentions. We may even find it hard to describe what we actually do *want*.

"Will," as our sense of choice and existential freedom, emerges as a systemic property from the experience and interactions of both our intentions and our attentions. The gestalt is our sense of "will power." We feel it as, "I can choose and then attend that choice." Generally, when we sense a weakness in our "will power" the problem will lie at the higher levels, not the lower.

Herein lies the importance of this analysis.

By recognizing these facets of "will," or volition, we have a set of principles and a technology for using the leverage points that actually govern our ability to "run our own brain," take charge of our states, and exercise the gestalt experience of "will power." We can now begin to utilize this Eighth Secret of Personal Mastery as we apply a principle of alignment.

> **Mastery emerges when we align our *attentions* with our higher level *intentions*.**
> *Within every thought we think, we have both an attentional content or focus and an intentional design. If we do not **intentionally** take charge of our attentions from a higher level, our attentions will drive us and often run us ragged. Conversely, when we take an Intentional Stance from our meta-outcomes, personal genius becomes easy.*

So, whenever an attended concept or set of representations in our mental map does not seem to work in terms of making us more resourceful in moving on in life, we can now immediately shift our focus. We can identify our higher and highest intentions and then align our everyday attentions to them. Or we can establish new and higher positive intentions which will then govern new attentions. This will de-energize old attentions, slay demons, tame dragons, and create a powerful new focus of excellence in life.

All of this creates a new focus in how to address and deal with our neuro-linguistic constructions or programs. If we attempt to deal *only* with *attention*, without considering *intention*, we will never find the leverage point that can transform the entire system. And that will make change very hard.

This would be like trying to watch a television screen and making sense of it while somebody in another room has the remote control and is channel surfing! Imagine that. You could drug the person (give them ritalin) so that they would go slower, and not make their internal pictures so quickly or hear their internal voice speaking so rapidly. Or, you could look around for *who* has the control—remote control. Look for the one with the smirk.

Why do some people have difficulty controlling the "stream of their consciousness?" Why does their attention shift and turn and twist and jump and do somersaults? Before we toss everything in the bin labeled, "Genetic," "Biochemical," or "Inherent Deficiency," perhaps we should at least briefly explore *intention*. Perhaps we should at least question the higher *frames of references* of these people. Undoubtedly, since mind-body work together as a system, each influencing the other, genetics do play a role, and so do eating habits, medicines, health practices, exercise, *and thoughts* in the form of ideas, beliefs, values, understandings, etc.

Actually, *everybody* has the ability to become distracted and to do internal *channel surfing* with their minds. Don't you? And suppose you add a little stress, some negative experience that feels like we didn't get closure on it, some conflicting values, etc., then try to concentrate! Or, even better, experience mom and dad fighting and arguing and screaming about not having enough money, calling you names for being a kid and making mistakes, spilling things, forgetting things, telling you that you are stupid, and then go to school to study something that you don't care about in the first place. Then try to effectively concentrate.

The *concentration of attention* which shows up as an intense *focus*, a zooming-in on some subject and staying with it *needs* a strong *intention*. It needs something like interest, excitement, fun, skill-developing, etc., that will make you feel good. This, by the way, describes the heart of what we call "genius." It also needs a higher frame of safety, security, relaxation, freedom, etc.

Can (or does) the person who has been diagnosed as suffering from ADD (Attention Deficit Disorder) go into a state of intense concentration of attention with anything? A video-game, TV football, a *Star Trek* movie, a game of tennis, etc.? If they can, then they are probably among those who *only seemingly* have a deficit in their attention. They actually suffer much more from *intention deficit*. They lack a strong *intention* or reason for staying with a school subject. More likely, they have not really developed *a strong enough why*. Unlike the person who strongly *wants* some particular knowledge or information, and knows precisely what they will do with it, how it will enrich their life, what it will make them, etc., the person with *intention deficit* does not have a clue.

So, accordingly, they don't seem to care ... about Mathematics, English, Geography, History, etc. But just give them a video-game that all their friends play and watch them access a state of *total concentration of attention*. This does not describe a case of some genetic lack or deficiency. This does not describe someone whose brain does not work well and who needs to be medicated.

In this we can now sort out another key difference between our *intentions* and our *attentions*. *Attention* seems to operate in a passive way. It seems to passively attach itself to things. It waits for something to "grab its attention." *Intentions* operate in a much more proactive and directive way. It operates as a higher state of mind that says, "I want ..."

Unless we take charge of our *attentions* by setting up higher level frames of references (our executive and meta-states) attention will simply get into a "channel surfing" mode. It will race here and then there. It will be grabbed by this movement, that color, and this compelling representation. Like a wild and undisciplined monkey, it will be all over the place playfully checking things out and staying with none for long.

Consider the powerful persuaders who design commercials. What incredible artists at "capturing attention" by vivid, dramatic, and surprising sights and sounds. They turn on loud dramatic sounds that demand that we look up to see what's happening. "Made you look!" they say. They use the most momentary pictures of provocative and curious sights that leave us on the edge of our seats or a cliff just waiting for more. They change the view every couple of seconds. And, a steady diet of that kind of way of thinking can invite us to install inside of our own representational screen an ever-shifting "commercial consciousness."

Conversely, when we *align our attention* **to our higher intentions**, then we use (and commission) our motivations, reasons, values, beliefs, higher level interests, etc. to govern and control our *attentions*. Doing this empowers our inner executive states as it simultaneously establishes our personal mission and purpose. Then, as an attractor in a self-organizing system, the higher level *intention* (and intention of that intention, etc.) become our highest level "program."

Aligning Attention with Higher Level Intentions

In order to *align* our attentions with our intentions, we have to go higher to first make our intentions explicit. Once we do that, then we can bring those intentions back down to set a new *attention* that will serve the higher frames. Since attention comes and goes, aligning it so that it notices, pays attention, goes into sensory awareness, focuses, etc. on what will serve our intentions well and which will offer us more choices and potentials puts *attention at the service of intention.*

To do this, you may first have to *give yourself permission* to **live in the new attention** (the Permission Frame). That may mean permission to step out of your Comfort Zone so that you can allow the new intentions to become the higher level *attractors.* As you do, you give the higher executive frames an opportunity to become your self-organizing attractors in your entire mind-body system. And because this will take time, give yourself permission also to take the time necessary to *intend your new attention.*

Directionalizing Your Neuro-Linguistic Energies

When you engage in this *meta-level alignment process,* you thereby activate the Ninth Secret for Personal Mastery. In NLP, we have a saying that partly expresses this principle. It goes, "Energy flows where attention goes." Directing your mind-body attention inherently directs your neurological, mental, emotional, personal *energies.* To this saying, we now add another element or dimension that transforms it into a neuro-semantic principle.

Secret #9

Energy flows where attention goes as determined and governed by intention.

Our attentions at the primary level actually work in service of our higher level intentions and intentions-of-intentions. These intentions may, or may not, be conscious and explicit. Yet they govern experience. Now aligning our attentions to our higher intentions gives us the power to focus our energies of mind, body, emotion, and spirit so that we develop our personal genius.

A Neuro-Linguistic Exercise for Attending New Intentions

The following exercise offers a practical way to set some new intentions and intentions-of-intentions. Use it to develop your "will power" without all of the stress and strain that has traditionally been connected with such. You can use this exercise by yourself or have someone coach you through the process. You can use it by simply thinking about some activity that you do, but not with the power and focus that you really want; or by thinking about some activity that you want to do, but seem to never get around to.

Step 1: Identify what you want.

Regarding a particular domain (i.e. work, home, sports, fitness, relationship, etc.) ask, "What do you want?" From this identify your first level intention or intentions. "What do you seek to experience, accomplish, feel, or create in life by means of the things you *think, feel, say, and do?"* Describe and specify with precision your desired outcome.

Step 2: Identify your higher or executive level "wants" all the way up.

After the first set of outcomes, inquire further, "What do you want from that want?"

"What do you seek to accomplish by achieving your first level intentions?" "Why do you want to go for such things?" "How will getting these things enrich your life?" "What will they do for you?" Identify fully the desired outcomes of your desired outcomes.

Continue this process of meta-questioning your intentions until you begin to loop around the higher intentions or just repeat them in different words. When you do that, you have generally "reached the ceiling" of your constructions.

Step 3: Diagram the structure of your intentions and intentions-of-intentions and compare them to your attentions.

To keep track of the higher executive levels, use a circle or ellipse for your *primary state* intentions and attentions. This will specify the first order things "in the back of your mind" (intentions) and things "in the front of your mind" (attentions). "What do you *attend to* on a regular basis every day?"

Then use a circle or a "frame" line to indicate each higher level of desired outcomes which set the higher frames of your life.

Step 4: Design and Redesign your executive levels and intentional Meta-States.

When you have finished the elicitation and diagramming, step back into a witnessing and observing state. This will create the space wherein you can *Quality Control* your experience. "Run an ecology check" on these levels of mind that you have uncovered. Do they serve you well? Do they enhance your life? Do they set the direction and orientation that you want your life to go in? Do they empower you in bringing out your personal excellence?

If not, then redesign them by identifying and specifying what you do want.

Step 5: With a set of higher level intentions and intentions-of-intentions, set into your highest executive self to establish and install these as your Intentional Stance.

"As you consider these positive intentions and higher level positive outcomes, do you really want these for your life?" (Yes)

"Are you willing to let these govern your mind-and-emotions?" (Yes)

"Are you willing to accept the discomfort and unpleasantness of stepping outside of your old comfort zone and continually affirming and practicing these new intentions until they 'take' and become your executive intentional states?" (Yes)

"Is there any part of you that would object to letting these higher frames rule and govern your life?" (No)

"So you really want these?" (Yes)

"No, I don't think you do!" (Yes I really, really do!)

"So go inside and make an agreement with your highest executive self to commission these frames to take over and become your Intentional Stance in life."

Step 6: Future pace and reframe all objections.

If you get a "Yes" to the objection question, then identify the objection. "What's the objection or fear? What part of me hesitates to take this intentional stance and let these higher positive outcomes govern my life?" Frequently, it's just the dislike of being out in a new place, outside of the old comfort zone, and a sense of the unfamiliar.

If there is an objection, dovetail the meaning of that objection into one of the intentional states. For example, suppose a facet or part of your mind says, "I'm afraid that if I seek to live in a Win/Win way with others, people will take advantage of me." We can then ask generically, "What *resource* would you need in order to not let those with ulterior motives take advantage of you?" Then we can build in, "Taking my time and checking things out before making decisions," as a frame or policy for how to interact with others in Win/Win ways. We can build a policy like, "Win/Win or no deal." Or, "Upfront and on the table communications or no deal."

Finally, future pace. "Step into the higher intentional frames and imagine taking this as your attitude, motivation, understanding, intention as you move through the world tomorrow, next week, and in the months to come. Notice how this intention or these intentions transform how you think, feel, and relate." "And as you step into this higher positive intention, and the next intention-of-intention and experience this executive state fully and completely, and in just the way you find it most compelling and resourceful, imagine operating in your everyday life from this place ... And just enjoy the transformation that occurs because of it. And don't you really want to be this way now and wouldn't you like this to become your *way of being in the world* from this day forward? ..."

Summary

- We set *policies* not only in businesses, governments, and families, but we all establish *policies* in our minds about how to do things. These *rules* for coping and mastering the environment, for relating, feeling, thinking, etc. operate as yet another set of executive or meta-states that powerfully affect our everyday life.
- To truly *take charge* of our lives and develop our own personal excellence, we need to flush out, detect, examine, and consciously choose our own executive policies for living and being.
- *Secret #8 for Personal Mastery:* Mastery emerges when we align our *attentions* with our higher level *intentions*. Within every thought we think, we have both an attentional content or focus and an intentional design. If we do not **intentionally**

take charge of our attentions from a higher level, our attentions will drive us and often run us ragged. Conversely, when we take an Intentional Stance from our meta-outcomes, personal genius becomes easy.

- *Secret #9 for Personal Mastery:* Energy flows where attention goes as determined and governed by intention. Our attentions at the primary level actually work in service of our higher level intentions and intentions-of-intentions. These intentions may, or may not, be conscious and explicit. Yet they govern experience. Now aligning our attentions to our higher intentions gives us the power to focus our energies of mind, body, emotion, and spirit so that we develop our personal genius.

Specialized Terms:

Modal Operators: Words that describe *our style of operating, or modus operandi* in the world.

Teleology: The study or thinking about "last things," where things are going, the *end* results of our choices and actions.

The Tenth Secret
of
Personal Mastery

Secret #10

Beliefs that govern our perceptions, states, health, skills, etc. are thoughts embedded in a frame of confirmation.

Thinking a thought will not do much neuro-linguistically, and especially neuro-semantically, until we embed it in a frame of confirmation. We build empowering beliefs that send commands to our nervous system when we bring thoughts of confirmation to bear on some thought. We destroy and eliminate toxic ideas that limit and sabotage us when we bring disconfirmation to our thoughts.

Chapter 7

Installing Executive Policies and States

Making Executive and Meta-Levels Stick

When it comes to Meta-levels, it's Beliefs all the way up ...

Having just a mental *policy* does not equate with having it installed as your actual operational procedure. You can have, even talk profusely about, wonderfully creative and powerful policies and yet not experience them as your actual way of doing things. This means that *setting, deciding, choosing, and intending* the policies as your strategies is only the first step. After that you have to get them installed into your very neurology.

So, *how* do we do that?

The processes and patterns for aligning meta-level intentions and intentions-of-intentions in the previous chapter puts into our hands one very powerful way to actually *install* things. This chapter provides some other processes that will similarly *install* executive policies so that they indeed become our operational programs.

Re-Directionalizing Consciousness to Set a New Orientation

When we *make a decision*, our choice for a certain path *orients* us so that we begin to move in a certain direction. At the same time, doing this establishes a certain set of personal policies. Thereafter, every choice we make simply reflects that orientation. Your orientation in life today speaks about previous decisions that you have made. And, of course, reflect your higher level *intentions*. In this way, deciding, choosing, and intending incorporates the actual intentions and meta-intentions as the *governing policies* of our life.

As we now recognize these interconnections and the implicit policies within our choices, orientations, sets, etc., this informs us that when we directionalize our consciousness (or redirectionalize it) we thereby establish and install them as our personal policies. Recognizing that we can now ask:

- What *policies* have you programmed into your brain regarding where it should go?
- Have you ever discovered some orientation of your brain, emotions, consciousness that doesn't serve you very well?
- Would you like to learn to "swish" your brain off into more enhancing directions that would operate more generatively?

The *Swish Pattern* describes a "tool" (or human "technology") by which we can essentially, "tell our brain where to go" and program it so that it automatically goes there. This pattern essentially involves finding (or creating) a set of representations that begins the old swish and then connecting it to a new swish so that you end up going off (mentally-and-emotionally) into a direction of resourcefulness. The term "swish" here originally came from *a whoosssh sound,* like the sound of blowing wind, or even the sound of saying "swish" with a long emphasis on the last "sh" sounds. It really means nothing except it vaguely reminds one of "switching" the brain from one reference experience to another, and it anchors the process by the uniqueness of the term and the way it's pronounced.

Swishing Your Brain to a More Resourceful Way to Respond

The following pattern offers a way to install a new way of responding, a new set of procedures and a new policy, with respect to an old stimulus or trigger. You can use this basic process on any behavior that tends to operate automatically as if in a Stimulus-Response pattern. We have found that it works really well for nail-biting, unconscious eating patterns, smoking, etc. Many of the original NLP books provide extensive refinement of this pattern, especially Andreas and Andreas (1987, 1989).

Step 1: Identify an old trigger that you want more choice and resourcefulness with.

First identify anything that "sets you off" into the unresourceful direction. As you do this, you may need to *backtrack* from the state of feeling "out of sorts," unresourceful, frustrated, etc. and then track back to whatever stimulus triggers that mood. If this program has operated for a great many years so that it has become entirely unconscious, you may need to first simply begin noticing and journaling when and where you get into those undesirable moods or when those uncontrollable habits seem to take over.

What sets off the old direction? What sight, sound (tone, volume, pitch), sensation (touch, pressure, movement), word (phrase, idea), etc. evokes or provokes the unwanted response? Identify it. Typically, it will involve one of the last things you have awareness of just prior to getting into that unpleasant disposition. If you don't know, then simply choose one of the last things. Notice how you represent it in terms of your pictures, sounds, and sensations.

Now that we know (or can use) an internal representation, that sets aside this picture, sound, word, etc. for a moment. We first need to do some more preparation.

Step 2: Design engineer a new identity frame.

The next step in preparation involves creatively *imagining **the You** for whom this stimulus is "no problem."* Make a picture of yourself—the future, resourceful *You*. As you design and edit this image, see *the You* that is fully empowered to handle the stimulus. As you do, feel totally free to design into that image any resource that would empower you. You might want to see yourself as proactive, thoughtful, assertive, centered, resilient, relaxed, peaceful, loving, intelligent, etc.

Edit into your internal picture of that *Empowered You* any and all qualities that make this seem real, believable, and compelling to you. Hear that You speak ever so resourcefully. Watch him or her move about, breathe, gesture, etc. in ways that further makes the previous problematic stimulus "not a problem."

Step 3: Step in and test the resource frame.

When you have done this, fully and completely, step into that snapshot or movie of that *resourceful You* to test it. How does it feel when you step in and *become* that person? How would you like to *move through the world* from that self-image? When you step into that future You with all of those resources, does it make the previous trigger or problem seem like nothing?

If you don't find this representation strong or compelling enough, step back and make your pictures and sounds brighter, closer, bigger, etc. Then add in the other qualities that will cue your brain and body that this empowered You can handle it. "Piece of cake!" This thought exercise gives you the opportunity to wildly, courageously, and imaginatively design engineer *the person you would like to be.*

If you still have problems, is there anybody you know for whom that trigger would be "no problem?" What if you imagined some fictional person, television or movie personality, world renowned leader, etc.? Imagine that person encountering the trigger stimulus and handling it with total ease. Now step into that imagined person and *be that person in your own unique way.* If that doesn't give you a rush, keep repeating it until it does.

Step 4: Embed the Resourceful You into the old stimulus.

With that image of *the totally resourceful You,* now step out of it and just observing it, let the resourceful You image shrink down to the size of a dot ... a little tiny black dot and put that dot in the center of the other picture. You can now see the picture that previously provoked you into those unresourceful feelings and behaviors but now with a difference. Now you also see that there's a dot in the middle of that old picture, perhaps on your boss' nose, an unseeable little dot in the middle of a room, or whatever. You know it's there. You know what lies hidden deep inside it. And you know that whenever it explodes out and fills the screen of your mental theater, that you will *step into it and feel all of the resources in it and know that it is inviting and compelling you to become that person.*

Step 5: Get ready, set, go—Swish!

Having connected the two pictures, we now need only to let the first image lead to the second. So, beginning with the

trigger picture that has evoked unresourcefulness, *and* seeing the dot representing *the Resourceful You,* in just a minute
you will want to do two things simultaneously.

As you let the unresourceful picture fade away into the background very, very rapidly, you will immediately see the movie
of *the Resourceful You* explode from out of the dot in the center
and rapidly move forward toward you as it totally fills the
entire screen. This fading out of the old and the exploding of
the new will occur *at the same time* and *very quickly*—in about
the time of one second. It will happen about as long as it takes
to say *Swish!*

Okay, ready? *Swish!*

And as the new image now fills the screen, just enjoy it for a
moment, absorbing all of the powerful feelings and thoughts
that it evokes in you.

Step 6: Swish five times and feel resourceful.

Having done this once, now *clear the screen of your mind.* Look
around the room. Count from 37 downward. Spell Mississippi
three times. Do something to interrupt this mental work.

Then, when you have a clear mental screen repeat this *Swish*
pattern five more times, clearing the screen after each one and
fully enjoying the rush of having your mind-emotions send to
the empowering resourceful images of the future You.

Figure 7:1

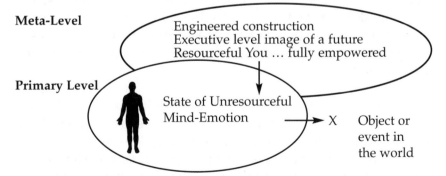

Swishing your brain this way (kind of like swishing around mouth-
wash after brushing your teeth) provides your meta-level brain
with a *program* that directionalizes your brain so that it will go in
a new direction to an old stimulus. As it does, it implicitly sets up

numerous policies. Making some of these explicit, we have actually established several new mental-emotional policies:

- You can and will take charge of *where* your brain goes. "I will no longer tolerate just letting my brain run loose and putting me into some funky place that does not serve me well at all."
- "I can and will reorganize any old neuro-linguistic program that directionalizes my brain which does not serve me well anymore."
- "I can and will set up *directions* for my mind-and-emotions to go that will work in a generative way to bring out the best in me."
- "I owe it to myself to become the world's best expert in getting the best out of myself. I accept that responsibility as a sacred privilege."
- "I can keep rehearsing the image of *my resourceful self* for whom various tasks, interactions, triggers, challenges no longer knock me down."
- "My ongoing development of personal mastery lies in my hands—a responsibility I willingly accept."

Setting Policies via Installing Confirmation Frames for your Ideas

As we grow up and move through life, we inevitably come to represent experiences and make sense of things through various domains of understanding. As we do this, we create understandings and ideas. From this we make decisions and beliefs. The early *mapping* that we do (which takes these forms) thereafter serves as our *model of the world* which we use to navigate people, events, and circumstances.

We turn our internal movies (representations) into a solid phenomenon that we call "beliefs" when we move to a meta-level and *validate* the thought. This provides a structural distinction between a mere "thought" and an energized "belief." A *thought* simply consists of internal sights, sounds, and sensations that we represent. We can *think* any thought we want to think without any fear or danger of *believing* it. We just "think" it.

How then do you know when you *believe* something and that you distinguish it from just thinking it? The answer lies in your answer to the following questions. Do you say *"Yes!"* to it? Or do you say *"No!"* to it? Or perhaps you say, *"Maybe. It could be, but then again, it could not be that way."* In other words, what higher level frame do you have the thought embedded in? Do you have it embedded in ideas and representations of *confirmation* or of *dis-confirmation?* Or do you have both, and continually swing back and forth?

Yes, No, and Maybe represent our meta-level choices with regard to our thoughts. Think the following thoughts—represent them fully and completely. Then notice the *response* (yes, no, maybe) that you go to *in reference to* the thought. When you do, you have moved to a higher logical level—to a thought *about* a thought.

> "Ice cream is good for you and the best thing in the world."
> "Adolf Hitler was really a good man with some good ideas."
> "The way to succeed in business is to get the goods on others."
> "The idea of Win/Win negotiating is the coward's way."
> "Treating people with respect and dignity creates good will and the kind of communication atmosphere that promotes effectiveness"
> "Men are out for one thing."
> "You can't trust a woman to do a man's job."

It's the Confirmation Level that makes the Difference

The difference between *representation* or a mere thought and *belief* then lies in how we move to a meta-level and then *validate* a thought (a belief), *dis-validate* a thought (disbelieve), or waver back and forth (a doubt). When we move to a higher level to *think about the thought*, we then gather the necessary and sufficient evidence and reasons to believe. When we don't have enough evidence or proof, then we doubt, or kind-of-believe (weakly believe). When we have counter-evidence or facts and reasons that argue against the idea, then we disbelieve, doubt, or waver. All of this describes *the structural form* of these phenomena.

This structural analysis of the meta-levels that set frames for our thoughts is not merely an exercise in abstraction. Understanding the very structure of beliefs immediately provides direction and insight about *how to build up more positive and empowering beliefs* and *how to de-energize and de-frame old limiting beliefs*. It's that important. And this highlights the Tenth Secret for Personal Mastery.

Secret #10
The beliefs that govern our perceptions, states, health, skills, etc. are thoughts embedded in a frame of confirmation.
Thinking a thought will not do much neuro-linguistically, and especially neuro-semantically, until we embed it in a frame of confirmation. We build empowering beliefs that send commands to our nervous system when we bring thoughts of confirmation to bear on some thought. We destroy and eliminate toxic ideas that limit and sabotage us when we bring disconfirmation to our thoughts.

Setting Executive Frames of "Yes" and "No" for Ideas that Ramble around in the Head
The key to turning a mere thought, some idea or conceptual understanding, into a full-fledged *belief* lies in the frame that we embed the thought within.

> If we embed it in a frame of "could be," it makes the idea possible.
> If we embed it in a frame of "wish it was," it makes the idea a wish.
> If we embed it in a frame of "doubt," it makes it a doubtful idea.
> If we embed it in a frame of "that's crazy, weird, improbable," then the idea loses its power and becomes a curiosity.
> If we embed it in a frame of "confirmation," then it turns the idea into a "belief."

The higher level frame totally governs the nature of our ideas. Deframing and/or building up beliefs then can work as simply as moving to a higher executive level and setting a frame there of *Yes, No, or Maybe*. An idea is just an idea until we put it in some frame. The structure of the frame determines the conceptual gestalt that will result: whether belief, doubt, disbelief, possibilities, fantasy, etc.

Now at the primary level, any "thought" that we can entertain in our mind, we can represent with more reality, compellingness, and vividness. Yet to merely have big, vivid, colorful, three-dimensional, and close pictures does not create "beliefs." To have a *belief*, we have to do something more. We have to make a meta-move and *confirm it* with a great big *"Yes!"* As we do this, we may, in fact, have to utter such confirming *Yeses!* to the idea until it becomes, not just a thought, but an energized belief. Doing this, in turn, establishes numerous policies about how to live, act, think, feel, etc. These policies result from the implicit assumptions and pre-suppositions inherent in the belief.

That's the theoretical format that describes the structure of a belief. Now let's utilize it in practical ways in order to make it work for us in terms of personal mastery. (For more on the structure of beliefs, see *The Structure of Excellence*, 1999, Hall and Bodenhamer.)

META-YES-ING
A Quick Change Belief Transformation Pattern
As *preparation* for this incredibly powerful executive level process, take a few minutes to carefully complete the following lists. This allows you to executively decide what *ideas* and *concepts* you want and don't want in your mind. Knowing that beliefs operate "like commands to the nervous system," evaluate the thoughts that you want to give *that much power* to in your mind-body system. After all, there are toxic beliefs that can really poison your mind and body.

- *Make a list of empowering ideas.* Do you know of any enhancing and empowering beliefs that you would really like to have running in your mind-and-emotions? What positively captivating ideas do you know that govern the experiences of people around you that you respect? What ideas enable and support those who seem to achieve excellence in their particular field of study?
- *Make a list of dis-empowering, limiting, and self-sabotaging ideas.* What limiting beliefs do you have which get in your way? What ideas or concepts trip you up and bother you? (i.e. ideas about work, authority, manipulation, relationships, finances, etc.)

Just Utter an Executive "Yes" to the Idea

With this *Meta-YES-ing pattern,* we put into your hands a very powerful human technology; one that utilizes the very structure of beliefs. By it, you can now de-commission any belief or idea that sabotages your success, gets in your way, limits your choices, or that reflects an old idea that has become unuseful. With it also, you can now commission any idea or concept that you hear or read about that would increase your effectiveness.

Step 1: Access a strong representation of Disconfirmation.

We begin this process by clearing out some room in our mental space. Some new ideas cannot, and will not, "go in" or "take" due to the fact that some other idea (as a belief frame) prevents it. If you believe that you're not a good learner, that learning is hard, that it's a waste of time trying to learn new things, etc., then you'll find it next to impossible to install the opposite belief. The old limiting belief negates and discounts it. When you attempt to stick into your brain an idea like, "I am an excellent learner," "Learning is a piece of cake," "I can learn anything," when you have a negating frame, you obviously make the transformation from one to the other very difficult.

Traditional psychology has looked at that and *assumed* that there were deep, unconscious "reasons" for this stuck state. "It goes back to the way your mother treated you." "You must have been traumatized in childhood by a teacher." With the Neuro-Linguistic and Meta-State Models we do not need to posit all of that or spend a lot of time "finishing 'unfinished' business." (Actually the old business is finished, we just dislike the way it finished!)

By postulating that we made some very limiting and unuseful maps from some earlier experience (regardless of what they were), and that those maps became our executive belief frames, we can now work much more directly with those levels. "Does it serve you well?" "Does it bring out your best?" (Ecology checking questions.) If not, then let's disconfirm them. Let's blow them out. Let's de-commission them.

To do this we first access a strong and vigorous example of saying *"No!"* to something. It doesn't really matter what, just some instance of saying *"No!"* that has a lot of intense neuro-linguistic energy within it. So make sure that the person's

"No" looks, sounds, and feels congruent and that it truly fits with the person's beliefs and values. I like to invite people to stand up and utter the **"No!"** and to really get into it. When the person expresses a strong *"No!," anchor* this resource experience of congruently, firmly, and definitively saying *"No!"* to something.

Step 2: Specify the limiting belief to de-commission.

Ask the person to identify *the limiting belief* which they no longer want to run their programs. Assuming that they have already thought through the disadvantages of the belief and how it does limit them, question the belief thoroughly. Ask about *how* it limits them, *when, where, in what way,* etc. Asking such questions that index the usefulness or unproductivity of a belief assists the person in deframing it, loosening it up, and preparing for the belief transformation. So find out how it has not contributed to their well-being, how it has messed things up, etc.

Further, as you notice how the person represents the belief, pace the positive intentions (secondary gains) that drive the belief. In other words, what did the person seek to accomplish of value for themselves by thinking or believing in that way?

Step 3: Utter a strong and intense Disconfirmation to the limiting belief.

Structurally, we here *meta-*"No!" the limiting belief. Begin by asking the person to access their strong and powerful *"No!"* As he or she does, then have the person apply it fully to the limiting belief. In this way, the *"No!"* takes a meta-position to the old idea.

This process can just as equally work by inviting the person to first *go meta* to that belief, and then, *about* that belief, to utter their strong and powerful **"No!"** Regardless of the syntax and order of the process, make sure that the person utters the *"No!"* congruently, intensely, and repeatedly.

"And you can keep on saying *No!* to that limiting belief until you begin to feel that it no longer has any power to run your programs."

"And how many more times and with what voice, tone, gesturing, do you need to totally disconfirm that old belief so that you know—deep inside yourself—that it will no longer run your programs?"

Step 4: Access an incredibly powerful case of a Confirmation.

We now want to get an incredible strong representation of saying *"Yes!"* to something. Repeat the process as in Step 1, only this time do it with all of the internal representations and neurology of **a confirming "Yes!"** to something. Begin by getting an emotional Yes, after that you can access a matter-of-fact Yes. Once you get the confirmation state, reinforce it by asking about it, and amplifying it so that the person has an intense experience of his or her *"Yes!"* Again, anchor this state and all the neurology that goes along with it with a touch, by the way you say *"Yes!,"* and where you gesture to as you say the Yes.

Step 5: Elicit a full and precise description of the desired empowering belief that the person wants to commission.

Fully elicit from the person the **enhancing belief** that he or she has decided to commission as part of their programming. "What specifically will you think and say to yourself as you express this new belief?" Write out the language of this new compelling idea that the person finds supporting. "How would this empower you?" "How would it enable and enhance your life?" "Where, when, with whom, in what way?" Get several versions and make sure that the person finds the expression of it compelling.

Step 6: Utter a strong and intense Confirmation to the new expansive belief.

Structurally, we now want to *meta "Yes!"* the enhancing belief. After the deframing of the old belief, and the opening up of space for a new way of thinking and believing, we can now invite the person's mind to swish to the new content that would support them.

Invite the person to fully re-access the enhancing belief and then to *go meta* to it and *validate* it with a great big *Yes!* Or, with the state of *"Yes!"* vibrating from every fiber of their mind-and-body, have them feel that in relation to the new enhancing thoughts. Again, after connecting the executive level *"Yes!"* to the new thought, invite the person to repeat it with intensity and congruency. "And how many more times do you need to say '*Yes!*' to that idea so that it becomes your way of thinking and feeling as you move through the world?"

Step 7: *Finish the process by future pacing the new empowering belief.*

As you imagine taking this way of thinking and understanding things with you as you work, relate, etc., just notice how it changes things for the better and makes life a whole lot more fun and productive.

Setting Policies by Deframing and Reframing Meanings

Not only do we have hidden and unconscious *policies* for how to live, act, relate, etc., stored in decisions and beliefs, but we actually have them incorporated within or behind *every attribution of meaning* that we construct. We have them within or behind every operational frame-of-reference. This makes these hidden *policies* ubiquitous. They are everywhere!

Actually, this simply represents yet another way to talk about our "beliefs." In that sense, beyond the primary level of thoughts, *it's beliefs all the way up.* We have beliefs about ourselves, others, the world, what's important ("values"), purpose, destiny, etc. And each belief sets a meaning frame. It may be a belief or frame about what something "is" (identity), what something means, or what causes other things (causation). In this, we can pick literally anything as a topic and when we explore what it *means* to us, we thereby begin to make explicit the meaning frame and therefore various hidden policies that may govern our lives.

What do the following *mean* to you? What do you think and believe about these items?

- Speaking up to your boss.
- Expressing your negative emotions.
- Expressing your positive emotions.
- Conflicting with a peer.
- Negotiating for a better arrangement with someone.
- Expending lots and lots of energy to get something done.

- Making a mistake.
- Asking for help.
- Talking about your sexual feelings.
- Expressing ambivalence, reservations, or uncertainty.
- Showing affection.
- Etc.

Frames of Meaning—It's Frames All the Way Up

Step 1: Begin by asking the meaning question.
"What does this *mean* to you?" "And what else does it *mean?*" Sometimes you have to shift terminology and use various synonyms to get to this. "This sounds significant to you. In what way does it seem important and valuable to you?" "This must carry a lot of weight for you. Just how do you find it so significant?"

Step 2: Move up and ask about the meaning of the meanings.
"What, when you think about X (the first level meaning), does that mean to you? What importance or significance does that hold for you?"

In this elicitation process, clearly distinguish in your mind whether the responses you receive are other *thoughts* (ideas, understandings, cognitions, etc.) about the thing or *the emotion* of it (how the person feels about the thing), or what the person wants to *do about it* (a problem-solving solution). The *thoughts* given may just repeat the first thought—*in different words.* That does not make it a meta-level frame *about* the first, but just another way of expressing it.

For example, if you find that someone thinks that being "friendly" and "sharing" with colleagues at work "makes them vulnerable," then what does "being vulnerable" mean to that person? Suppose he says, "It means I could open myself up for being taken advantage of." In saying this, the person has simply repeated the same thing by merely using different words. The person is expressing the same idea as "being vulnerable."

So use the new language and keep asking the same meta-meaning question. "What does it mean to you that you could get hurt?" At this point, you can also expect people to also give *emotions* or *actions*.

"I wouldn't like that." (An emotion).
"I would want to avoid that." (An action).

Neither of these are meta-level answers either. One describes what the person feels in the state of vulnerability. The next expresses how a person wants to respond. *Feeling* and *acting* are two expressions *of* state, something characteristic of every state and every meta-state. Typically, most of us find it hard to truly stay with the meaning frame-of-reference, our meaning attribution. Why? Because our human consciousness seems more motivated and oriented to *do something about things* (actions) or to *register the emotional feel* of the experience (emotions). These imply and presuppose that we operate from a problem solving frame and emotional frame more often than stepping back and checking out the higher meaning frames within which our reality is embedded.

When this happens, simply validate the response, acknowledge it, and then repeat the meta-level question.

"Yes, I can imagine that you would like to avoid that, and you would like to avoid it because it would mean ... what?"
"Yes, I'm sure you'd like to get out of there. And when you do, you do so because it means what to you?"

In this way you can slowly identify the meanings and layers of embedded meaning layers that comprise the fabric of the person's reality—within which numerous policies operate. And when you discover unuseful, unnecessary, limiting, or dysfunctional policies, you can de-construct them and then reframe them. These skills thereby give us the ability to order and reorder our reality formats and cognitive routines so that they serve us more effectively.

"But It's the Rule"

We began the previous chapter seeking to flush out the "rules" and "policies" within our executive states. Doing so enables us to look more closely at our mapping about how to act and what to do as we encounter events, situations, and ideas in the world. In this process, you can now begin to make your rules more explicit so that you can have more choice.

What are your rules for making cold calls, asking for a raise, negotiating, speaking up to an authority figure, etc.? What kind of experiences do you have permission for versus a governing prohibition standing over you? Are you allowed to do this or that? Is it ok? Do you deserve it?

Summary

- We all have internal *policies* in our heads for how to think, emote, speak, act, relate, etc. These internal mental rules get installed in us as we grow up, become aware of the world, draw conclusions, make decisions, and develop beliefs.
- Our policies can and do become outmoded and irrelevant over time. This necessitates that we have the ability to make them explicit so that we can update them from time to time.
- To re-set executive policies or to establish new enhancing executive policies, we can *swish our brains* to new and more resourceful ideas. We can tell our brain to go to higher level frames that encode our future resourceful self.
- We can also recode old beliefs by embedding them in a frame of disconfirmation and transform great and inspiring ideas so that they become our new empowering beliefs. We need only to bring a powerful state of confirmation to bear upon them.
- Secret #10 for Personal Mastery: The beliefs that govern our perceptions, states, health, skills, etc. are thoughts embedded in a frame of confirmation. Thinking a thought will not do much neuro-linguistically, and especially neuro-semantically, until we embed it in a frame of confirmation. We build empowering beliefs that send commands to our nervous system when we bring thoughts of confirmation to bear on some thought. We destroy and eliminate toxic ideas that limit and sabotage us when we bring disconfirmation to our thoughts.

The Application Secret of Personal Mastery

Secret #11

Mastery emerges through application.

We will never experience personal mastery if we do not implement and apply what we know. Even the greatest and grandest and most compelling ideas achieve nothing if we fail to act upon them.

Chapter 8

Executing Executive Decisions

The Art of Implementing Great Ideas

"If you want people to buy, you've got to make it practical!"
(Robert Olic, Marketing Consultant)

Suppose you have *identified* your *inner executive states and powers.* Suppose further that you have *developed* and enhanced those meta-level frames-of-references that govern your life. And suppose finally, that you have *commissioned* them to set all kinds of empowering policies (beliefs, rules, principles) to really crank up *the vitality and charm* of your daily life ... Pretty good stuff, huh?

But why leave it at that?

What would it be like if you also had a higher level program in your mind for **implementing** such empowering decisions? After all, *if* for whatever reason, you somehow failed to actually *implement* all of those new life-enhancing decisions, what good would that do you? What value would that serve? How much would you then experience as improvement in your daily life?

These rhetorical questions underscore the utter importance of **implementing skills** in our lives. Without *skills for implementing knowledge,* and putting decisions into practice, all attempts at self-improvement amount to nothing. What personal mastery would that represent? This means that ultimately *the ability to translate enlightening concepts into some practical everyday life* absolutely determines whether our efforts at learning, growing, developing, and reaching for personal excellence will amount to anything.

- *How* then do we make it practical?
- *How* do we translate the shifts and transformations at meta-levels into useful everyday responses?

To answer these questions, we will seek in this chapter to make explicit the actual mechanisms (the neuro-semantic mechanisms) in the brain and nervous system that facilitate practical implementation of executive decisions, states, beliefs, and frames. You will learn about *the implementation power* that you will find in such processes as rehearsal, habituation, feedback, future pacing, etc.

Implementation—What a Great Idea!

- What marvellous insight, idea, or truth would you like to *implement* into your "way of moving" through the world?
- What empowering belief would you like to *install* in your everyday way of thinking and perceiving?
- What invigorating decision would you like to have ready access to as just "your way of doing business" on a daily basis?

This describes a basic problem that plagues most of us. We typically *know* more than we *do.* Have you find that true for yourself? Actually, this highlights one of the *dangers* of knowledge. We can confuse knowledge, insight, theories, models, and understandings with actual *skill.* We can know all kinds of wonderful things that would tremendously improve our lives, but lack the ability to *come through* in putting those great ideas into action.

In this, we need not substitute or confuse *intelligence* for *implementation.* We need both. We need great and inspiring ideas of the mind that we can *implement* in our bodies and actions. Yet a great many highly intelligent, even brilliant, individuals who know all kinds of life-transforming things seem to suffer from a lack of **D.Q.** (Doing Quotient). At least their D.Q. does not come close to matching their I.Q. Actually, given the important connection between knowing and doing, all *effective knowledge* involves following through, acting on, and putting the knowledge to practical use. We call this *implementing.*

Mere knowledge of a subject does not necessarily equate to, or even create, *skill* with that understanding. This means that implementing, following through, and *installing* intellectual knowledge into actual behavior represents true "personal power." The term *power* here means "the ability to *do* something." In this context, such *power* refers to *taking effective action in the world* to make things happen so that we fulfill our values and obtain our desired outcomes. This means "making real" (real-izing), actualizing, and manifesting our thoughts, ideas, visions, values, and beliefs.

Knowledge should lead to action, should it not? The intelligence and wisdom that we develop by processing information, developing awarenesses, creating understandings and models ought to empower us to live more effectively. Yet, by itself, it does *not*. Knowledge by itself does not automatically translate to potential skill or capacity.

Why not? Because *human neuro-semantic reality* does not operate in a strict **Stimulus** —> **Response** (S-R) way. *Mind* mediates S-R. *Consciousness* filters, modulates, and governs how we **Respond** to a **Stimulus**. As a result, knowledge does not automatically lead to action—which actually represents a very good thing.

In humans, we can think, and think, and think, and indeed, never get around to doing anything about what we know. We *pause*. We can stop and pause between an initiating Stimulus and consider it. Between the S and R we have a space for freedom of choice. In this *space* we can even try something out *in our mind* before we do it. This state of *thoughtful mindfulness* enables us to mentally rehearse prior to real-time activation.

This *conceptual space and moment* represents, at the same time, both our glory and our agony. It speaks of our *glory* in that the S-R gap of mind provides us with what the lower creatures do not have— higher level thoughts and choices about *how* to respond. We can mull things over. We can ponder. We can sit back and think, and gather more information, and play with it in our minds. We can talk about things to others. We can run virtual reality scenarios. We can put it aside for awhile and come back to it later with new resources. We can do all kinds of things in our mind *without* having to act it out.

Of course, we can also over-do this. When we over-do this, it can become an *agony*. Then we end up experiencing *patterns of inaction,* procrastination, delay, hesitation, inertia, self-contempt, confusion, etc. so that we never get around to taking effective action on our understandings. This can cause us to miss opportunities, fail to develop skills, and get into habits of self-sabotage and ineffectiveness.

In our responding, all stimuli has to pass through consciousness (except for our neurological reflexes). This means that we can hold back from putting ideas into action. We can disengage. We can spend our days filling our heads with information without ever doing anything about it. We can become eggheads whereby we learn more and more while becoming increasingly incompetent in applying it in the real world.

Given this, *what does it take* in order for us to develop *implementation power and skill?* What do we need in order to implement the executive decisions of our inner executive? If consciousness *per se* represents an insufficient cause, then what kind of consciousness provides us with this ability?

The Eleventh Secret of Personal Mastery

Secret #11
Mastery depends upon application.
We will never experience personal mastery if we do not implement and apply what we know. Even the greatest and grandest and most compelling ideas achieve nothing if we fail to act upon them.

Discovering Your Strategy For Implementation
Would you like to discover your own strategy for implementation so that you can evaluate it in terms of effectiveness? Take a few moments, right now, to take a deep breath and relax as you recall a time in your life *when you effectively implemented* some piece of knowledge, understanding, or insight ...

In doing this, find several memories where you pulled off the feat of effectively putting some valued "understanding" into action. Start with something small and simple. Perhaps someone told you that they would appreciate it if you opened a door for them, and so you simply did. Or someone offered you a valued idea and you mindfully acted on it.

Perhaps you discovered that to avoid munching on junk food late at night, you should simply not buy it in the first place, or stock it in the house for easy access. And then you did that very thing—you chose to refuse to stock up on it the next time you went shopping.

Recall your memory fully and completely so that you *see what you saw* then, *hear what you heard,* and *do so* until you begin to *feel what you felt.* Allow yourself to experience that memory of implementing with honest and unconscious completeness. Now as you do, fully allow yourself also to notice the body sensations (kinesthetic) of acting on the information, the self-dialogue that you used by which you prompted yourself to do it, the kind and quality of images that danced before your inner theater, etc. Further, as you do this, do it with the realization that this will only enhance your ongoing ability to effectively implement your executive decisions. Stop now and do this.

Your Own Non-Implementation Pattern

To contrast *how you run your own brain* for implementing with the experience of non-implementing, think about some recent event in your life when you did not implement something. Pick something that you knew very well that you *should* put into practice, and that you really wanted to, but for whatever reason, you did not. What did you *not* come through with? Now recall that instance fully and completely as you did the other experience. Do it from the perspective of *being there.* You will know that you have succeeded in this when you re-experience the memory as if seeing out of your own eyes and hearing out of your own ears. S*tep into the movie* in your mind so much so that you feel the sensations that you felt then ...

Next, contrast these two programs. This will enable you to specify the very leverage points which will enable you to activate your *implementation state of mind.* What occurs in your awareness when you implement a decision or commitment which fails to occur when you do not implement? What occurs in the non-implementing state that you do not repeat when you implement knowledge? As you check out this information, check for such *distinctions and features* of your representations as the following variables.

- *Auditorially:* Tone of voice: volume, quality, sound of the internal sounds
- *Linguistically:* Words used in internal dialogue: What do you say in each experience?
- *Visually:* images: color or not, how close or far, fuzzy or clear, where located?
- *Kinesthetically:* felt sensations elicited at different stages in the process.
- Number of steps in the process
- Looping around and around a thought, or the lack of looping
- Clarity of Values
- Clarity of Outcomes

One young man, Jim, said that he had lots of internal dialogue and internal chatter in his head when he did not come through with acting on something. He would hear himself explaining and reasoning and thinking and convincing himself about why he did not want to come through, did not feel ready to act, or felt apprehensive about acting. In his awareness, he would see, hear, and feel things that he did not want to experience. Sometimes he would feel himself looping around and around.

> "Why do I have to do this?" "I wish I could get out of this!" "It seems so hard!" "It's so overwhelming!" "I'm not clear about how to get this done." "What if I fail?" "What if she gets angry?" Etc.

By contrast, when Jim effectively implements, he has a much quieter internal mental world. He has a clear and sharply focused mental image of the idea that he thinks about implementing. If what he wants to do has several steps or stages to it, he internally represents those steps in a coherent way that moves fairly quickly like a movie. Then he feels congruent about wanting to do it. He does not talk very much to himself at that point. What languaging he does use involves shorter and more succinct statements.

> "What a great idea!" "I feel really excited about this!" "This will make things much more effective." "Just do it!" "Go for it!"

At the sensational level, he feels energized with an optimal amount of muscle tension. His breathing feels strong and energetic as it comes from low in his stomach in a relaxed way. Mentally, he has a sense of clarity about what he does and how he goes about doing it. Emotionally, he feels confident about doing it as well as competent in pulling it off.

Also, when you do this, notice the supporting beliefs between the two states of mind. What do you *believe* about taking action? How much pain and/or pleasure have you attached to implementing your ideas? What painful or pleasurable experiences have played a formative role in deploying your insights? These all speak about higher frames-of-references (Meta-States) and so will govern the experiences.

Mechanisms That Facilitate Implementation

Several mechanisms play a role in facilitating our power of implementation. These include an awareness of the old action programs, a meta-awareness of how well or how poorly those programs worked, an awareness of our own thinking and processing of information, appreciating the value and power of implementing, deciding to implement, mentally rehearsing the new idea to habituate new programs, imagining how it will play out into the future (future pacing), etc. These neuro-linguistic processes help us build an inner executive to run the learnings and knowledge that we want to become our "programs."

Awareness of the Old "Action Programs"

We all come equipped with an *urge to act* on strong, compelling ideas. We have a genetic makeup so ordered. Our energy system inherently moves us to need satisfying responses. Our "old brain" unfailingly drives us to fulfill our desires, whether hard-wired or learned.

You can observe this *urge to act* in the raw in the newborn baby. Notice how the baby immediately and automatically *acts on* whatever it "thinks." The infant feels an urge and acts on it. The entire repertoire of infants, in fact, consist of crying, sucking, shaking, and other autonomic nervous system responses.

What does this mean? This means that we all come into this world **implementing.** We implement urges, *e-motions* (motions resulting from our evaluations), desires, and ideas that cross our minds. No wonder young mothers and fathers can experience a baby as very demanding. They do what we humans have been wired to do. Using their primitive consciousness they attempt to satisfy their needs. And they will rage and tantrum, smile and coo to get what they want.

Later, as adults we develop a more extensive set of behaviors in our repertoire, even though we still feel those *urges to act.* Now, however, they show up primarily as *e-motions,* rather than primitive and uncontrollable drives. *Emotions,* as somatic movements, urge us with pushes and pulls to act. In fact, the first and primary thing we all tend to register in consciousness involves our emotions. We "have a feeling" about doing something. [*soma,* "body," as in *somatic.*]

The old brain creates this general sense of the *urge to act.* The old brain that runs our autonomic nervous system pushes us to go after our "needs." Whatever we *think* we need, and so cue our nervous system, we then experience *urges* for the same. It becomes our "programming."

This experience can also create all kinds of problems for us. While children, we did all kinds of "crazy" thinking, believing, and conceptualizing that today shows up as mere out-of-conscious *urges.* No wonder that in the process of becoming "fully human and fully alive" (John Powell), we have to use our new brain to *think* and to *re-think.* Doing so enables us to temper, qualify, update, and reality-test our old thinking. We can now check out our old thoughts to see if they serve us very well.

What *e-motions* as energy drives operate in you? What drives push and pull on you and seek for you to express them? What programs do you now, automatically and unthinkingly, implement? These make sense given your learning history and experiences while simultaneously they may also undermine your well-being, health, success, and peace of mind.

The *action programs* developed in our early years often become less and less effective over time. No wonder we need to keep updating our programs and installing new resources. Ineffective and non-productive behavior arises whenever we become uninformed about those old programs or when we fail to reality test them.

What old *action programs* still run your programs? Do they serve you well? Do they enhance your life? Listen to your languaging patterns.

Awareness of Thinking

When we become *aware of* ourselves and our thinking or emoting, we move to a meta-level. This grants us greater perspective and vision. It enables us to meta-think and meta-comment on our old *action programs.*

Suppose you find the following old program:

> "I should always do whatever comes into my mind." "I should have whatever I want right now!" "I won't, for one moment, let people or events get in my way of satisfying my desires."

When someone uses their thinking to so reason, it will lead to action programs of *impetuousness.* In bringing thoughts-and-feelings of impetuousness to bear on ourselves, we set ourselves up for that very experience.

On the other hand, suppose you built some mental paradigms that attached pain to implementing? Have you got "pain" attached to taking action? If you implemented your ideas, then what? What would that *mean*? Would it mean "being impetuous, taking a risk, making yourself vulnerable, risking failure, endangering your safety, possibly making a mistake, etc.? Suppose you had the following ideas deeply ingrained within you. Would this not program you for perpetual waiting, procrastination, hesitating, phobicking, etc.

> "I must take care to think everything through and never, but never act on my ideas without lots of thinking time." "It's

always dangerous to act." "I never could do anything right for mom or dad. So I learned to not do anything until I can do them perfectly." "When you do things, you will always upset someone. So the safest policy that I know—do nothing that might upset others."

The conclusions that we draw as we create our mental mapping (Model of the World) determines the *emotional energies* generated by our nervous system. Then that governs our states. Such mental mapping represents our most basic and pervasive powers.

As an engineer, Alfred Korzybski labeled this *"abstracting"*—the summarizing and concluding ("thinking") that our nervous system/brain does in creating our *perceptions* and *thoughts.* He used his logical level model, *The Levels of Abstraction Model,* to show that both *science* and *sanity* depend upon *consciousness of abstracting.* Such meta-awareness, in fact, empowers us with choice about whether our mapping serves us well or not.

Appreciation for Implementing

Since *what* we seek to implement involves *cognitive knowledge,* we have to develop some *clear ideas* about our desired outcomes. What idea, belief, decision, understanding, etc. do you want to "put into action"?

How much do you appreciate the value of putting a given idea into action? What will it do for you? How do you deem that important? We certainly do not want to put a program to action where we implement just anything or everything. We want discretion in our implementing, as well as wisdom. Doing this increases our sense of *readiness to implement.* We *want* to implement because we understand its value and we confirm its significance.

Further, the more complex the idea, the more readiness we will need in order to implement. We can easily implement expressing concern, opening a car door, picking up after ourselves, can we not? We find such ideas, and their corresponding behaviors, easy. But what about implementing a truly big project—going back to college, writing a book, maintaining an exercise program, learning to speak more assertively, changing careers, etc.?

You've got *an idea*. Your thoughts and plans about that idea excite you. You want to put it into action. You have a clear sense of how to do it. Now make sure that you have *an intense enough appreciation* for it. From 0 to 10, how much importance do you see in it? Make a list of all the values. What other values could you attribute to it to juice up your appreciation?

Has your appreciating yet reached the level of a *passion* for you? Does it feel truly *urgent* to you? How much more urgency do you need to feel about it in order to act on it? Apply this to cleaning the kitchen, doing sit-ups, finishing college, reading, etc.

If you don't feel passionate about it yet, then mentally edit your internal maps so that it looks, sounds, and feels more compelling, more attractive. Add more clarity to it. Attribute more importance to it. Amplify how you represent it. "Blow it out of proportion." If you know how to catastrophize, awfulize, terriblize, and magnify things, then you know how to make something bigger than it is. You have everything you need to *juice* this one up as well.

As your overall objective, aim to attach *massive pleasure* to acting on your highly valued insights. As you do, you will condition your neurology to feel good about taking action.

Deciding to Implement

Have you actually and consciously *decided* to implement something? We frequently do not implement because we have never actually made the decision.

"Yes, I wish I could put this into practice!" "I think I might put this into practice tomorrow."

Instead of *deciding decisively*, we merely wish, hope for, or long for. One man told me:

"I have half-a-mind to join that health club and to stop smoking."

"You have half a mind to do this? What would it be like for you if you had a full mind about this?"

"Actually, it would be great. If I had a full mind about this decision, then I would be focused and clear, and doing it wouldn't be much of a problem."

"That makes it sound like a tremendous resource for you. So I'm wondering what you would have to do to have a full mind about this?"

"Well … I don't know, I guess I would have to make a decision to really do this."

"And can you imagine doing that?"

"Yes, I can …"

"And…?"

"Well, I couldn't use my excuses."

"So what dragon pops up in your mind about being of a full mind regarding this decision?"

"What if I fail? I guess I'm afraid of failing."

"And 'failing' means what—that you would have one or ten slip-ups or that somehow you would think that maybe smoking isn't all that bad for you, in fact, you think it's positively good and healthful for you?"

"No, nothing like that. I wouldn't go there. I'd just be afraid that if I slipped up I might never get back on track …"

"Really? Never? … ever? Is that truly your frame-of-reference?"

"No."

"Then what do you need to do right now, this day, and for every day hereafter in order to truly make an empowering decision about this?"

To make a true decision, a decision that you will find empowering and definite, and lasting, you will need to decide about such things as:

- *What* specifically do you want to do.
- *How* specifically will you get it done.
- *When* and *where* will you do it.
- *With whom* you will do it.
- *What* resources you'll need to help pull it off, etc.

Fully develop your mental map and then *definitively decide* to go for it. To take effective action will necessitate that you develop sufficient mental clarity about these things. Otherwise you won't know *what* to do, *when, where,* etc. Get your *executive decision* specified in clear, behavioral terms.

One of my executive decisions for years has been to climb the Colorado fourteeners—the fifty-four mountains in the state that measure more than fourteen-thousand feet above sea-level. *Knowing how* to do this involves understanding the details of preparing to go to the high country, the things to bring, how to organize the trip, how to stay in shape for such hiking and climbing, etc. The more involved and intricate any outcome, the more you need a well-developed plan. Break it down into all of the pieces involved. Then chunk those pieces into bite-size bits. Sequence them so that you can make a flow-chart of the process.

Your mind is almost "made up" about something. You have a piece of insight. So now make that knowledge *power*—make a plan and commit yourself to put it into action. Making a true decision (beyond a mere wish) means you "cut off" (de-cision) other options. This boils down to saying *"No"* to some things so that you can say completely *"Yes!"* to other things. You do this by specifying and focusing on one specific thing. No matter how small a response, make a decision to act on it. Never, but never leave the scene of an insight without taking some action—even if this means only writing it down or talking about it with someone.

This describes and grants you the key to true *personal power* in the sense of acting on your goals, beliefs, values, etc. To have created these executive decisions and understandings and to *not* put them into practice will actually work to undermine your powers. When you know and want to take action, then hear a congruent and strongly compelling voice say, *"Just do it!"*

You don't need to make it any more complicated then that. William James (1890) in *Psychology: A Briefer Course* wrote about this thing:

> "Never should we suffer ourselves to have an emotion at a play, concert, or upon reading a book, without expressing it afterward in some active way. Let the expression be the least thing in the world—speaking genially to one's grand-mother ... but let it not fail to take place.

> "If we let our emotions evaporate, they get into a way of evaporating.... When a resolve or a fine glow of feeling is allowed to evaporate without bearing practical fruit it is worse than a change lost; it works so positively to hinder the discharge of future resolutions and emotions."

Psycho-neurologically, to *act* on a thought, resolve, or understanding *empowers* it. George Weinberg in *Self-Creation* described this:

> "Every time you act, you add strength to the motivating idea behind what you have done." (p. 5).

Actions reinforce cognitions. Every time we act on, or implement, an insight, we drive that insight deep into our very neurology. The physiology and neurology of the action incorporates the information and program into us. This represents a basic programming principle in our nature and explains why what we *do* can so deeply affect us.

This explains why and how we can use the *"As If" Principle* or the Pretend Frame to walk ourselves through various behaviors (even when they do not feel comfortable or "real"). We can do so until we get used to them, until they become real to us. Such intentional acting allows us to then encode the learning into our very muscles and cells.

William James developed his famous Theory of Emotional Control, along with Karl Lange, on this realization.

> "If you check or change the expression of an emotion, you thereby check or change the emotion itself. Do the thing you fear to do, and do it repeatedly until the fear diminishes. Feelings follow action. Action seems to follow feeling, but really action and feeling go together. By regulating the action (which is under the more direct control of the will), you can indirectly regulate the feeling (which is not).

> "The sovereign voluntary path to cheerfulness, if your spontaneous cheerfulness be lost, is to sit up cheerfully and to act and speak as if cheerfulness were already there. If such conduct does not make you feel cheerful, nothing else on that occasion can. So to feel brave, act as if you were brave, use all of your will to that end, and a courage-fit will very likely replace a fit of fear."

Develop a Bias for Action

Let's take this a step further and *develop a positive bias for action*. In Western cultures, most of us have grown up with the dichotomy between *learning* and *doing*. Consider how this applies to reading. Most people treat "reading" as *mere* information gathering, disinterested learning, processing of data, etc. When it comes to down-to-earth, practical stuff that makes up everyday life, they even think it incredible that they could find anything practical "in a book!"

This dualistic paradigm as a way of thinking about "book learning" and "real-life learning" pervades the thinking of most people. So what? As a result, the very idea of *reading to learn how*, or reading experientially, even strikes people as weird and unreal.

> "How did you learn to do that?"
> "I read it in a book."
> "Naw! No way!"

Yet people who read to *not* implement, who read *to escape*, who read to *pass the time*, etc., often end up reading without really comprehending, learning, getting it, changing. How well do you read? Does the experience of "reading" somehow seem bookish and "not real" to you. Or does it seem, at least, "not practical for real life"? If so, then you have learned this dichotomy all too well. Now if you want a paradigm shift that will totally alter your sense of reality, and your world of meaning, *shift to the idea of implementation reading and thinking*. Set this as your frame-of-reference about reading.

> "Information, learnings, and understandings always and inevitably have practical and daily implications in my life. How will this idea impact upon my life tomorrow? Where could I use this belief? In what context would this understanding change things?"

Develop your own ability to *think implementation*. Let the idea, "How can I use this?" become your perceptual program. Do this by planting the indexing questions deep into your consciousness.

How, when, where, what, in what way, with whom, etc.?

When you do this, then you will *constantly explore and play* with how to practically use things. It will become part of your very perception.

- How could I use this information?
- How could I put this into my way of relating to people?
- Where would this come in handy?
- With whom would I like to share this information?
- What else could I do with this insight?
- What other part of my life can I apply this insight to?
- Who can I discuss this information with?

This paradigm shift presupposes many empowering ideas. It presupposes that you can *translate ideas into practice at your choice*. It presupposes that you never meet or deal with *mere* ideas, but always *ideo-dynamic* ideas. *Ideo-dynamic* speaks about the energetic nature of ideas in our nervous system to effect the internal signaling and communicating of our body. It presupposes that by taking a proactive stance regarding data, we become a lifelong learner, thinker, applier, translator.

Would you like a great and empowering frame to use when you read? *Assume that you will present the key ideas to somebody later today or tomorrow.* Read everything for the purpose of sharing it with someone. In fact, actually pull some people into your life to share ideas with. Read just enough to get some new and exciting ideas, and then stop and implement it in some way.

In a recent training in the northern part of England (Harrogate), an Australian gentleman went from table to table in a pub one evening after a Meta-States Training sharing the insights that he developed during the day.

The attitude of sharing the good things you discover in order to empower them will bless you immensely. It will also turn on your motivation for learning. It will expand your perspective, increase your memory, and deepen understanding. Getting into this implementation mode will make you a better friend and conversationalist. You will stop treating ideas promiscuously—delving in here, playing around there. Rather than promiscuous playing, always seek to find some way to put knowledge into action.

An Implementation Plan with Ongoing Feedback
Many times we begin to implement an idea or plan, but then come up short when we experience some trouble, resistance, or frustration. We start, but then back off whenever things get tough. We let negative feedback rein in our horses and stop us dead in our tracks. When this happens, however, we don't stop completely. Instead we can simply take the difficulties as feedback and then incorporate our refined learnings and distinctions into our plans.

If you begin to "diet" (or start a rather more conscientious, healthy way to eat) and then find that you slip up when someone asks you out for lunch, you have a great piece of information to use as feedback. You need a contingency plan in your eating for handling such. Use it to build into your implementation strategy the ability to feel delighted that someone asked, and that you have the ability to say "No" gracefully, or would love to eat a salad.

Taking feedback as *information* for fine tuning your strategy enables you to troubleshoot your commitment to some action plan. This increases your flexibility for shifting to "Plan B" while holding on to your vision and commitment.

What undermines your implementation of any given X?

If you perfectionistically judge whatever you do as fallible, imperfect, and "not good enough," then you will probably procrastinate by putting things off until the last minute, lazying around doing nothing while wishing you had more energy, mentally overwhelming yourself with all the things you have to do, guilting yourself about being bad, looping unceasingly—these represent fabulous ways to mess up your implementation skills.

Welcoming Feedback In A Positive Way

Once you begin to *swing into action* and deploy your resources in translating knowledge into action, you can expect some rough sailing. After all, expecting that our very first translation of an idea into action will spring forth full-grown, complete, and without any need for improvement, doesn't seem useful or realistic. After the initial action steps, we will need to give it repetition, practice, continual ongoing failing, so that we can perfect it.

Welcome *the translation process.* The first appearance of every great idea typically shows up in an under-developed state that needs improvement. As we seek feedback about how we can improve it, then we can go to work honing and sharpening it. In terms of *competency*, any new development of knowledge and skill begins with the stage of unconscious incompetence. We don't even know about our incompetence. Next, as we become aware, we experience conscious incompetence. For most people, this represents an extremely unpleasant and uncomfortable place. Many people will not tolerate it at all. They will not give themselves a chance for mastery. Those who do, however, will eventually get to the level of conscious competence. They understand something and can pull it off. As this habituates, it will eventually become unconscious competence.

Figure 8:1

Levels of Competency

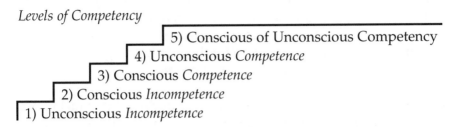

5) Conscious of Unconscious Competency
4) Unconscious *Competence*
3) Conscious *Competence*
2) Conscious *Incompetence*
1) Unconscious *Incompetence*

No baby just stands up after crawling and takes off walking with the skill and expertise of an adult or an Olympic runner. The infant's *concept* of walking takes many ups and downs before we see the idea expressed elegantly. Before that happens, the child will abundantly practice in rising and falling until he or she learns that delicate balance that we call "walking."

To become a high level implementer necessitates that we make a good adjustment to *error signals*. By welcoming such feedback and using the information for improvement, we won't be put off by imperfection. We can reframe "failing" (an unspecified verb) and the noxious sounding nominalization, "failure," as *feedback about what we discovered does not work so that we can move on to trying other things.* "Failure" means we just have not found the solution *yet*. We don't have to associate it with any other meanings. Doing so empowers us to not get put off by the trial and error method of learning.

Developing a positive attitude about feedback involves seeing it as "the key information that I need for more effectively translating my knowledge into action." Without this frame of reference, we will only wreck ourselves on the shoals of "failure," personalize it, and get into some really grouchy states. But with this reframe, we can move on to asking profound questions:

— "What can I learn from this that will help me?"
— "What else might contribute to turning this around and reaching my goal?"
— "Who else knows how to pull this off that I could consult with?"
— "What books address this subject that might give me some insights?"

The Japanese use the term **kaizen** to describe the process of *continuous improvement* by small, incremental changes. *Kaizen* refers to the slow, but ever increasing improvement that occurs over time when a person aims to improve things every day by .05%. Business consultant and theorist, Edwards Deming, recommended this as a powerful quality control process.

Every time we fail to put some executive decision into practice, we have "a rare and unprecedented opportunity" for self-discovery and for fine-tuning our processes; by tracking down the causes or contributing factors that undermined the translation.

- What specifically sabotaged implementing this knowledge?
- What internal and external factors?
- What beliefs or emotions?

Ellen J. Langer (1988) and associates conducted some experiments with regard to the ability to *use information*. The variable she played around with concerned *how* individuals received the information. Some received information *in absolute terms,* others in absolute terms but as "one possible model," and others in *probability terms* (it "could be" this way).

Those given the information in the format of absolutism (in both versions) "were not mindful enough to notice when a made-up case did not fit the model at all." Conversely, those who received the information in probability language realized that the information would "be true only under certain circumstances" and *did incredibly better in using and applying the information* (*Mindfulness*, p. 128).

This experiment tellingly reveals the danger of closing one's mind, becoming mentally rigid, and forgetting to index when, where, who, what, how, etc. It alerts us to how we can sabotage our power of coming through when we slip into the toxic thinking of *the deity mode of absolutism.* When we use the language of absolutes, we speak about things in the static sense of permanence.

Albert Ellis (1976), the psychologist who developed RET (Rational Emotive Therapy), described various kinds of thinking patterns that create cognitive distortions: black-and-white thinking, awfulizing, catastrophizing, maximizing, etc. This highlights how the more we think and talk in rigid, all-or-nothing terms, the less likely we will gain new and surprising insights into the applications of our present knowledge.

And no wonder. *Creativity* necessitates a more playful attitude, a less definitive approach, a greater willingness to experiment, to test, to play around with ideas and thoughts, to tolerate uncertainty, to get excited by the unknown, etc. By using a more tentative languaging, we empower ourselves to create and invent new approaches and understandings.

Future Pacing

What would stop you from implementing your knowledge? When we vividly imagine ourselves taking effective action at some future time, we *future pace* the idea and "run the program" in a virtual reality. Doing this frequently provides a simulation environment for new learnings, awareness, ideas, and resources.

What do you need in order to even more effectively put your knowledge into action? More physical energy and vitality? Memory aids to keep focused and on target? A more pleasant environment? Whatever you find, future pace that piece into your internal movie and notice the effect that has.

Start with a primary state, any primary state and then access, amplify, and apply *implementation thoughts-and-feelings* to it. After you do that, now add in just whatever other resourceful ideas, memories, imagination, etc. that will allow you to enrich and qualify your style of implementation.

Summary

- Implementing our executive decisions involves setting up a higher frame which empowers us to make the decision to implement great ideas. This then equips us with the ability to take a *proactive stance* in life. It enables us to take responsibility for our thoughts-and-feelings and how we use our powers of speech and behavior.

- The implementation frame further enables us to *design engineer* the kind of behaviors, programs, experiences, states, beliefs, etc. that we desire.
- *Secret #11. Mastery emerges through application.*
  We will never experience personal mastery if we do not implement and apply what we know. Even the greatest, grandest, and most compelling ideas achieve nothing if we fail to act upon them.

The Alignment Secret
of
Personal Mastery

Secret #12

The personal mastery of focus and power comes from alignment with all of one's higher or executive frames of mind.

When we align all of our higher frames of minds—our valuing, understanding, believing, identifying, deciding, etc., we find that we can direct our powers of attention according to our higher intentions. This creates a laser beam type of focus

Chapter 9

Aligning Conflicting Executives

*Eliminating Internal Conflicts Resolving
the Wars of the Managers*

"A house divided against itself shall not stand."
(Abraham Lincoln quoting Jesus of Nazareth)

Conflicts happen. Not infrequently, even great businesses fall apart and the people who pioneered them end up destroying what they created. What's the culprit behind this? It typically results from unresolved conflicts. The bosses, supervisors, and top management get into a mode of fuming and fussing, and in the end, they incinerate their dreams and hopes. So their vision goes up in smoke. This is not good.

If there's power and focus in alignment, when people hold a common vision, when they co-dream a future, there is an equally destructive power when people get at odds with each other. When that happens, *misalignment* creates all kinds of friction, misunderstanding, and fights about meanings, beliefs, values, identity, and direction. People in different departments begin to compete with each other as if they were enemies. People at different levels take actions that contradict the very purposes and agendas of the company. This reduces the overall effectiveness of the group as it also wastes time, energy, and resources. An even worse evil arises from this as it creates a hostile environment for everybody. This makes it more difficult for people in all departments and at all levels to work at optimal productiveness.

A similar thing can happen in *human personality* that undermines personal mastery. Different parts or facets of ourselves can get into inter-departmental wars with each other. One part of us becomes "an enemy" to another part. And, as it happens with a business, so it can happen in personality; destructive forces are then unleashed that sabotage and ruin our higher hopes, dreams, and visions.

So what's a multi-dimensional being to do? We can take *a time out*, identify the source of these conflicts, and begin a mediation process for aligning and re-aligning the inner "parts" which have become alienated and conflicted. This kind of troubleshooting will mean several things in terms of developing our own *inner executive*. Among other things, it will mean that we will need to:

- Find the saboteurs to our executive parts that won't follow instructions
- Get beyond the communication blocks and misunderstandings
- Design and facilitate conflict resolution between these parts
- Negotiate new arrangements that bring congruency and integrity
- Develop an overall team spirit between all of the parts.

When Inner Executives become Dysfunctional

It's no surprise that a company's CEO can become dysfunctional, and even go bonkers. The same can happen to our own inner CEO. In the movie with Dolly Parton, *9 to 5*, we enjoyed observing a great example of a dysfunctional, red-neck, black-and-white thinking, self-centered CEO who needed to be hog-tied and de-commissioned. And so it happened!

- When a business' CEO goes over the edge of sanity into unsanity or even insanity, what results would we expect?
- How would something like that affect the company's everyday functioning?
- What are the factors that could create this kind of problem?

Numerous things can sabotage our inner executive states from functioning effectively. We noted in the previous chapter the sabotage factor of simply *failing to execute* our executive decisions. In this chapter, we will focus on the disordering that occurs through inner conflict, misalignment, and incongruency. These things create a dysfunction of the inner executive and of the executive states so that they do not, and cannot, operate effectively.

Trouble-shooting Meta-State Problems

The following pattern offers a process for trouble-shooting, updating, and refining our current executive and meta-states so that we keep our inner executive states current, relevant, functional, and in good health. As a diagnostic list, the following *Signs of Conflict* offer us a way to run a quick diagnostic on our overall system.

Signs of Conflict and Internal Stress:

- A "part" of me thinks-or-feels one thing while another "part" feels something different.
- Procrastination
- Stress and tension
- Conflicting thoughts-and-feelings
- A sense of embattlement with others
- A sense of competition with others
- Looping around and around, feeling stuck, and at an impasse
- Defensiveness
- Can't get oneself to act, feeling de-motivated
- Negative thoughts-and-feelings about a higher level state
- Existential negative emotions (guilt, shame, fear)

Detecting the Internal Conflict

You know you have an internal *battle* going on when you feel "at odds with yourself." This occurs whenever one part of you wants to accomplish one thing, yet another part keeps interrupting you so that it prevents you from staying focused. This kind of *internal conflict* illustrates a lack of alignment between facets of mind, between different meta-level structures.

To flush out misalignment within different facets of yourself, you need only to quiet yourself and to simply turn inward. As you do, ask yourself something like, "Does any part of me object to a goal, objective, outcome, or criterion?"

After asking this question, simply allow any and every thought in the form of internal pictures, sounds, words, sensations, memories, imaginations, etc. to arise and play out on the screen of your awareness. As these "automatic thoughts" begin to intrude, simply pay attention to them as internal communications and signals. As you give yourself permission to just notice the thoughts and messages "in the back of your mind," you will begin to detect the meta-level frames of beliefs, orientations, states, etc. that create the inward incongruency and ineffectiveness.

We can also use another process for flushing out and detecting various *dragon states*. We can use sentence stems about self-expectancy. For example, read the following sentence stem: *When I think about failing to accomplish an important goal, I can expect myself to* ... Now go with that thought. Where do your thoughts, feelings, and physiology take you? Write that sentence stem out on a sheet of paper and then write five or more sentence completions. What emerges as you do?

Whatever you can **expect** of yourself (of your thinking, emoting, and behaving) tells you about the higher meaning frames that govern it and within which it is embedded. Your mental and emotional responses to certain events arise because you have given the event certain meanings. So when you *backtrack* to the thinking, perceiving, understanding, meaning-making, etc. that governs the responses and the state of consciousness, you will find the determining executive state or states. And, of course, when you find such, you also find all of the rules, policies, procedures, and meanings that drive the state.

Do you feel you have some mis-alignment or incongruency? Try your hand at the following *sentence stems*. As you do, write each on a blank sheet of paper and then as you access a relaxed, playful, and curious state, begin to let the thoughts in the back of your mind generate five to twelve completions to each stem. As you do this, do so in the realization that there is no right or wrong answer or way to respond. Set the frame that there's no shame or blame here. Instead, seek only to flush out and detect the various structures in your higher mind. So if you find some unpleasant frame, just note that it exists and governs. Just witness it. Nor does it really matter how such constructions of perceiving got created. It's enough to detect such so that we can then move to a higher level of choice.

Figure 9:1

Sentence Stems for Flushing Out Self-Expectancies

- When disappointments occur, I can expect myself to think or feel …
- When someone rejects me, I can expect myself to think or feel …
- When someone criticizes me, I can expect myself to think or feel …
- When someone insults me, I can expect myself to think or feel …
- When I catch a character flaw in myself, I can expect myself to think or feel …
- When I feel angry, I can expect myself to think or feel …
- When I feel afraid, I can expect myself to think or feel …
- When I feel grief and sadness, I can expect myself to think or feel …
- When I feel guilty, I can expect myself to think or feel …
- When I feel weak or vulnerable, I can expect myself to think or feel …
- When I feel disappointed, I can expect myself to think or feel …
- When I feel tired, I can expect myself to think or feel …
- When I feel grumpy, I can expect myself to think or feel …
- When I feel stressed, I can expect myself to think or feel …

Such *self-expectancies* typically tell us about some of our executive states that have got into a looping pattern. We start feeling "bad" in some way, perhaps angry. Then we feel guilty about our anger. Then we feel ashamed of our guilt of our anger. Or we feel hesitant about making a call to a customer, and then we judge it as a sign of our ineffectiveness or flawed nature. Then we feel frustrated and upset about our inadequacy. And so it goes. We spiral around and around in a loop of negativity, victimhood, discounting, or self-contempting. In the second book on Meta-States, *Dragon Slaying: From Dragons To Princes (1996, 2000 second edition)*, we referred to such painful and torturous states that undermine our effectiveness and empowerment as *dragon states*.

In these structures of mind, we essentially *turn our psychic energies against ourselves.* We do this by bringing *negative* thoughts and feelings **against** ourselves. Rather than accepting the events that occur and welcome them into awareness so that we can learn from them and use them to spur us on, we reject them, hate them, despise them, judge them.

Yet in spite of the good intentions of this maneuver, it actually puts us *at odds* with reality, with the reality of events, with our own mental-emotional reality, and with social reality. So while we typically do this to reduce pain and to protect ourselves, it usually comes back to haunt us. Reflexively, we simply bring the rejection and judgment back to bear upon our own state. This builds up a very negative meta-state that revels in shame and blame. It starts with rejection of our anger, then hatred of our fear, guilt of our anger, stress about our shame of our frustration, etc. This does not describe a very celebrative way to live.

Explore the Meaning Frames of our Executive States

When we move up to a higher level of "mind," we bring thoughts and feelings to bear upon some experience or state and this creates *the meaning* of that experience. It sets the frame. Doing this establishes a mental paradigm and reference system by which we think and experience it. It establishes how we value the given experience.

In the previous exercise of flushing out *self-expectancies*, we essentially flush out the **meaning frames** within which our behaviors make sense. We can also do this in other ways. For example, we can more directly ask, *What does it mean for you to feel...?* "What does it mean for you to feel anger?" Disappointment? Guilt? Frustration?

The structure of this "magic" involves a simple association. We *bring* shame to bear on our *anger*, for example. Relationally, the *shame* thoughts and feelings stand at a higher logical level to the *anger* and so it operates as the frame for our thinking and experience with regard to the anger. We could say that the *shame* state has become the *conceptual context* into which we have *embedded* the experience of anger. Now, every time we experience *anger* (whether appropriate or inappropriate), we experience it as *a shameful thing.* "How dare we?!" The shame qualifies the anger to thereby transform it into "shameful anger."

To understand any executive state running your programs and controlling your sense of congruence or incongruence, simply get into the habit of asking *the meaning question.* You can inquire about **the meaning** of something in numerous ways.

> — What does that mean to you?
> — What significance does X hold for you?
> — When you think or feel Y, what other thoughts and emotions come to mind?
> — What meanings do you give to X?
> — What have you learned to attribute to X?

Exercise for Alignment Processes—Integrating Meta-Levels

The following process has been named *The Spinning Icons* pattern by Nelson Zink and Joe Munshaw (1996). It comes from their work in NLP that allows a person to "chunk up" the scale of abstraction and to create new and more empowering generalizations (i.e. beliefs, ideas, understandings, decisions, etc.) for navigating a territory regarding which we feel in conflict. This process works especially well when we can hardly even put words to our internal conflicts and do not consciously know what to do. It enables us to develop new resources for personal integration that we may not understand consciously. The new synthesized generalization that it can evoke will then serve as a new and more resourceful map. We can now use this as an Advanced Outcome Alignment pattern for working with polarities.

Step 1: Access two primary states or experiences that internally feel at odds.

What two ideas, understandings, beliefs feel at odds within you and that creates conflict for you? What parts do you not have peace about? Perhaps it involves some idea like: "It's bad to be materialistic," or "The desire to succeed in life and win lots of toys." Perhaps, "I can't stand criticism," or "To stand out from the crowd and take risks involves exposing myself to criticism."

Identify two "parts" or facets of your experience that seem to be at odds with each other. Describe each part individually until you have a clear understanding of these two un-integrated facets.

Step 2: Turn the Primary States into Abstract Symbols.

Go meta to each of the states or experiences and generate an iconic image, cartoon, or symbol. "What could represent the first state for you?' "What would you like to use as a symbolic representation of the second state?" Notice the quality, location, and features of these two images or symbols as you describe them fully.

Step 3: At a level meta to the two iconic images, begin to let the two images slowly exchange locations.

Mentally imagine putting the images of the two icons into each other's place so that they exchange places. For example, you could put "materialism" in the location of "desire to succeed" and vice versa. After they have exchanged places, let them continue to exchange places faster and faster until they blend and create a synthesis. Move your eyes back and forth as you watch icon 1 and icon 2 exchange places.

Figure 9:2

Meta-States and Meta-Levels

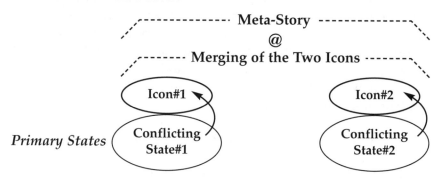

@ = about

Step 4: *Stop and tell a Meta-Story.*

Once the two images have merged and mixed and become confused, stop. Then immediately begin to tell a story about the new merged or merging image. Or you could make up a proverb, invent a poem, express a motto, koan, etc. Tell a story *about* the synthesis of the merging of the two parts. The more you don't know *what* to say, the better—produce an immediate, no waiting, no hesitating response.

Step 5: *Future pace and integrate.*

After the story has emerged and been told, inquire of yourself how the story or proverb may be relevant to the difficulty and internal conflict. Invite the symbol to come into yourself and then to store it inside you so you can take it with you into your future.

Aligning Meta-States

The following process provides a way to align our higher executive states. It allows us to be able to align and utilize the various meta-level structures of our executive states. As a result, it will generate within you an overall sense of feeling integrated, congruent, whole, and well. I have adapted this pattern from Robert Dilts' work with the Neuro-logical levels, Andreas' work regarding Core States, and Roye Fraser's original work on Generative Imprinting. The following offers a new reformatting so that it clearly reveals a meta-stating process.

Step 1: *Identify a Primary State Sensory-Based Experience where you want more alignment.*

Think of a behavior where you would like to have more personal alignment, congruency, and integrity. What activity do you engage in that you consider very important that sometimes lacks the full range of congruency, power, and focus that you would like to have? Make a list of excellences in your area of expertise, around which you would like to develop your internal congruency.

As you do, describe this behavior, activity, experience in sensory-based terms. Describe it from a video-camera perspective of *the specific behaviors* that you would actually see, hear, or sense.

Where do these primary level behaviors occur? *Where* do you do this? (Environment)

Step 2: Identify the Primary State mental-emotional skills and abilities (or Capacities) which enable you to do this.

How do you use your thinking-and-feeling to pull off this skill? What strategy or strategies do you deploy in doing this? What strategies support and empower these skills? How do you know *how to* do this? Where did you get this *know-how?*

Step 3: Identify the Meta-Levels of Beliefs and Values that support and empower this. **(Beliefs/Values)**

Why do you engage in this? What beliefs guide this behavior? Specify all of the crucial beliefs that run these behaviors, in terms of beliefs about the activity itself, you, the context, what makes it work, its significance, etc. What importance does this hold for you?

Step 4: Identify the Meta-State of Identity which emerges from this for you. **(Identity)**

Who are you that you engage in this behavior? What does engaging in this behavior say about your identity? *Who* does this make you? Do you like yourself doing these activities?

Step 5: Identify the Meta-State of Purpose and Destiny that then arises. **(Vision, Mission, Spirit)**

How does this fit into your overall sense of destiny and purpose? Describe in a couple of sentences your own personal sense of purpose and destiny. When you step into this state and these activities, fully and completely, what do you experience?

Figure 9:3

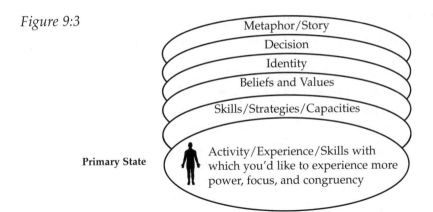

Step 6: Make a Clear-Cut and Decisive Decision for this skill and experience.

Have you decided for this? Have you totally and definitely made a decision to operate this way, live with these insights, to make this your way of being in the world?

Step 7: Describe these Meta-Levels of Meaning with a metaphor or story.

What metaphor or story encapsulates this state with its multi-layered levels? As you just naturally let it emerge ... notice also other things that might emerge: sounds, colors, shapes, music, light, etc. As you do this, let one of these things serve as a symbol, icon, story, or metaphor for the entire experience. Now imagine taking that with you everywhere you go.

Step 8: Integrate fully by Bringing the Higher Levels to Bear on the Lower Levels.

As you even more fully step into this awareness and experience it completely, snapshot it and honor it and let it enrich all of your levels ... and now imagine bringing this back down the levels, letting it collapse into the lower levels to thereby enrich them. How do you now experience the behavior, environment, etc. when you bring this higher level with you? And you can bring each of these levels, in turn, to bear upon your everyday state, can you not?

Meta-Stating With "the Miracle Question"

The following process originally developed as *"The Miracle Question"* of Steve de Shazer (1980) in his groundbreaking work in the field of Brief Therapy. I have here utilized it and reformatted it somewhat in order to use a semantic frame whereby a person can *totally step aside* and *out of* a problem space (or state) and then into a new space (or state) of solution thinking. By doing this, we can invite a person to engage in an *entirely differently kind of thinking*. Setting up this miracle frame empowers us to move forward using some solution-oriented thinking. This pattern utilizes fully *the "As If" frame* in order to construct a new outframing perspective.

Step 1: Identify a problem.

Begin by asking for a problem state where you want more choices and responses: "What prevents you from getting on the highway of life and living in a vital, happy, and ferocious way?" "What holds you back?" Make a list of all of the words and beliefs that arise. Or, think about some *conceptual category* that you don't like. Use the sentence stem, "I don't like...." then fill it with some concept, issue, problem, etc. (i.e. cause, time, relationships, justice, power, dependency, independence, manipulation); or use the sentence stem, "The category that really rattles me is ..."

Step 2: Identify your Beliefs-about-beliefs.

What do you believe *about* that problem? What meanings do you give to it? What thoughts-and-feelings automatically come to mind when you think about the problem? Just let them come as you free-float and simply observe the thoughts that arise in relation to the subject.

Step 3: Sketch out the Meta-Level Structure of the experience.

Fully identify and make explicit the meta-state structure that results. When you first do this, it will help if you get a sheet of paper and diagram the structure of this fully. This will bring about a new level of clarity about the mental layers of thoughts-and-feelings into which the problem has become embedded. Continue to do this until you get to the top of the levels of abstracting.

Step 4: Run an Ecology-Check about the Meta-Beliefs.

Does this kind of thinking-feeling about this problem or issue truly help you? Does it make things better for you? Does it lead to a greater sense of resourcefulness? When you respond over and over with a growing sense of clarity, *"No, it does not!"* then amplify this state of the sense of *"No, it does not help to think about things in this way: it makes things worse."* We will use this rejection energy as a propulsion force *away from* the old problem frame and state so that it will propel on into a place where you can try on some new kind of thinking.

Figure 9:4

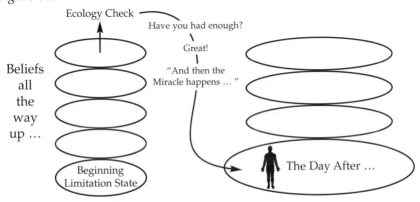

Step 5: Imagine the Opposite.

Close your eyes and imagine, just for the purpose of this mental experiment, that a miracle happened tonight while you slept. Imagine it. A miracle happens while you sleep. So that in the morning, when you awaken, you will know that a miracle has occurred, but won't have a clue as to *how* it occurred. And as you fully imagine that you will wake up in the morning thinking-and-feeling in a completely different way, you can anticipate also how that will radically change things. And right now, just take your time so that you can do it thoroughly and vividly ...

And as you dream upon your pillow you may want to wonder, really wonder about what kind of thoughts and feelings, beliefs and states you would like to have in your life in order to truly and powerfully just explode into tomorrow with grace, power, love, passion, and confidence. And when you experience those states, what would that state presuppose in terms of even higher level thoughts and feelings? What supporting meanings and beliefs would empower this? And, how would you represent this?

Now, as you open your eyes, this day after the miracle, begin to describe things ... A miracle has occurred, and you don't know *how* it has, but you can begin now to describe how you recognize that it has. What's different? How will you know that something has changed? How will others notice it in you?

The Essence of Alignment

To align conflicting and differing parts, we find it usually highly instructive and constructive to first find out about *the positive intention* of the parts.

> "What does this or that part—whether a belief, idea, understanding, value, emotion, drive, etc.—seek to accomplish of value and importance?"

If we start from this basic assumption, then we do not make the mistake of assuming that the various parts and facets of our personalities *"are"* bad or evil. Certainly, sometimes these facets of ourselves (or others) may create a lot of problems, cause a lot of disruption and disorganization, and even initiate evil and harmful things. But that doesn't make the part itself bad.

Do you have a part of you that knows how to criticize? Of course you do. Do you like this part of you? Do you celebrate and enjoy this facet of your mind that can notice something not totally efficient and say so? Or do you hate and despise this part? Do you condemn, judge, and reject this part? The thoughts and emotions you bring to bear on this facet of yourself, of course, establish the next level up layer or state *about* the experience. And if you get caught up in hating and rejecting it, especially without understanding its function, purpose, and *positive intention*, then you will create only an internal war which will promote more misunderstandings.

So first, explore its value. What does it seek to accomplish of value and importance? Why do you criticize anyone anyway? Do you not seek to make things better? Do you not want to offer a piece of advice that would eliminate the difficulty?

Most of us criticize in order to make things better. We want to offer new insights; we want to improve quality; we want to expand the choices of the person, etc. Yet what typically happens when we criticize? People feel attacked, insulted, put-down, and rejected.

In fact, the *art* of effectively offering a critique so that it doesn't sound like a criticism, but sounds like insightful information to improve things represents a pretty high level *communication art*, wouldn't you say? What we call "criticism" is usually the lack of this artful communication—a blunt attempt at showing someone we care.

Yet once we move to a higher level and identify *the positive intention behind* the activity, thought, emotion, communication, etc., we can step into **an agreement frame** that brings together the parts that conflicted and differed on the primary level. This illustrates *the very essence* of creating and inventing alignment whether within ourselves or between people. Once we move to a level higher than or meta to the specific warring parts, we can find a space where we agree. We all want *that*.

This means that **alignment**, along with integration and congruency, usually involves turning around and undoing the demonizing of the parts. One way to do that involves searching for the positive intention. And, sometimes, we will have to move to level after level until we find a level where the intention strikes us as positive and contributing.

Another way to do that involves asking another kind of question. Namely, "Upon what *value continuum* can we put this vice?" This utilizes what Aristotle wrote about in his *Ethics* regarding "the golden mean." Vice as evil and hurtful things, he noted, tends to arise from *a value* (something good and valuable and useful in and of itself) and *over*-do it or *under*-do it. Thus the value of *relaxation* becomes a vice—hurtful, unuseful, damaging, and problematic, when we over-do it. Then it becomes "laziness." It becomes equally a vice when we *under-do* it. Then it becomes "chronic tension," and "workaholism." Aligning thus involves finding *a golden mean* (as Aristotle described) that allows us to tap into the values and usefulness of something while maintaining *balance* with other aspects and the whole system.

Psychosynthesis

Roberto Assagioli (1965) has developed *psychosynthesis* as a process for the purpose of synthesizing and aligning things psychologically. This process brings together two dichotomized experiences and unites them into a larger frame of reference. As a result this creates *a synthesis* which facilitates personal integration and integrity. Use this pattern to obtain a higher level *agreement frame* about two or more frames that seem to conflict with each other.

Step 1: *Identify a state of pain, distress, suffering.*
> Pick any negative emotional state. Name the problem that feels like the misalignment of meta-level Executive States. This could include the gestalts of impatience, fearful hesitation, confused fear and anger, etc.

Step 2: Describe the essence of the state as a value.
> Now take the "problem" that you may have felt as a "vice" or badness or wickedness and put it on *a "value" continuum.* Step back and view the problem as *too-little,* and then as *too-much* of something, of some value. As you do, *what* value does the problem represent which you have *under*-done it or *over*-done it? This utilizes the productive assumption that every "vice" represents some virtue in an out-of-balance form. For example, we can view "anger" on a continuum of *caring* and then see it as too much caring about something, too much involvement, ego-investment, etc.

Step 3: Identify the current Meta-States about the value.
> What do you think and feel *about* this experience or state? What do you think and feel *about* a behavior or emotion at one of its extremes? Identify the frames of reference that you have put around the "problem." In what ways has the frame itself contributed to the problem?

Step 4: What gestalt of thoughts and feelings arise from the total configuration?
> Identify the overall configuration of thoughts-and-feelings that arise from that frame *about* that particular experience. When you view the problem as a vice and then bring various other rejecting or hateful thoughts and feelings to bear upon it, what then emerges in personality? Does this make things better or worse?

Step 5: Identify a new resource and Meta-State the old Meta-State.

Begin with the resources of acceptance, seeking to understand, "a positive intention drives this," "this represents only a value out-of-balance," etc. Bring these kinds of thoughts and their corresponding feelings to bear on the problem. As you do, notice now what new gestalts arise. Begin now to explore additional resources. "How else would I like to meta-state the problem?" "What other frames-of-reference would I like to put around this that would temper and transform it?"

When The CEO Gets His or Her Act Together

We began this chapter by acknowledging that a governing CEO can become incongruent, dysfunctional, out-of-alignment, and needs to get his or her act together. To that end, we have focused on various alignment processes and patterns. This has enabled us to identify yet another secret of personal mastery, namely—

Secret #12

The personal mastery of focus and power comes from alignment with all of one's higher or executive frames of mind.
When we align all of our higher frames of mind—our valuing, understanding, believing, identifying, deciding, etc., we find that we can direct our powers of attention according to our higher intentions. This creates a laser beam type of focus.

Summary
- In alignment, we pull ourselves together so that we become focused and integrated regarding our values, beliefs, identity, mission, etc. This leads to the personal power of congruence.
- Feeling various parts of ourselves clash and clang makes it difficult, if not impossible, to respond in a powerfully focused way. When a civil war rages within, it prevents us from being clear.
- Several profound processes support becoming integrated and whole. We can utilize our highest executive state to bring this about. Now we can make high level decisions for *not tolerating* internal conflict and for *refusing* to stay stuck.

- "The Miracle Question" enables us to construct representations of *life apart from the conflict.* This empowers us to re-arrange higher level values, beliefs, and understandings.
- **Secret #12: The personal mastery of focus and power comes from alignment with all of one's higher or executive frames of mind.**
  When we align all of our higher frames of minds—our valuing, understandings, believing, identifying, deciding, etc., we find that we can direct our powers of attention according to our higher intentions. This creates a laser beam type of focus.

The Self-Organizing Secret
of
Personal Mastery

Personal mastery emerges only when we engage our higher executive levels of mind as self-organizing powers.

Because the higher frames govern, determine, modulate, and organize the lower levels, when we set the highest frames and take charge of managing our highest conceptual contexts, we order our neuro-linguistic self-organizing system so that it operates for our well-being. Using this top-down approach then leads to personal mastery since it enables us to manage our higher levels of mind by controlling our higher conceptual frames.

Chapter 10

Managing Higher Levels

Put Your Meta-Mind to Work for You

"Speak to the Controller's Controller."
(Dr John Grinder)

In some companies we find multiple levels and layers of management. The Post Office, for example, has eighteen levels of government employees. This translates to managers of managers, and managers of managers of managers, etc. When these levels are rigid, closed, authoritarian, buck-passing, etc. then *bureaucracy* typically emerges. When a system is governed by the process of "passing the buck," "the Peter Principle" (being promoted to a level of incompetency, from Peter Lawrence), protecting the *status quo*, operation by rules and regulations, tons of paper work, inefficiency, etc., then the bureaucracy that emerges tends to be disempowering, dysfunctional, and de-humanizing.

If we create an effective layering of leadership and management, then communication and responsibility flows easily and efficiently as messages move up and down the levels. As a result this creates a sense of group spirit that leads to productivity and human development.

A similar thing occurs in human personality. As we have noted in the previous chapters, our self-reflexive consciousness sets in motion a layering of our levels of mind. We have not only a primary mind, but also layers of meta-consciousness. We think about our thinking, we feel about our feelings, we communicate about our communications, etc.

As previously noted, from this arises systemic processes and emergent qualities. This works to our detriment when we have a

213

closed-system. If we set a frame that allows no new feedback, no testing of our frame, no updating, we can get stuck in looping around in self-sabotaging and self-fulfilling prophecies. This also works to our benefit. We can set frames that activate and enhance personal mastery that bring out our personal genius for greater productivity and effectiveness.

Contextual Frame of References

Meaning begins at the primary level as we simply link and associate things together. What any thing, event, word, or experience *means* then depends upon what have we *connected* with that item. What does a job mean? It all depends. What idea, feeling, memory, or concept have you *connected* to your "job"? It could mean freedom or slavery. It could mean productivity or dehumanization, it could mean an expression of talent and skill or it could mean being used.

Here we have first level *meaning.* It is the meaning of linkages and associations. Yet *meaning* does not stop at that level. We then create *meanings-about-our-meanings.* The Second and Third *Secrets of Personal Mastery* highlight this power of our self-reflexive mind:

Secret #2

Mastery emerges as we discover our Higher States as Our Executive Operations. *We humans never just think—we think about our thinking, and then think about that thinking. Our thoughts-and-feelings forever and inevitably reflect back onto itself to become more and more layered. Therefore, the secret of personal mastery lies in discovering our higher thoughts-and-feelings and choosing those that serve us well.*

Secret #3

Our Reflexive Consciousness Enables us to always Layer yet another Level upon our current Model of the World. This gives us the ability to always step outside of our frames-of-reference and go right to the top—to our highest executive states. We do not have to be stuck or limited any more than we want to be. We can always outframe. This gives us the ability to truly Take Charge of our mind, emotions, reality, and destiny.

When we make a meta-move to our *associative meanings*, we create *contextual or framed meanings*. So beyond the conditioned *meanings* of associations at the primary level, we have *context meanings*. When we move here, we move into our *conceptual world*—a world of ideas, concepts, beliefs, and abstract understandings. It is a particularly human world and defines us as "a semantic (or meaning-making) class of life."

This move transports us to our conceptual frames of reference. Here *ideas set our frames*. Here *ideas* create "realities." Here we enter into a semantic environment of the mind. And in this semantic world, we find meanings emerging from the larger level frames-of-reference.

We see this developmentally in the way all of us learn to become human. The first *context* that we experience comes from our immediate family. There we become socialized by the language and the rules of the culture. Yet the family exists only as a small unit and exists itself within a larger context—the town or city community, which exists inside of an even larger context—the state or nation, which exists within an even larger context—the human race; and this exists within a certain time frame—the twenty-first century, etc.

Contexts within contexts within contexts.

Whatever you *know* also exists within a layered hierarchy of contexts. What you know about *dog* and about the word *dog* has arisen from the contexts that you've experienced with such a referent. It also exists within the context of the English language. And that exists within the larger context of how that language grew and evolved over the centuries.

We never know what anything *means*, or what any given person *means* by his or her use of a given term until we know the mental contexts out of which they come, to which they refer, and those from which we come. This makes our mental, semantic contexts extremely important. To lack this understanding prevents us from truly knowing a person. In this, *contexts and contexts-within-contexts* determine and control most of the meanings that run our lives.

So, to truly develop personal mastery we now need to add the Thirteenth Secret.

Secret #13

Personal mastery emerges only when we engage our higher executive levels of mind as self-organizing powers.

Because the higher frames govern, determine, modulate, and organize the lower levels, when we set the highest frames of all and take charge of managing those highest conceptual contexts, we order our neuro-linguistic self-organizing system so that it operates for our well-being. Using this top-down approach then leads to personal mastery since it enables us to manage our higher levels of mind by controlling our higher conceptual frames.

Managing Higher Levels

We have maintained throughout this book that mastering personal power results from *a top-down approach*. This explains and underscores the critical questions that we have been raising:

- *How* can we manage the higher levels?
- What processes and techniques enable us to take charge of our inner executives at these various levels and manage them?
- Where do we have leverage points with regard to these internal management levels?

In the previous chapters, the secrets of personal mastery put into our hands practical insights, technologies, and skills that enable us to use the Meta-States Model to develop everyday excellence. These *Secrets of Personal Mastery* have also given expression to numerous meta-level principles, for example, the principle, *"the higher level governs and modulates the lower levels."* We now know that we can manage states and executive states by simply setting higher frames. All we have to do is use our reflexive mind to *set a frame*. When we do, we can establish an express purpose, a semantic context, and an operational idea or belief. When we do that, the frame then becomes *a self-organizing attractor* for our neuro-linguistic system of mind, body, and emotions. This commissions that higher level state of mind to govern our actions, thoughts, feelings, and behaviors in terms of that frame. It's that easy, it's that profound, it's that magical. So, *on to the magic.*

Building an Internal "Controller"

How would you like to install a high level *Controller State* in your mind? Suppose you could install *a high level executive frame of mind* so that you would not have to "think" so much everyday about your own personal mastery? What if … and this is the wonder and marvel of the following process … what if you could incorporate a higher part of your mind so that it self-organizes your entire mind-body system for personal mastery? What if you could commission it to make that its entire purpose? Would you like that?

I originally discovered the following in the work of Grinder and DeLozier (1983). As co-founders of NLP, Dr John Grinder and Judith DeLozier worked on *prerequisites for personal genius* during the early 1980s. Their book, *Turtles All The Way Down*, later presented a transcript of some of these trainings. In it, they focused on the subject of managing states through the use of "logical levels" and higher level *Controller States*.

In the context of considering the prerequisites for personal genius, they argue that the best way to control one's *commitment states* involved using "logical levels." In developing this pattern, they relied heavily upon Gregory Bateson and so extensively quoted him regarding both the theory of logical levels and how to use them. To this end, they used the realization that when we move to a higher level, we can then set up or establish the frames, rules, criteria, boundaries, understandings, etc. for personal genius. Doing so facilitates our ability to model genius, because from there we can commission an internal "Controller" or Executive state of mind to govern our commitment states at lower levels.

The original Grinder and DeLozier process for doing this was quite involved, theoretical, and complicated. Using the latest processes in the Meta-States Model, we have streamlined it into the pattern that follows here.

Turning the Primary Level "Demon" Loose

We begin this process by identifying two commitment states at the primary level that we really love and which brings out our personal genius. What intense and passionate states do you sometimes access that you really love?

Have you ever felt *totally committed* to anything?

> As you allow your mind to identify something (or someone) to which you might like to become committed, notice your representations of this commitment.

> What would it feel like to experience a time and place where you become so totally focused on *one thing* that "time," "space," "environment" and even your "self" just vanishes away ... now ... as you fully experience again a commitment state to something—a movie, a conversation, a ball game, a tennis match, rock climbing, making love, learning something that totally fascinated and ... obsessed you ...

Numerous theoreticians have described and labelled the experience of *a totally committed and passionate state.* Glasser (1976) described it as a "positive addiction," Csikszentmihalyi (1991) more recently has labeled it a state of *"flow."* The ancient Greeks called it "demon" (diamonia). Grinder and DeLozier (*Prerequisite for Personal Genius,* 1987) similarly described it as a "demon" state, meaning a state where you become completely and totally focused in a positive way. They write,

> "That's what demons are. They're so narrow-band focused that the whole resourcefulness of the organism is expressed at that single point. That's why you can just ease your way through otherwise very difficult situations." (p. 219)

Also, quoting Casteneda's Don Juan adventures, they described it using the metaphor of *"being a warrior."*

> "If you observe warriors at any moment you will find that they are completely, passionately committed to whatever it is that they're doing at that moment in time ... although the warrior will do diverse, even unrelated kinds of things, the

warrior acts with utter congruency and a passionate commitment ..." (p. 164).

"Castaneda proposes the worthy opponent—a person or a
context which serves as a stimulus for the child to make a
full mobilization of resources." (p. 208)

In all these descriptions, we have *"genius"* described as *an intensely focused, and concentrated state of consciousness characterized by passion, commitment, flow, intensity, purposed, conscious-and-unconscious
alignment, etc.*

And sometimes, just sometimes, to those who stand outside of this
state, and observe it in someone else, it can look like *madness*. So,
Judith DeLozier, quoting Castaneda, described it as "controlled
folly." (Consider the Meta-State that implies.)

Such intense demon states typically involve a *transformation* in
one's sense of self. Csikszentmihalyi described it as *self-forgetful-
ness*—a form of self-transcendence. Grinder (1987), following
Bateson, described it as an *extension* of self.

"When you were driving race cars you made that complete
demon commitment. You had to be good. In that context
your consciousness let go and allowed you to extend your
definition of self to the tires...." (p. 79)

In this totally committed state, one's mind focuses in such a
narrow-band of consciousness that it generates an altered state.
One senses the road through the tires—one's sense of self extends
out to the tires. Strange. And yet a commonplace experience.

And Then the "Demon" Vanishes

If "one of the prerequisites for effective personal organization is
the ability to make clean, one-hundred percent commitments at
each stage of whatever activities you engage in during the day"
(Grinder, 1987: 164), then what happens when something interrupts or contaminates that state?

We *lose that one-hundred percent passionate commitment.*

Hasn't that happened to you? Have you not been caught up passionately in something when all of a sudden something interrupted your state of mind? Now if you could easily and quickly just *step back into it*, there really wouldn't be any problem. But often, the interruption totally throws us off course. Frequently, we find it impossible to recover that wonderful flow state of commitment and consciousness to one passion. No wonder this is an important and common concern. How often and frequently we seem able to lose our states of flow! So many things can interrupt, contaminate, and interfere with them. Our states of focused concentration can get interrupted with such ease and frequency.

The problem then that many of us have with our "demon" states of excellence, commitment, passion, flow, "addiction," etc. lies in how one of these states will sabotage another, or how other less intense states or experiences will interrupt them. John Grinder noted that self-interruptive behavior functions as a dead giveaway that we have "overlapping demons."

> "How many of you are self-interruptive in your activities? Isn't in fact the normal situation one in which you're trying to single track and things have not been carefully sorted, or you do not have controllers to make the choices about their appropriateness and you get intrusions?" (p. 170)

> "One of the most important functions that we are responsible for as individuals in a fragmented technological society is clean state switching." (p. 164)

Do you know about self-interrupting states? If you can experience an intense state of concentration—totally engaged in reading, running, conversing, problem-solving, nurturing, watching a movie, playing ball, playing with a child, etc. *and lose it* just as completely—then you undoubtedly know this experience intimately.

> [This use of the term "demon" pre-dates its later usage in referencing something "evil." In the third century B.C. the term "demon" designated genius. The ancient Greeks referred to Socrates as having a "demon" as they acknowledged his wisdom, intelligence, and genius. So how did it come to refer to "evil," "destructiveness," and "demonic"

experiences and persons? It probably took on these conno-
tations due to the fact that whenever we over-do any
genius (giftedness)—it becomes unbalanced and untem-
pered. Without restraining influences, the giftedness
becomes destructive, or "a demon," to us. Peter's gift of
expressiveness and quickness to talk, became "a Satan" to
Jesus when his brain ran ahead of his reason (Matthew
16:22–23).]

Developing Resources

Okay, so what do we need in order to develop more **clean state
switching?** How can we build some "controllers" that will guard
our states of focused *flow*?

Obviously, we first need the ability to sort and separate between
our states. Then we can choose more appropriately *when* to invoke
our "demon" states of total concentration. Then we will not contaminate or dilute one state with another. We need the skill to step
into, and out of, states, to have good separators or boundaries
between them. We also need the ability to move to a meta-level
and to manage or control our "demon" states from that level.

Grinder describes this,

> "Every state has associated with it a class of physiologies
> and if you have the sensitivity in your physiology you can
> use it as a way of very efficiently moving from one state to
> another and keeping one sorted from the other. The con-
> troller at a higher logical level is responsible for clean state
> switching—another way of describing the well-formedness
> condition of non-overlapping demons." (p. 166)

To do this, we have to learn how to *become "impeccable in our state
shifts."* Further, according to John, "the easiest way I know to
accomplish that is *to make use of logical levels."* (p. 165, italics
added). Doing this allows then us to *"double-track"* without getting
lost, experiencing amnesia, getting stressed, frustrated, worn out,
or contaminating our states. If we experience the overlapping of
our demons:

"with their tremendous commitment and passion, you better justify it because in almost every case I've ever run across you get diminution of quality, a "reduction in the demon-like qualities of both because they're at cross-purposes." (p. 174)

Using Logical Levels at a Meta-Position

If you read *Turtles All The Way Down,* you'll discover that Grinder and DeLozier heavily emphasized the conceptual work of Gregory Bateson with regard to logical levels and "going meta." In their workshop, as reflected in their book, they made multiple readings from his classic work, *Steps Toward An Ecology of Mind* (Bateson, 1972). This enabled them to put an emphasis on Bateson's use and development of logical levels and self-reflexive consciousness. *Turtles,* in fact, represent one of the few NLP books that deals extensively with these subjects outside *Meta-States.*

John Grinder illustrated this by talking about getting interrupted from a focus by the news of some escaping horses. He says that the easiest way he knows to accomplish becoming impeccable in state shifts

"... is to make use of logical levels. The me that jots down that note, and then moves quickly to intercept the horses that are running across the field by this point, is of a higher logical level than the demon who was passionately committed to whatever that first-/second-attention interface task was and profoundly different at the same logical level than the demon who will now pursue the horses and enjoy gathering them and putting them back in the corral. Notice there is no sense of loss if you make a clean, residue-free shift. The only way you could experience loss or interruption or frustration or boredom or any of these funny words that we use for this phenomenon is by double-tracking ..." (pp. 165–166)

In the following process pattern for managing our executive levels of consciousness, I have adopted it from the seminar discussion and exercise description given by Grinder and DeLozier in *Turtles* (pages 167–179). As you use it, you will discover that it essentially operates as a meta-stating pattern for **managing** your *personal* *genius* by design-engineering "choices" and "controls" at a higher logical level.

Accessing Your Own Personal Genius Pattern

Step 1: Find and access two fully committed states.

From your personal history, identify and fully specify two commitment states that you have easy access to, and can quickly re-experience. Identify states of excellence and commitment that mean a lot to you.

Grinder suggested the following two constraints in choosing the commitment states to work with: a) Choose two states that come as close to a full 100% commitment as you can achieve at this point. b) Choose two states that lie within a common area: work, personal life, sports, intellectual area, etc.

Perhaps you can access a state of focused intensity in (1) long-term effective planning and reading/researching; or (2) doing gymnastics and riding horses; or (3) outgoingness at parties and social gatherings and talking on the telephone. In this way, the two states have some major things in common—they deal with social relations, they deal with athletic competency, artistic expression, or whatever.

Step 2: Appoint someone as your witness and coach who will calibrate your states.

The observer person will calibrate your two states and assist you in going "in" and coming "out" of the states upon cue. The witness will not need much information about the states. You can simply designate them as "State A" and "State B" if you like. As a meta-person to the genius accessing process, the witness will function as a lifeline for you and bring you back in case you get lost in the process or collapse into some unresourceful state. The witness will also give "Go" and "Stop" commands with regard to stepping in and out of various states.

Step 3: Practice accessing and shifting the first commitment state.

Begin by fully accessing State A and let your witness know when you have elicited this state by simply nodding your head or saying something like "I've got it," or "Yes." When you fully access it, then gauge the state in terms of intensity.

How much do you feel and experience it on a scale from 0 to 10 (with 10 being absolute)? The witness will, at this point, simply calibrate to that state by noticing your posture, breathing, eye-scanning patterns, muscle tones, etc.

If you do not have a very intense or strong state, the witness should coach you by simply asking questions about the state. When did you experience this state most intensely? See, hear, and feel that memory fully. Step back into it so that it seems that you are there again. What were you aware of?

Step 4: Practice breaking the Commitment State.

Upon the witness' cue, break the state and step out into a separator state. The "demon" state of your personal genius needs a total focus which separates it from any other state that might contaminate it. "Demon" states, by definition, will relate to *one thing*. By stepping cleanly out of that state—shifting focus of mind (internal representations) and body (physiological correlates) you learn to separate from the intense *Flow State* and leave it cleanly behind.

Step 5: Access and fully experience the second Commitment State.

Repeat the same process as Step 3 as you step into the second commitment state. Upon accessing this state, the witness will again snap his or her fingers to cue you as to when to break state. As you step into the separator state, the witness will continue to calibrate. Continue doing so until you can do so with a minimum overlap between the two states. You have reached the desired level of achievement when you carry over no residue in mind or emotions from one state to the other, but can cleanly separate and break between them.

Step 6: Create or discover an Executive at a meta-level.

Many people already have, at a meta-position, a part that controls these commitment states. At the level of this "controller" or "executive" meta-state you make choices which determine the appropriateness of going into this state or not. From this state, determine *when* and *how* to switch into the commitment states. Decide in what contexts you would find it appropriate to do so, and in which context you would find it inappropriate.

To set up these arrangements, move to a meta-position to your genius state. From this meta-position, find or create a facet of yourself that will perform the role of a controller. Grinder and DeLozier write,

> "It's the controller's job to draw the line. You go, 'You, lovely as you are, you operate on this side,' ..." (p. 172)

> "Context, context—the controller determines the context for the demon." (p. 176)

In this way, you commission a part of yourself to monitor and gauge the appropriateness of accessing your genius state in a given context. Language with yourself so that you have a sense of choice about contexts, times, places, etc.

If your executive self (or controller) doesn't want to do this, simply go meta to the first line controller. "Talk to that controller's controller" (p. 173). How do you do this? By simply moving up another logical level, to the thoughts and feelings you have about those decisions, and then, from there setting up a new frame there. Your Executive States, as controllers, set the "cage" for the demon.

> "The cage for the demon is the context it accepts. And there it can just get in and kick. Notice the tremendous freedom you get through this organizational structure ... there's no self-interruption because the controller handles the switching. The controller can use time driven variables, or completion of tasks, for example, as a way of knowing when to switch out of the state. The controller is responsible for setting the context and enforcing it and determining when to unleash the demon within the context." (p. 171)

Have you ever feared giving in to a passion, commitment, overwhelming vision, or genius of yours? Have you feared that if you did so, it would "take over" and it would drive you mad or crazy? Perhaps you feared that it would take over and get out of control. In such cases, such *fear* of the experience of commitment serves to keep us from getting into the focused intensity. We fear our passion. We feel suspect of our excitement. So we inhibit our genius.

With clients of addictions, I usually draw a continuum line that stretches from the two poles of "undriven" to "totally driven." I sketch out a vertical line of dashes that intersects the horizontal line to separate the domains of **want** and **need**. To the left of the line, we experience healthy passions. To the right, we experience and suffer unhealthy addictions.

Figure 10:1

Continuum of Desire

Desire and Passion		Obsession	
No Desire	*Healthy Commitment* >	Increasing Intensity	Compulsion "Must have" it *Unhealthy Addiction*

At the meta-level, design your executive Meta-State by asking the following questions. Most people will generally need to provide such information for their Executive States. As the controlling part understands the demon's intent, it comes to trust it and work with it.

- What intent drives this commitment state?
- And what intention drives that intention?
- What does this particular demon or genius seek to pull off?
- What aesthetic improvements might you recommend to qualify the committed behavior so that you could program it to operate with even more quality and efficiency?
- What other behaviors could you substitute, consistent with the intent of the genius state, that would make the performance efficient and up to quality?

Benediction

John Grinder ended his pattern about prerequisites of genius with this benediction:

"May your houses be full of wonderful demons. These demons cannot afford, in doing the kind of powerful, aesthetic job they need to do, to be worried about whether it's

time to go to dinner or what 'spousie' will think or whatever. The constraints that they live under have to be set and
maintained by the controller. It is not the job of a demon to
know its limitations. It is the job of the controller to set and
enforce ... those particular constraints which define the
area of operation for that demon. The controller holds the
key and secures agreements from the demons that when
released they will operate within their appropriate contexts. The cage for the demon is the context it accepts. And
there it can just get in and kick. Notice the tremendous freedom you get through this organizational structure. There's
no self-interruption because the controller handles the
switching...." (pp. 170–171, italics added)

Outframing

Throughout this work, we have repeatedly referred to an essential
meta-level process that we call *outframing*. Outframing refers to
the wondrous ability to *step aside from* a given experience and its
frames-of-reference and to *go above it all* to set an entirely new and
more enhancing frame.

When we reframe, we exchange one frame for another. We thereby make a lateral move and say, "It doesn't mean *this,* it means *this
other thing.*" When we *deframe,* we pull the component pieces that
comprise the structure of an experience apart. We find out all of
the individual facets and components of the *mind languages* (our
internal pictures, sounds, sensations and words along with their
qualities) and syntax that make it work so that we can then *mess it
up.* Here we make a vertical move *downward.*

Outframing involves a jump to a higher logical level so that the
resultant thoughts, feelings, and ideas relate to, and about, everything below it. So when we "run an ecology check" on an experience, we engage in an outframing move.

- "Does this experience serve you well?"
- "Does it enhance your life or empower your actions?"
- "Does it make for increased productivity, efficiency, or
  effectiveness?"
- "Would you recommend it to others?"

So with running a Reality Check on things. We bring thoughts and feelings about checking out, testing, and objectively evaluating the realness of something to bear on some experience.

"When you step back from this, how much validity would you attribute to this way of perceiving? If we invited several objective witnesses to look this over and make their evaluations, what would they say about it?"

When we outframe with *acceptance,* we bring acknowledging thoughts and feelings to bear on the experience. This doesn't mean that we particularly approve, like, or condone the experience. It means only that we *face it* or acknowledge it for whatever it is. We look its existence in the face without blinking or going into denial. It takes a certain strength of ego and internal permission to simply acknowledge reality without letting our wishes, magical thinking, and passions blind us. We may not like paying taxes, but we accept it as a fact of economic reality. We may not like the aging process in our cells, yet we acknowledge the existence of such. We may not like or desire many other facets and constraints in various realities, yet instead of making ourselves an enemy to *what exists,* we adjust ourselves to it by first of all acknowledging it.

In such *outframing,* we set up one of these ideas, conceptual understandings, beliefs, or awarenesses as a "floater state" or higher executive state so that it *sets the ultimate frames* for our experiences. This endows such cognitions to become our presuppositional states and ultimate paradigms about life, ourselves, and others. In this way, we manage our highest expressions.

Summary
- We can use Neuro-Linguistics and Neuro-Semantic processes to set executive states for managing our own personal genius. This enables us to control the genius within so it doesn't become a runaway demon. This makes us balanced and integrated persons.
- Achieving this level of management over our powers and commitment states enables us to live out our dreams and values more fully. It then empowers us to just "get out there and kick!"

- To manage one level of mind, we can simply go to the next level and set a frame that will enhance our life. Doing so creates a frame or "cage" for the primary levels of experience.
- **Secret #13: Personal mastery emerges only when we engage our higher executive levels of mind as self-organizing powers.**
  Because the higher frames govern, determine, modulate, and organize the lower levels, when we set the highest frames and take charge of managing those highest conceptual contexts, we order our neuro-linguistic self-organizing system so that it operates for our well-being. Using this top-down approach then leads to personal mastery since it enables us to manage our higher levels of mind by controlling our higher conceptual frames.

Chapter 11

Executing for Ongoing Development

Minding Your Meta-Mind

*"At the submicroscopic level we might more accurately
talk not of 'things' changing, but of change 'thinging.'"*
(Robert Pula)

"You cannot step twice into the same river."
(Heraclitus' student Cratylus)

*"You must be thoroughly convinced of the
process character of nature."*
(Alfred Korzybski)

Suppose that you have so efficiently constructed and commissioned your inner executive states that they enhance your life in the most powerful way possible. Suppose that you have ordered and aligned all of your higher executive states so that the structure of your excellences truly brings out your best. Even with that progress, it doesn't guarantee future progress. What will *guarantee* ongoing future developments and progress: keeping today's Inner Executive informed, updated, current, and *in touch*.

In large companies the Chief Executive Officer (CEO), along with his or her staff of executives, can get so much *out of touch* with the people they manage, even the market they work with, including the current technologies or processes, that they can sabotage the health of the business. In the 1980s, *Management by Walking Around* became one suggested process by which management could overcome this problem. By just "walking around" and mingling with the troops, the idea was that employees and manager could interact, learn, stay in touch, etc. Failing to do this typically isolates the executive from the most relevant and important information—customers.

In even more remote times, kings would sometimes dress as paupers to mix and mingle with their subjects in order to see what life was really like in their kingdom and what the people truly thought of the king and his administration.

How does this translate over to *personal development?* How can we do that to keep our personal genius alive and growing?

In terms of personality and the structuring of mind-and-body *states*, we know that higher levels govern and determine the everyday experiences. But if we lack an efficient and easy flow of information within the human system, the higher levels can become isolated and often habituated to default to the old programs. And given the ongoing process world of change and ever-new emergent realities in which we live, this will inevitably make our Inner Executive states more and more irrelevant and out of touch. We have become effectively organized for a world that no longer exists.

To address this we need only to set *ongoing learning, discovering, and development* as our orientational frame. Without ongoing discovering, we condemn our inner executive to the prison of current understandings, beliefs, values, paradigms, and procedures while the world moves on. If we perpetuate this way of moving in the world that doesn't constantly update things, we build a static structure that over-values the old, the true and tested, the secure, etc. There's a flipside to this. As we become less and less flexible, adaptable, fluid, and open, we become less sensitive to the new, less aware of the relevant, and more limited in responding.

What then? Once we have identified, developed, and installed our inner executive, we need a flexible structure that facilitates an ongoing development and progressive transformation. We need an inner executive that can not only live with change, and the increasing rate of change in a process world, but also respond to an attitude of openness, creativity, and vitality to change.

Mapping the Process Universe

The genius of Alfred Korzybski emphasized that we live in *a process world* of continual change. This may not seem apparent when we look at the mountains, rocks, bridges, and roads. At least, not in the moment. But when we step back to view even these "solid" and "unchanging" things from the viewpoint of time, we can begin to appreciate the forces of change that govern the world.

Indeed, we live in a process universe where we can always count on things changing. We see this with a vengeance in the microscopic life and even more so when we get to the sub-microscopic level. At that level of awareness, we suddenly become acutely aware of reality as a "dance of electrons." Here, at the level of quantum physics and mechanics, the principle of uncertainty predominates.

This highlights the importance of establishing an inner executive that will not allow us to become closed, rigid, insensitive, and inflexible. In fact, staying open and flexible not only keeps our thinking, emoting, and responding more current and relevant, it keeps us younger and more vital. We commit an act of suicide whenever we shut down our receptivity to the ever-changing world.

Preventing Dullness

Stephen Covey utilized a particularly relevant metaphor in his work on *highly effective people* and families around this theme. In speaking about the importance of maintaining an ongoing development in the face of change, he described "sharpening the saw." It lies in the nature of things that when we use a saw or take an axe to a tree, it will become dull over time. With every whack of the axe, the blade becomes duller and duller. It becomes less efficient. In some ways, it may seem non-productive to stop whacking away at the tree and to take time to sharpen the blade.

The same occurs in the process of maintaining our own personal empowerment. Sometimes we have to stop what we're doing. We have to get away from the tasks of everyday life. We have to take a break in order to refresh the vision and rejuvenate the spirit. Staying sharp in mind and emotion, in spirit and body, entails a willingness to step back to keep updating and refreshing the highest level frames that govern our overall purpose, mission, and vision. This truly prevents dullness.

To stay current and up-to-date, we must commit ourselves to the very idea of ongoing development, improvement, and training. Only in this way can we keep our blade sharp. This refers to the never-ending process of learning, growing, exploring, etc.

Keeping your Inner Executive Sharp

Staying *sharp* involves several things: maintaining a training schedule of those components that enable us to stay at our best. Most people seem to easily recognize this in the physical realm, and just as easily fail to recognize this in the inner realms of mind and emotion. Yet *staying sharp* and maintaining our edge necessitates a discipline there as well.

Taking inventory on a regular and consistent basis also helps. Monitoring our current progress and level of skill enables us to operate with a higher degree of awareness. Stagnation begins to set in when we *take things for granted.* Recognizing where we are and constantly setting new and compelling goals pulls us into our future. This speaks about the need to constantly be *refreshing our vision* so that we don't grow stale or stagnate.

Meta-Stating with Flexibility and Tentativeness

Given that the nature of the world involves ongoing change, this makes the ability to flexibly adjust to the ever-changing conditions around us highly valuable. We can expect things to change. *Change* is the only constant in a world of flux where, at the sub-microscopic level, reality exists as "a dance of electrons." Developing a good adjustment to the constancy of change enables us to "ride lightly in the saddle" with a flexibility about the tentativeness of all of our maps, ideas, beliefs, and progress.

To meta-state such thoughts-and-feelings of flexibility, openness to change, adaptability, willingness to keep growing, learning, and developing empowers us in coping. It enables us to adapt "the spirit of a child" in wonder, awe, appreciation, seeing things freshly, etc. With this attitude then we can ask such creative questions as:

- What else is there?
- What am I missing?
- What questions am I not asking?
- What am I taking for granted?

Meta-Stating with Ongoing Feedback

Another factor that contributes to keeping our cutting edge and to staying sharp is a good relationship to feedback. In our ongoing training and implementation, we need to experiment and practice. This gives us new feedback data that we can then use to hone our skills and refine our responses. Our openness to feedback enables us to get the most out of our experiences. Then we can let the feedback *tune us up.*

1) Access a Mind-Emotional State of Openness to Feedback.

Think about a time when you received feedback openly, freely, and even with excitement. You received it, it "tuned you up," and out of it you learned how to respond in a smarter way that made you even more effective.

2) Amplify the Openness to feedback State and Anchor it.

As you sense and feel the openness, allow that feeling to grow and to increase and as you do, connect it to a gesture, movement, word, etc., to anchor it.

3) Tie the Feedback to your desired outcomes.

What is my outcome, design, and objective? Feedback has meaning and significance only in relationship to a goal. When we coach someone else by giving them honest and helpful feedback, we do so with regard to a specific outcome. We provide an objective reflection about how much "on target" the person's words or actions were. All feedback should serve some goal.

4) Translate the Feedback so that you have specific behavioral descriptions.

This will enable us to avoid *personalizing* or interpreting any feedback as having anything to do with our identity. It's *not* about us. It's about our speech or behavior. It's about some actions or responses that we are engaged in. So seek for *behavioral* feedback, and refuse to receive judgmental or evaluative feedback that is not coded in *See, Hear, Feel* (VAK) terms. This will prevent all *evaluations* and judgments. When we coach, giving *sensory based* feedback enables us to offer useful information.

> "As you fired off the anchor on her arm, I noticed that you put your fingers down about $1/4$ of an inch from where it seemed you set the anchor a moment ago."

5) Keep the Feedback tentative and seek validation.

Sometimes we not only take "feedback" too personally, but we receive it too quickly and fail to check it out. After all, all feedback does not contain the same quality of information. High quality feedback that carries weight and offers us a chance to hone our skills provides empirical data along with how the information is evaluated. To avoid assuming that every feedback is accurate or useful, we have to inquire:

Who is giving it?

What state are they coming from?

That's why we "practice" in the groups—to find out the edges, limits, response patterns, etc. of things. Also, affirm things which are done right and powerfully as well as things that need more fine tuning.

> "In view of eliciting the learning state (objective), you paused only two seconds for her to recall a memory, and just when her eyes defocused, you jumped in and asked her to make the picture brighter (sensory based), I got the impression she needed more time to process … Did you need more time?"

In this respect, remember also that helpful feedback is typically timely.

Meta-Stating Implementation

The ability to actually *implement knowledge* represents a higher level state that enables us to stay sharp. Having a meta-state pattern wherein we operate from a frame of always seeking to apply information to ourselves so that we can be congruent empowers us to encounter information and make it our own. Once we have set our own frame for *the installation* of information, then we have the ability to use and replicate excellence.

Now we can take new learnings, insights, processes, patterns, and models and *get them inside of ourselves* so that they make a difference in how we think, feel, talk, behave, and relate. This puts into our hands the ability to transfer ideas into actual life and to execute our action plans.

In this regard, take any or all of the following resource states and meta-state yourself with them.

1) Clarity of understanding of the process.
  • Have I represented it with vividness and clarity in my mind?
2) Intensity of emotion and energy for the new skill.
  • Do I feel a need for it or feel excited about it?
3) The Fittingness of the New Frame for our life situation. Alignment.
  • Does it fit?
  • Is it aligned with our highest values and visions?
  • Am I willing to let this become a part of my identity?
4) Responsibility: Ownership, Initiation.
  • Have I taken personal responsibility *for* transferring the skill into my life?
  • Have I owned the learning?
  • Am I willing to take responsibility for making this part of my life?
5) Willingness to experiment and play. Experimenting and active involvement in role-playing groups.
  • Am I willing to play around (experiment) with the new skill, pattern, or model until it becomes second-nature to me?
  • Am I willing to play around in respectful ways in the small groups using the role-playing scenarios to get this installed in my behavior?
6) Repetition of the skill or pattern.
  • Will I work with this often enough so that it becomes habitual?
  • Will I playfully repeat it enough so that I can do it in my sleep?
7) Future Pacing.
  • Have I imagined vividly how this will play out in my life in the future?

9) Skill Reinforcement in groups as experiencer, coach, and meta-person.
  • Will I take responsibility to get the most out of the group experiences and enable the others to get the most out of it for themselves?
10) State Extending Exercises.
  • Will I delight myself with the playfulness of extending the parameters of the new states and meta-states that I create?
11) Empowering, Sensory-Based, and Immediate Feedback.
  • Am I willing to learn how to give and receive the kind of enhancing feedback that makes for reinforcement and installation of these skills?

Mind-To-Muscle Pattern

Ultimately, ongoing personal mastery arises from the ability to turn highly informative, insightful, and valued principles into *neurological patterns*. As with typing on a keyboard, the original learning may take a considerable amount of time and trouble in order to get the muscle patterns and coordination deeply imprinted into one's muscles. Yet once we have practiced and trained to that extent, then *the learnings become incorporated into the very fabric of the muscles themselves*. This then allows us to lose conscious awareness of the learnings and let the muscles run the program. At that point, we have translated *principle into muscle.*

The same holds true for expertise, excellence, and mastery in all other fields, from sports, mathematics, teaching, to surgery, selling, and public relations. We begin with a *principle*—a concept, understanding, awareness, belief, etc., and then we translate it into *muscle.* I have found this especially true in our modeling projects regarding resilience, leadership, wealth building, selling excellence, learning, etc. From that I have put together the following process that I now use in all of The Neuro-Semantic and Meta-State Trainings.

This pattern is designed to create transformation by moving up and down the various levels of mind so that we map from our understandings about something from the lowest descriptive levels to the highest conceptual levels and back down again.

1) *Identify a Desired Principle.*
This principle could be a belief, understanding, value, secret, law, etc. Any awareness will work. Pick something that you want to incorporate into the very fabric of your muscles. Specific the concept or principle by stating it, or even better, writing it down as clearly, succinctly, and compellingly as possible.

> What do you know or understand or believe about X that you want to set as a frame in your mind?
>
> Describe your theory or theoretical understanding in a paragraph or two. Write it as succinctly and compelling as possible. Begin with the line, *"I understand ..."* or *"I conceptualize ..."*

2) *Describe the Principle as a Belief.*
Now use the semantic environment, *"I believe ..."* and complete the sentence by rephrasing the concept and understanding as a personal declaration of a belief.

> You believe what?

3) *Reformat the Belief as a Decision.*
Once the belief is stated in a way that sounds convincing and is stated succinctly so that if feels compelling, reformulate the personal belief so that it takes the form of a personal decision. Finish the following semantic environment, *"I will ..."* or *"I choose to ..."*

> So, given that you believe that, you will do what?
>
> What will you choose to do?

4) *Rephrase Belief-Decision as a State or Experience.*
> When you fully experience your concept—>belief—>decision as an emotional state, what will you experience?
>
> How will you feel? Complete the semantic environment, *"I feel ... and I experience ..."*
>
> What are you experiencing?

5) *State the Actions that you will take as an Expression of this Translation.*
> Finish the following semantic sentence stem, *"The one thing that I will do today as an expression of this concept, belief, decision, and state is ..."*
>
> You will do that? What other step will you take?
>
> Will this specific action enable you to execute your principles?

6) *Step into the Action and Go Meta Repeatedly.*
As you fully imagine carrying out the one action that you will do today ... seeing what you will see, hearing what you will hear, and feeling what you will feel as you do it ... now move up through the levels ... into the State from which this action emerges, naming the State and experiencing it fully, owning the Decision, Affirming the Belief with a powerful *"Yes!"* as you do, and stepping up even higher in your mind into a full awareness of your reasons, understandings, concepts, and principles that drive this way of being in the world ... and as you step into that place fully, now bring it back down again ... noticing how it transforms everything even more and creates an even greater sense of empowerment.
Repeat this several times, future pacing as you do.

Summary
- In a process world of ongoing change, the adventure into *Personal Mastery* never ends. It keeps developing as we explore ever-new pathways.
- Shifting attention to enjoying the process and appreciating the experiences along the line grant us yet another facet of personal mastery. We do not wait for or demand flawless perfection, just the enjoyment of growth and exploration.
- To stay sharp, alive, and vigorous then we develop a good relationship to feedback and tentativeness by accessing the wonder and openness of a child's playful sense of awe.

Where Do We Go From Here?
The range of applications for personal mastery—for accessing and empowering your *Inner Executive*—has really no end. Even the sky is not the limit for you.

Appendix A

A Brief History of Meta-States
The Mind Mastery Model

Neuro-Linguistics, Meta-States, Neuro-Semantics

The Meta-State Model used in this work originated from several sources, the most important one designed by an engineer who arrived on the shores of the United States early in the Twentieth Century totally disgusted with The Great War of Europe. Having seen first-hand the destruction and insanity of the First World War, he wondered how the human sciences could be so primitive and regressive compared to the revolution and advancement going on in the hard sciences (engineering, mathematics, physics, etc.).

This curiosity then lead to several central questions:

- Why do we, as a race, progress in an ongoing development, generation after generation, in the "hard" sciences?
- What explains the ability of those fields to continually improve upon the previous generation's contributions, and refine models and technologies?
- What causes us to be so regressive and primitive in the "soft" social sciences that involve communication, relationships, politics, etc.?

This put Alfred Korzybski to wondering and questioning about people, human "nature," the structure of communication, etc.

- What *enables* us to progress so rapidly and effectively in the engineering sciences?
- What *prevents* us from progressing in the social sciences of psychology and sociology?
- Why can we not build human structures, institutions, and processes that offer ongoing development and the highest human engineering possible?

- *What would it take* so that we could begin to *engineer* excellence in the human sciences as we have in physics, mechanics, chemistry, medicine, etc.?

Modeling Human Modeling

As an engineer, Korzybski thought about *what specifically* we do when we advance the sciences; he realized that we first of all *create a model.* We invent a process, pattern, flow chart, diagram, map, paradigm, etc. We also construct some kind of *an explanatory theory* to order our thinking.

Science, he noted, operates and advances by setting forth a model, then testing it, refining it, retesting it, and so on. Coming from the engineering field, Korzybski thought in terms of the *map/territory* distinction. We create a map about the structure or process of how something works. Korzybski also noted that true and evolutionary progress occurs because we do not have to start afresh in each generation and reinvent the wheel. The hard sciences progress so quickly because each new generation is able to begin where the previous generation left off. What they have learned and discovered can be passed on. What makes this possible?

Symbols. We can pass on our knowledge, learnings, and discoveries by *encoding them in a symbolic system.* We can avoid old trial and error learnings from experience by developing and refining ever better *mental models* (maps, theories, scientific procedures, specialized languages). This describes the very heart of "the scientific attitude." We develop an idea, state it as a hypothesis, test it, experiment with it, use feedback to refine it, and continue to do so until we have a full-fledged proven model that works. This generates accelerated learning.

Korzybski (1921) labeled this development process by a special name: *Time-Binding.* Because we can encode the learnings of previous generations and pass those concepts on to the next, we can bind "time." We bind "time" (or actually, *the learnings* that occurred in previous "times") using our symbols, just as plants bind chemicals to their experience and animals bind *space* to their experience. As he described the *functional operating* of plants as *chemical-binders*, and animals as *space-binders*, he describes humans as *time-binders*.

Of course, as an engineer, you know that he felt that he just had to know the essential "nature" of the materials and substances with which he worked. Engineers have this thing about getting acquainted with their materials. It makes sense. When we engineer something using bricks, that typically differs from how we would engineer something else made out of wood, or steel, or limestone, and especially if we used jelly or pastry. *Materials* do make a difference.

Korzybski decided that he needed to figure out the "nature" of humans. Ultimately he boiled "human nature" down to the basic ideas that you still find in the field of General Semantics and Neuro-Semantics today:

1) ***Time-Binding.*** We are capable of binding the learnings of others in previous times. This leads to the use of neural and extra-neural devices (or tools) to extend our senses (telescopes, microscopes, dictionaries, books, computers, the internet, etc.).

2) ***Symbolic/Semantic.*** We are capable of binding "time" through the use of symbols into our very neurology (hence "neuro-linguistic" and "neuro-semantic" in nature). This necessitates that we distinguish signals from symbols, and recognize the levels of symbols in creating ever more conceptual mappings of the world (mathematics, music, computer languages, human languages, etc.).

3) ***Self-Reflexive.*** We are capable of mapping our maps, of engaging in reflective consciousness so that we can abstract at multiple levels, which then leads to self-programming of our minds, as well as the ability to make meta-moves regarding our experiences.

4) ***Systemic.*** Our thoughts-body-emotion operate in a systemic way inasmuch as the neuro-linguistic feed-back and feed-forward processes loop around in circuits of information, each one influencing the new set of responses.

Korzybski realized that the engineers and scientists who succeeded in creating new, practical, and cutting-edge products succeeded precisely because they ultimately developed new *symbol systems*. They refused to stay within the box of the old language systems. This enabled them to create even better *maps*. They typically discovered flaws and inadequacies in the old Aristotelian way of thinking, reasoning, and languaging things and so invented new Non-Aristotelian systems. *Engineering success,* whether in mathematics, bridge construction, modern technology, or human communications, relationships, and sanity, depends entirely upon accurate, practical, and enhancing *maps.*

Undoubtedly, this highlights the most crucial element of all which facilitates success and effectiveness in modern science. Namely, new and advanced *symbol systems*. In most fields, the engineers, mathematicians, scientists, chemists, etc. had to invent their own *language* and *terminology* in order to advance and test their models. When Korzybski discovered this, it lead him to a radical, yet very profound, insight about the very thing *preventing* similar success in the social sciences involving human communications, relationships, sanity, politics, etc.

> *The very way we talk and use language to express our understandings about human beings, functioning, thinking, emoting, behaving, relating, etc.—the symbol systems and language forms themselves prevent effective engineering of human relationships.*

Korzybski set out to begin *a new kind of engineering*. Beginning with his analysis of *the materials* with which he would build up new ways of functioning and relating, he first described his *time-binding* theory *(The Manhood of Humanity, 1921)*. As plants *bind* chemicals, and animals *bind movement*, so humans *bind "time"* by the use of *symbols*. For effective engineering for *time-binders and a symbolic class of life,* Korzybski (1933/1994) wrote his masterpiece, *Science and Sanity: An Introduction to Non-Aristotelian Systems and General Semantics.* This began the field of General Semantics. It was in those pages that Korzybski designed a model of "mind" which describes our *neuro-linguistic states* created by our mental mapping (i.e. "thinking," "reasoning," and "conceptualizing").

Run Your Own Brain—for a Change

Now, with a title like *Science and Sanity: An Introduction to Non-Aristotelian Systems and General Semantics*, you can imagine how popular it became. No wonder Korzybski's book never became a bestseller! Korzybski actually did not think that he had created anything all that difficult. He actually said that he wrote for "the intelligent layman." Yet even today, people with graduate degrees continue to exclaim difficulty in reading his book. This worked against him and in the end it prevented his incredible human engineering tools from ever getting out into the general public.

Then one day, many years later, something happened to change all of that. During the days of the Cognitive Revolution in psychology (1950s and 1960s), two men became captivated by the idea of *modeling excellence*. Having stumbled upon Korzybski's *neuro-linguistic model* of the mind and how to master it, they recognized its tremendous value. So, basing their work of modeling excellence on the map-territory distinction, Dr John Grinder and Richard Bandler created yet another field, *Neuro-Linguistic Programming (NLP)*.

The mouth-full terminology, *"Neuro-Linguistic Programming,"* actually refers to a pretty simple idea, namely, that the stuff in our heads govern the experiences we feel in our body. Or, our *linguistics program* our *neurology*. Our *mental mapping* about things operates as *programming* or patterning, and shows up in our body as our feelings, behaviors, ways of relating, etc. Neuro-linguistic means *"mind-body."*

NLP continued Korzybski's work and provided an even more extensive way of talking about *how* we can learn to *run our own brain* and *how* we can learn to run it more consciously and purposefully. They also created a new jargon for the field. Why? Because in every field that we want to master and become skilled in, whether baseball, hockey, mathematics, music, computer science, archeology, etc., we have to learn and use a specialized language. To try to work masterfully in the field without utilizing the specialized language leads to using vague, sloppy, and metaphorical words.

The Neuro-Linguistics of Bandler and Grinder, while containing a lot of specialized terms, has provided a new language for describing with more precision the very mechanisms by which we construct our internal maps and "realities." This now results in providing a way to use work more methodically with these forces, principles, and processes, and to create neuro-linguistic tools that become the *human* technology whereby we can design engineer our minds, emotions, strategies, and therefore lives and destiny.

What did NLP add to the engineering ideas and tools of Korzybski? It integrated into the *neuro-linguistic* model the new developments and discoveries in the Cognitive sciences, artificial intelligence, systems and cybernetics, communications, anthropology, and the best of Gestalt psychology, family systems therapy, hypnosis, and transactional analysis (TA). It also moved the model out of academic complexity and isolation.

Neuro-Semantics
Mastering and Managing Mind By Using our "Higher Mind" or Executive States

Then one day in the early 1990s, I happened upon an important facet of Korzybski's work. It happened when I was *modeling the structure of resilience*. What I discovered in the process was that we truly do not merely have *one mind*, but multiple "minds," and levels of "mind" about things. The state of resilience does not involve just one way of thinking about things. It involves more. It involves a higher mind that considers things about our everyday mind.

As I look back on that discovery, it now seems so obvious. Discover it for yourself. Think about some *setback* (i.e. a disappointment, frustration, change of plans, etc.) that you may have at one time experienced about an important goal in your life. What did you *first* think and/or feel about that? Probably you entertained ideas similar to the following:

"Why does this have to happen to mess things up?"
"Why does this always happen to me?"
"This blows everything. I'm as mad as hell!"
"I shouldn't have got my hopes up so high."
"How can I handle this right now?"

After you thought some of those thoughts and accessed some corresponding state of mind-and-emotion, what did you *then* think and feel? Did you *like* or *dislike* your initial response? And if you didn't like it, what higher level thoughts and feelings *about* that state did you elicit in yourself? What long-term beliefs do you have in your mind that support those ideas? And, *who are you* when you believe in some limiting thought? Who are you when your find your beliefs changing?

Realizing this, I went back to Korzybski's model of mind, the *Levels of Abstracting* (the Structural Differential). This provides the basic structure for the meta-levels model and for the Meta-States Model. I also turned to another twentieth century genius, anthropologist Gregory Bateson.

From these sources arose the mental mastery model of this work, **the Meta-States Model.** This model describes how *thought-and-emotion* creates our mental and emotional *states* and then loops back onto itself to create ever higher layers of mind. We have not only thoughts, but thoughts-about-thoughts, feelings about feelings. And after we have experienced whatever height of thoughts-and-feelings about something, we can then entertain a thought-and-feeling about that. As states arise from thoughts-and-feelings and then states-upon-states, a *system* of interactive forces arise.

For example, a person may first experience some fear in speaking up to someone—he may feel afraid of their reaction. But it doesn't end there. Suppose the gentleman then *thinks-and-or-feels* something *about* that state of hesitation and fear. Perhaps he then feels ashamed of himself for that. Or what if he felt angry for feeling that. Or again, he could experience disappointment or frustration about his fear of taking action. This second level *state* about the first level *state* means that, *conceptually*, the person has moved up a logical level and has created a frame-of-reference about the fear of speaking up.

Complicated? Complex? Yes, indeed. And yet this describes only the beginning. It vividly describes what we all do a hundred thousand times every day. We *layer* our thoughts-and-emotions on top of other thoughts-and-feelings.

None of this reveals anything new or mysterious. For centuries, philosophers have noticed and described this phenomenon of mind and human nature. *Self-reflexive consciousness,* they called it. Consciousness not only *goes out* to detect and create representations of the world, but it also *reflects back onto itself.* It also *applies* its representing, thinking, reasoning, and conceptualizing powers to its previous productions.

When we do that, we create for ourselves a *state-about-a-state or a Meta-State.* When we do so, we generate layers upon layers of "mind" about mind and set in motion a whole *system* of interactive internal feedback loops thereby enriching and complicating the functioning of "mind." Pulling together the ideas of Korzybski, Bateson, Bandler and Grinder, cybernetics, reality therapy, control theory, etc., I constructed a model to map out all of these interactions, today known as *the Meta-States Model.*

This model, built upon so many other formulations, now allows us to track our higher levels of mind. It takes us beyond the long recognized principle of the power of positive thinking. This model empowers us to first identify or detect our current executive states which govern our experiences and to then create new executive states that can turn everything around and program us for excellence. The most practical value in Meta-States lies in how it endows us with the ability to truly *take charge of our life at all levels.* The chapters that follow will sketch out an understanding of this model and provide step-by-step instruction on how to use this model to **empower your inner executive states as you develop the mental mastery that evokes your own personal genius.** Doing this will equip you so that you can *truly take charge of your life and your destiny* in new ways that will surprise and delight you. It will give you new keys for self-management, for state control, for understanding about yourself and others, for language elegance in persuasion, and for modeling excellence. While that may seem like a big promise, actually it does not describe half of the wonder and power that you will discover in *the Meta-States Model.*

Getting to the Higher Mind

The next level of consciousness involves the *first meta-level of awareness* (aware of our awareness). This kind of consciousness *transcends* the first by reflecting back onto the first; it makes the first awareness its object. We think about our thinking. We talk about our talking. We comment on our comments. Gregory Bateson (1972) noted in his own research and those of other researchers who demonstrated that highly intelligent animals can "think" at the first meta-level of awareness.

Yet with the human species, we seem to have an unlimited and never-ending ability to *go meta* (above) to ever higher levels of awareness. Korzybski (1933/1994) noted that the symbolic system of language empowers us to always say something about whatever we just said. Our *abstracting ability* goes on without end as an infinite process.

This *abstracting ability* also provides us with the basis for both science and sanity—"*science*" because we can posit a hypothesis, test it, reflect on the results and use it as feedback to postulate another hypothesis and so on. "*Sanity*"—because this ability to check out our mental maps with the territory that we seek to model enables us to make finer and finer adjustments and not become confused about the difference between territory and map.

We call this unique human power—*self-reflexive consciousness*, or self-reflexivity. So just as soon as you think or say anything—you will almost immediately have a thought-about-that-thought in the back of your mind. Frequently (if not usually) these *thoughts in the back of your mind* comprise even more significant information. Further, this *reflexivity* generates *higher levels of "mind."* As we layer thought upon thought, emotion upon emotion, idea upon idea, concept upon concept, etc., we generate a *system of consciousness*. This makes human consciousness *systemic* in its very nature.

It also makes us a *meta-class of life*. *Meta* here refers to going *above and beyond* something so that we then create something (a thought, emotion, idea) that is *about* something else. As these processes take us *up* into higher *conceptual realms*—realms of ideas and concepts, it makes us a *neuro-semantic class of life with self-programming* powers. This means that self-programming becomes a very real possibility for anyone who can "step aside" (so to speak) and observe the system as a system and then affect that system.

In systems literature, the ability to *think systemically* about the system has come to represent a whole new and higher form of thinking during the last half of the Twentieth Century. This has brought revolutions to the fields of Family Therapy, Business, Management, Artificial Intelligence and cybernetic systems, Government, Linguistics, etc. Peter Senge (*The Fifth Discipline*, 1990) has described *systemic thinking* as the key thinking pattern so essential for the Twentieth-first century.

The Layers of Mind

Sigmund Freud recognized the layering of mind. When he worked with a troubled person, he invited that person to simply experience the free intrusion of thoughts . "Say whatever comes to your mind," he coached them. He encouraged them to not suppress the thought, not to judge it, but to *welcome* the intrusion of the other thoughts hovering around a thought.

People with a natural knack for enabling people to feel comfortable, to relax, and to express themselves authentically also tap into this same structure. The primary thoughts and words that we use in our social relationships, in the roles and persona that we present to each other do not truly or deeply express the person. What a person *really thinks and feels*, what he or she may *truly wonder about, fear, anticipate, love*, etc. can be known only in a context of trust and relaxation ... one that embraces the person with "positive regard." This invites the *thoughts in the back of the mind* to come forward.

The *self-reflexivity* of consciousness creates both some of the most mysteriously wonderful as well as some of the most troublesome products in our experience. Consider the idea of learning to "run your own brain." Did you notice that this addresses at least two *levels* of you? It addresses *you* as a thinking and cognizing person (the brain part of you that you will run), and *you* as a higher level self who can *think* thoughts and give direction to your brain. How shall we think about the *Self* or *Person* who can, in some way, experience him or herself as having different selves, even different levels of "self?" Chapter 5 of this work explores and demystifies this concept using the richness of Meta-States.

Appendix B

Distinguishing Primary and Meta-States

Primary states differ significantly from Meta-States. The following identifies the most significant contrasts and specifies numerous meta-level distinctions. To effectively distinguish Meta-States and Primary States, use the following questions to focus your attention.

1) Is that response appropriate to the stimulus? Is it direct or indirect?

2) The nature of the emotion: Is it kinesthetic or conceptual? Does it lie in the body or in the mind?

3) What is the Aboutness of the state? Is it about an object out there in the world, a see, hear, feel object, or is it of another state (thoughts, feelings, etc.)?

4) Examine the kind of language used. What kind of language: sensory-based or evaluative?

5) From what perceptual position does the expression indicate, from first position or from any other position?

PRIMARY STATES	META-STATES
* **Simple/Direct**	**Complex/Indirect**
First-Level	Second/Third Levels, Etc.
No layers of consciousness	Several or many layers of consciousness
Immediate, automatic	Layer levels of consciousness/ Mediated by symbols
Synesthesia (V—K)	Meta-level synesthesias—the Collapsing of levels

* Primary Kinesthetics Meta-kinesthetics or "emotions"/Evaluative Emotions

(primary emotions)	—judgments coded in the soma (body)
Modality (VAK) and	*Affected* by Submodalities, but not driven
Submodality-Driven	**Linguistically-Driven** and Located
Kinesthetically Exper. +/-	No Immediate or localized
Associated!	Dissociated from primary emotions
Easily Anchored	Chains of Anchors—glued together by words
	Chains connected by multiple anchors
Intense to very intense	Less intense: more thoughtful, *"mindful"*
Strong, primitive, deep	Weaker, less primitive, more modified by cognition
Quicker, Shorter	Lasts Longer, more enduring, stable
Animal	Human: dependent upon
More Focused	symbol-using capacities
	Multiple-focuses simultaneously
One time learning	One time learning very infrequent
	Repetition generally **needed** to drive in and install
* **1st. Position**	**2nd., 3rd. or other multiple positions** consciousness expanded and transcendental
Thought @ world	Thoughtfulness/Mindfulness, Thought @ Thought
* **Object:**	**Object:**
External—in world	**Internal—in mind-emotions**
* **Sensory-Based Linguistics**	**Evaluative Based Linguistics**
Empirical Qualities	Emergent Qualities/properties: Having no lower-order counterparts
Somewhat projective	Highly projective
	Once Collapsed—begins to operate as a Primary State with a seamless logical-level synesthesia

@ = about

254

Appendix C

Emotions in Relationship to States and Meta-States

States differ. We experience lots of different kinds and qualities of states. State configurations come in all sizes and shapes. Just because you have accessed a *state of thoughts-and-emotions and physiology,* you may not access a similar state to someone else doing the same. In the Meta-States Model we have distinguished *three categories of states:* Primary States, Meta-States, and Gestalt States.

Primary Emotions Chart

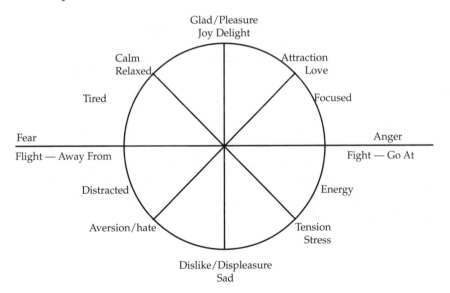

Gestalt States refer to a complex Meta-State configuration wherein the end gestalt of experience involves much more than just the sum of all the parts (ideas, feelings, states-about-states, etc.). For example, when we have boldness about our hopes/dreams plus commitment to face fears we have "courage." But "courage" may also arise from other configurations: outrageousness about hopes/dreams plus not-caring about embarrassment in the presence of others.

In gestalt states, we see the system principle of equilfinality at work. This refers to the fact that *in a system* we usually have many ways to get to the same outcome; how we have organism-as-a-whole evaluating/emoting. Here emergent qualities arise that we do not find in any of the parts, hence, it has non-addictive characteristics that induce what we might call a "feeling-as-a-whole."

Primary Emotions and Emotional States:

Dr Robert Plutchik (1980) defines *an emotion* as "a complex sequence of events having elements of cognitive appraisal, feeling, impulses to action, and overt behavior." In his book, *Emotion: A Psychoevolutionary Synthesis* he posited *8 primary emotions:* fear, surprise, sadness, disgust, anger, anticipation, joy, and acceptance (receptivity). He theorized the emotional process in terms of "a chain reaction"—

Stimulus Event → Cognition → Feeling → Behavior → Function

Threat by Enemy → Danger → Fear → Run → Protection

Loss of Parent → Isolation → Sadness → Cry for Help → Reintegration

He then mapped primary and mixed emotions: anticipation and joy > optimism; anticipation and anger > aggressiveness; joy and acceptance > love; acceptance and fear > submission; fear and surprise > awe; surprise and sadness > disappointment; sadness and disgust > remorse; disgust and anger: contempt. (*Psychology Today*, Feb. 1980, pp. 68–78).

Appendix D

Design Considerations from Meta-Stating Interfaces

What kinds of things happen when we meta-state ourselves and others? What kind of responses, consequences can we create by using various meta-stating patterns? In *design engineering of human states and meta-states*, we need to take into account the various interface effects of state-upon-state. The words in quotations ("…") provide examples of the *interface* between levels of states.

(1) Reduce painfully intense states. Some meta-states will reduce the primary state as in "calm about anger," or "doubt about doubt."

(2) Intensify states. Some meta-states will amplify and turn up the primary state as in "worry about worry," or "loving learning," or "anxious about anxiety" (hyper-anxiety), "loving love," "feeling calm about calm," "passionate about learning," "appreciate appreciation."

(3) Exaggerate and distort states. This increases the intensity factor. Generally, when we bring a negative state of thinking-feeling to bear on another primary state, we *turn our psychic energies against ourselves.* Examples: "anger about anger," "love hatred of (whatever)," "fear about fear," "hesitating to hesitate" (talking in a non-fluent way), i.e., stuttering, "sadness about sadness" (depression), "mistrust of mistrust."

(4) Negate a state. Examples: in "doubt about my doubt," I usually feel more sure. "Resisting our resistance;" in "procrastinating my procrastination," I take action and put off the putting off, so with "mistrust of mistrust," "ashamed of shame."

(5) Interrupt states. It so jars and shifts the first state, it totally interrupts it. It can arrest the psycho-logic. Examples include: "being humorous about seriousness," "anxious about calmness," "calmness about anxiety," "intentionally panicking."

(6) Create confusion. By getting various thoughts-feelings to collide and "fuse" "with" each other in ways that we do not comprehend. Example: "ridiculous about seriousness."

(7) Create paradox. By shifting experience to a higher and different level; it explains powerful techniques as "paradoxical intention" Watzlawick (1984): "Kant recognized that every error of this kind [map/territory confusion error] consists in our taking the way we determine, divide, or deduce concepts for qualities of the things in and of themselves" (215). Bateson (1972) defined paradox as a contradiction in conclusions that one correctly argued from consistent premises. Examples: the "be spontaneous now!" paradox, try really hard to relax, "never say never," "Never and always are two words one should always remember never to use." "I'm absolutely certain that nothing is absolutely certain." Title of book: *"This Book Needs No Title."* (Raymond M. Smallya, 1980)

(8) Create dissociation. Sometimes meta-stating causes dissociation from the primary state. If we dissociate dramatically enough, it may result in amnesia (switching states rapidly and without reference frequently produces amnesia and other trance phenomena). Examples: "distance from pain," "spectating about anxiety," "observing old trauma," "running an ecology check on the value of resentment," "having a ringing in my ears, but tuning it down until I don't quite hear it anymore, and wondering about that."

(9) Create the beginning of a new process. Getting us to *initiate* the first step of a new experience, can create a *new emergent experience:* Examples: "courage to have courage," "playful uncertainty," "learning how to learn," "feeling gentle and tender in the expression of my anger," "willing to become willing."

(10) Grab and Focus Attention to Swish the mind to provoke thoughtfulness in a different direction. As such it can arrest attention, overload consciousness, stimulate new thinking, and question axioms, beliefs, reasoning, memory, etc. (hence deframe). Examples: "calm about anger," "appreciative about anger," "lovingly gentle about anger," "intentionally becoming resistant to my own resistance."

(11) Induce Trance and trance phenomena. Most people experience third-order abstracting and above as "trancy." It invites one to "go inside" so much that the "inward focus" of trance develops as one engages, consciously and unconsciously, in an internal search for meaning. We especially experience meta-stating that shifts logical types *and* sets up double-binds as initiating trance. Examples: "And now I want you to rebel against thinking about just how comfortable you can feel if you don't close your eyes before you're ready to relax deeper than you ever have before, now. I wonder if you're going to fail to succeed at not going into trance at exactly your own speed or whether you won't."

(12) Create Gestalt States and Phenomena. States-about-states frequently generates gestalt experiences so that something new emerges from the process that we cannot explain as a summation of the parts, it partakes of a systemic and non-additivity quality. Examples: "suppress excitement" creates anxiety (Perls), "worry about what X means" typically leads to state of existential concern.

(13) Creates Humor. The jolt and jar of state-upon-state often results in the gestalt of humor (Plato: that which we experience as "out of place in time and space without danger"). It tickles our fancy, delights our consciousness, surprises, amazes, shocks, etc.

(14) Qualifies Experiences. The higher level state (i.e. the meta-state) qualifies the lower level experience. Example: "joyful learning."

(15) Solidify States and Frames. Bring confirmation, belief, conviction, valuing, importance, etc. to any frame and it will solidify it. "Saying *yes* to the idea that …"

(16) Loosen States and Frames. Bring questions, doubt, suspicion, wonder, etc. to a frame and it begins to loosen up. "Wondering and questioning whether the idea that … is really valid."

Appendix E

The Meta-Model

The Meta-Model began as a way of sorting out the linguistic distinctions that John Grinder and Richard Bandler noticed in the verbal responses that Virginia Satir and Fritz Perls used in working with clients. The model itself consists of *12 linguistic distinctions.* These distinctions enable a person to detect and identify places of *vagueness* in the very way that a person talks which may create all kinds of limitations. As a result, the person may move through life with an impoverished map.

At the surface level, the Meta-Model offers a way to respond to the lack of clarity and precision. The design? To elicit from the speaker more clarity and precision. In the process, this also facilitates a neuro-linguistic experience inside the person who hears the questions. Typically, the questions facilitate and coach the hearer to reaccess the internal referents. These are the frames of references by which the person creates meaning and makes sense of things. As the person does this, it enables him or her to fill in the details, to chase away the vagueness, and ill-formed structures, and to construct new representations. Overall, this enables the person to create a more precise and useful map. Bandler and Grinder described the Meta-Model questions and challenges as getting a person to create a more well-formed Model of the World.

The Meta-Model provides a list of twelve distinctions about language, along with numerous questions and responses. These cue us about *how to listen* to language as we and/or another person communicates. As we listen, we track over from the words to a mental representational screen in our minds where we can create a video-track of what we see, hear, feel, smell, taste, and say. What doesn't track over we inquire about. The non-trackable pieces fail to give us a see-hear-feel reference. The inquiry then enables us to obtain such missing information. We have extended the Meta-Model with additional linguistic distinctions in *The Secrets Of Magic* (1998).

The Meta-Model does not evaluate the goodness or badness of our mental constructions. It does facilitate an evaluation, namely, the sensory based data out of which we create our more abstract understandings. This model assumes that a fuller and richer map will work for us better than a map full of deletions. It assumes that *awareness* of our generalizations and alterations (distortions) gives us more control, choice, and power. Lack of awareness of *how* we have left things out, generalized ideas and beliefs, and formatted beliefs leading to identifying map with territory and the inability to step out of impoverished maps.

The linguistic distinctions of the Meta-Model fall into three categories of patterns.

> *1) Patterns of Deletion.*
> *2) Patterns of Generalization.*
> *3) Patterns of Distortion.*

Linguistic Deletions
1. Simple Deletions (characteristics left out) (Del.)
2. Comparative Deletions and Superlative Deletions (unspecified relations) (CD/SD)
3. Unspecified Referential Indices: Unspecified Nouns and Verbs (UN/UV)
4. Unspecified Processes — Adverbs Modifying Verbs (UP—adv.)
5. Unspecified Processes — Adjectives Modifying Nouns (UP—adj.)

Linguistic Generalizations
6. Universal Quantifiers (UQ)
7. Modal Operators (MO)
8. Lost Performatives (LP)

Linguistic Distortions
9. Nominalization (Nom.)
10. Mind-Reading (MR)
11. Cause-Effect (C-E)
12. Complex Equivalences (CEq.)
13. Presuppositions (Ps.)

Appendix F

The Meta-States Model

L. Michael Hall stumbled upon the Meta-States Model accidentally during a modeling project of resilience in 1994. Upon submitting it to *The International NLP Trainers Association* and winning the INLPTA's award for "the most significant contribution to the development of NLP" in 1994–1995, Dr Hall put the model in writing. This appeared in the book, *Meta-States* (1995). The following year, a Meta-States Workshop was transcribed and published as *Dragon Slaying* (1996). In 1997, *Meta-States Journal* began printing *Meta-State Patterns*.

As the Meta-States Model grew, other books were produced:

Mind-Lines: Lines for Changing Minds (1997) with Dr Bodenhamer which applied Meta-States to the conversational reframing patterns in NLP previously known as the "Sleight of Mouth" Patterns.
Figuring Out People: Design Engineering with Meta-Programs (1997), by Hall and Bodenhamer. Meta-States applied to the perceptual filters or NLP Meta-Programs
NLP: Going Meta—Advanced Modeling Using Meta-Levels (1998/1999).
The Structure of Excellence: Unmasking the Meta-Levels of Submodalities (1999) with Bodenhamer.
Meta-States Certification Training Manual (2000).
Advanced Neuro-Semantic Modeling (2000) Training Manual Selling Excellence (1999) Training Manual for selling and influence.
Wealth Building Excellence Using Meta-States (1999) Training Manual.
Defusing Hotheads: The Art of Defusing Hot, Irrational, and Stressed-Out People (1998).
Instant Relaxation: How to Reduce Stress At Work, At Home And In Your Daily Life. Debra Lederer (1999).

Personality Ordering and Disordering Using NLP and Neuro-Semantics (2000).
Frame Games: Persuasion Elegance (2000).
Frame Games Training Manual (2000).
Frame Games for Business Excellence (2000).
Frame Games for Fitness and Weight Management (2000).

The Meta-States Model grew out of the work of numerous theorists and disciplines dealing with such seemingly diverse domains as—

Language: General Semantics, Neuro-Linguistics.
Psychology: Gestalt, NLP, Family Systems, Cognitive-Behavioral Information Theory: Cybernetics, Computer science, General Systems.
Neurology: the Brain sciences, neuro-sciences.
Hypnosis: Ericksonian mind-body communication.

Appendix G

The Secrets of Personal Mastery

Secret #1
The road to mastery begins when we appreciate our "thoughts" as neuro-linguistic programs. *The foundation for personal mastery lies in the thought. What you think determines what you feel, how you perceive, your internal reality, in a word, your states. They also give you your initial road maps for navigating life.*

Secret #2
Mastery lies in discovering our higher states as our executive operations. *We humans never just think—we think about our thinking, and then think about thinking. Our thoughts-and-feelings forever and inevitably reflect back onto itself to become more and more layered. Therefore the secret of personal mastery lies in discovering our higher thoughts-and-feelings and choosing those that serve us well.*

Secret #3
Our reflexive consciousness enables us to always layer yet another level upon our current model of the world. *This gives us the ability to always step outside of our frames-of-reference and go right to the top—to our highest executive states. We do not have to be stuck or limited any more than we want to be. We can always outframe. This gives us the ability to truly Take Charge of our mind, emotions, reality, and destiny.*

Secret #4
A strong sense of vitality and mastery emerges from ownership of our basic neuro-linguistic powers. *A physical and mental sense of vitality, of being alive, and of learned optimism comes from owning, accepting, appreciating, and immersing ourselves in our basic powers of* **mind** *(thinking, evaluating, believing, valuing, understanding),* **emotion** *(caring, valuing, somatizing),* **speech** *(speaking, languaging, symbolizing, narrating), and* **behavior** *(acting, relating, incorporating, expressing).*

Secret #5
Mastery emerges from our power to detect and to set higher level frames. *Our neuro-linguistic and neuro-semantic powers blossom even more when we move to a higher level and use our thinking, feeling, speaking, and behaving to set a frame of reference.*

Secret #6
Whoever sets the frame governs all of the subsequent experiences as determined by that frame. *The ultimate power over human experience, states, perception, thought, emotion, skill, etc. derives from the higher level frames under which it operates. To understand the meaning and the dynamics within any thought or feeling state, we have to detect the governing frame.*

Secret #7
Installing new executive or Meta-State frames is as simple as linking ideas, thoughts, feelings, etc. together in an "aboutness" relationship. *When mind reflects on something so that it thinks about something in terms of something else, it creates meta-relationships, logical levels, and higher frames. It is as easy as that—as profound as that.*

Secret #8
Mastery emerges when we align our *attentions* with our higher level *intentions*. *Within every thought we think, we have both an attentional content or focus and an intentional design. And if we do not* **intentionally** *take charge of our attentions from a higher level, our attentions will drive us and often run us ragged, but when we take an Intentional Stance from our meta-outcomes, personal genius becomes easy.*

Secret #9
Energy flows where attention goes as determined and governed by intention. *Our attentions at the primary level actually work in service of our higher level intentions and intentions-of-intentions. These intentions may, or may not, be conscious and explicit. Yet they govern experience. Now aligning our attentions to our higher intentions gives us the power to focus our energies of mind, body, emotion, and spirit so that we develop our personal genius.*

Secret #10

Beliefs that govern our perceptions, states, health, skills, etc. are thoughts embedded in a frame of confirmation. *Thinking a thought will not do much neuro-linguistically and especially neuro-semantically until we embed it in a frame of confirmation. We build empowering beliefs that send commands to our nervous system when we bring thoughts of confirmation to bear on some thought. We destroy and eliminate toxic ideas that limit and sabotage us when we bring disconfirmation to our thoughts.*

Secret #11

Mastery emerges through application. *We will never experience personal mastery if we do not implement and apply what we know. Even the greatest and grandest and most compelling ideas achieve nothing if we fail to act upon them.*

Secret #12

The personal mastery of focus and power comes from alignment with all of one's higher or executive frames of mind. *When we align all of our higher frames of mind—our valuing, understanding, believing, identifying, deciding, etc., we find that we can direct our powers of attention in accordance with our higher intentions. This creates a laser beam type of focus.*

Secret #13

Personal mastery emerges only when we engage our higher executive levels of mind as self-organizing powers. *Because the higher frames govern, determine, modulate, and organize the lower levels, when we set the highest frames and take charge of managing our highest conceptual contexts, we order our neuro-linguistic self-organizing system so that it operates for our wellbeing. Using this top-down approach then leads to personal mastery since it enables us to manage our higher levels of mind by controlling our higher conceptual frames.*

Bibliography

Bandler, Richard, and Grinder, John. (1975). *The Structure of Magic, Volume I: A Book about Language and Therapy.* Palo Alto, CA: Science and Behavior Books.

Bandler, Richard, and Grinder, John. (1976). *The Structure of Magic, Volume II.* Palo Alto, CA: Science and Behavior Books.

Bandler, Richard, and Grinder, John. (1979). *Frogs into Princes: Neuro-Linguistic Programming.* Moab, UT: Real People Press.

Bandler, Richard, and Grinder, John. (1982). *Reframing: Neuro-Linguistic Programming and the Transformation of Meaning.* Moab, UT: Real People Press.

Bandler, Richard. (1985). *Using Your Brain for a Change: Neuro-Linguistic Programming.* Moab, UT: Real People Press.

Bateson, Gregory. (1979). *Mind and Nature: A Necessary Unity.* New York: Ballantine.

Bateson, Gregory. (1972). *Steps to An Ecology of Mind.* New York: Ballantine.

Bodenhamer, Bobby G., and Hall, L. Michael. (1997). *Time-Lining: Patterns For Adventuring In "Time".* Wales, UK: The Anglo-American Book Company.

Bodenhamer, Bobby G., and Hall, L. Michael. (1999). *The User's Manual For The Brain: The Complete Manual For Neuro-Linguistic Programming Practitioner Certification.* Wales, UK: Crown House Publishing.

Csikszentmihalyi, Mihaly. (1991). *Flow: The Psychology of Optimal Experience.* New York: Harper and Row.

de Shazer, Steve. (1988). *Clues: Investigating Solutions in Brief Therapy.* New York: Norton.

de Shazer, Steve. (1991). *Putting Difference to Work.* New York: Norton.

de Shazer, Steve. (1994). *Words were Originally Magic.* New York: Norton.

Dilts, Robert; Grinder, John; Bandler, Richard; and DeLozier, Judith. (1980). *Neuro-Linguistic Programming, Volume I: The Study of the Structure of Subjective Experience.* Cupertino. CA: Meta Publications.

Grinder, John, and DeLozier, Judith. (1987). *Turtles All the Way Down: Prerequisites to Personal Genius.* Scotts Valley, CA: Grinder and Associates.

Glasser, William. (1976). *Positive Addiction.* New York: Harper and Row.

Hall, L. Michael. (1995). *Meta-States: Self-Reflexiveness in Human States of Consciousness.* Grand Jct. CO: E.T. Publications.

Hall, L. Michael (1996b). *Dragon Slaying: Dragons to Princes.* Grand Jct. CO: E.T. Publications.

Hall, L. Michael. (1997). *NLP: Going Meta into Logical Levels.* Grand Jct. CO: E.T. Publications (in spiral book format).

Hall, L. Michael, and Bodenhamer, Bobby G. (1997). *Figuring Out People: Design Engineering with Meta-Programs.* Wales, UK: Crown House Publishing.

Hall, L. Michael. (1997a). *Neuro-Linguistic Programming: Going Meta—Advanced Modeling Using Meta-States and Logical Levels.* Grand Jct. CO: E.T. Publications

Hall, L. Michael. (1998). *The Secrets of Magic: Communicational Excellence For The 21st Century.* Wales, UK: Crown House Publishing.

Hall, L. Michael, and Bodenhamer, Bobby G. (1999). *The Structure of Excellence: Unmasking the Meta-levels of "Submodalities."* Grand Jct. CO: E.T. Publications.

Holland, Norman N. (1995). *The Brain of Robert Frost: A Cognitive Approach to Literature.* London: Routledge.

Howard, Pierce J. (1994). *The Owner's Manual for the Brain.* Austin, TX: Bard Press.

James, William. (1890). *Principles of Psychology.* Vol. 1. New York: Henry Holt Co.

Korzybski, Alfred. (1933/1994) *Science and Sanity: An Introduction to Non-Aristotelian Systems and General Semantics,* (5th. Ed.). Lakeville, CN: International Non-Aristotelian Library Publishing Co.

Lederer, Debra with Hall, L. Michael. (1999). *Instant Relaxation: How To Reduce Stress At Work, At Home And In Your Daily Life.* Wales, UK: Crown House Publishing.

Metcalfe, Janet, and Shimamura, Arthur P. (Eds.) (1994). *Metacognition: Knowing about Knowing.* Cambridge, MA: The MIT Press.

Index

About the Author

L. Michael Hall, Ph.D.
E-mail: Michael@neurosemantics.com
NLPMetaStates@OnLineCol.com
www.neurosemantics.com
www.learninstitute.com
Neuro-Semantics®
P.O. Box 9231
Grand Jct. Co. 81501
(970) 523-7877

Dr L. Michael Hall is an entrepreneur who lives in the Rocky Mountains in Colorado. As a psychologist he had a private psychotherapeutic practice for many years, and then began teaching and training—first in Communication Training (Assertiveness, Negotiations, Relationships), then in NLP.

He studied NLP with co-founder, Richard Bandler in the late 1980s and became a Master Practitioner and Trainer. He wrote notes for the trainings at Bandler's request, and edited *Time For a Change*. As a prolific author, he has written and published more than two dozen books including *The Spirit of NLP* (1996), *Dragon Slaying, Meta- States, Mind-Lines, Figuring Out People, The Structure of Excellence, Frame Games*, etc.

Michael earned his doctorate in Cognitive-Behavioral Psychology with an emphasis in psycho-linguistics. His doctoral dissertation dealt with the *languaging* of four psychotherapies (NLP, RET, Reality Therapy, Logotherapy) using the formulations of General Semantics. He addressed the Interdisciplinary International Conference (1995) presenting an integration of NLP and General Semantics.

In 1994, Michael developed *the Meta-States Model* while modeling *resilience* and presenting the findings at the International NLP Conference in Denver. He has hundreds of articles published in *NLP World, Anchor Point, Rapport, Connection, Meta-States Journal*.

Michael is the co-developer, along with Dr Bob Bodenhamer, of Neuro-Semantics having co-authored a unified field model using the three Meta-Domains of NLP. They initiated *The Society of Neuro- Semantics,* and have begun to establish *Institutes* of Neuro-Semantics in the USA and around the world. Elvis Keith Lester joined the team in 1998, and then established the *LEARN Institute of Neuro-Semantics* in Tampa, Fl.

Today Michael spends his time researching and modeling, training internationally, and writing. Recent modeling projects have included modeling excellence in sales, persuasion, accelerated learning, state management, wealth building, women in leadership, fitness and health, etc. These are now Meta-State Gateway Trainings.

The Society of Neuro-Semantics®

L. Michael Hall and Bobby Bodenhamer trademarked **Meta-States** and **Neuro-Semantics** in 1998, and along with E. Keith Lester have formulated *The Society of Neuro-Semantics.*

Trainings available

Meta-State Trainings —

Accessing Personal Genius: Introduction to Meta-States as an advanced NLP model (three days). This training introduces and teaches the *Meta-States Model* and is ideal for NLP Practitioners. It presupposes knowledge of the NLP Model and builds the training around accessing the kinds of states that will access and support "personal genius."

Advanced Modeling Using Meta-Levels: Advanced use of Meta-States by focusing on the domain of modeling excellence. This training typically occurs as the last four days of the seven-day Meta-States Certification. Based upon the modeling experiences of Dr Hall and his book, *NLP: Going Meta— Advanced Modeling Using Meta-Levels,* this training looks at the formatting and structuring of the meta-levels in Resilience, Un-Insultability, and Seeing Opportunities. The training touches on modeling of Wealth Building, Fitness, Women in Leadership, Persuasion, etc.

Secrets of Personal Mastery: Awakening Your Inner Executive. This training presents the power of Meta-States *without* directly teaching the model as such. The focus instead shifts to *Personal Mastery* and the *Executive Powers* of the participants. Formatted so that it can take the form of one, two or three days, this training presents a simpler form of Meta-States, especially good for those without NLP background or those who are more focused on Meta-States Applications than the model.

Frame Games: Persuasion Elegance. The first truly *User Friendly* version of Meta-States. Frame Games provides practice and use of Meta-States in terms of frame detecting, setting, and changing. As a model of frames, Frame Games focuses on the power of persuasion via frames and so presents how to influence or persuade yourself and others using the Levels of Thought or Mind that lies at the heart of Meta-States. Designed as a three-day program, the first two days present the model of Frame Games and lots of exercises. Day three is for becoming a true Frame Game Master and working with frames conversationally and covertly.

Wealth Building Excellence (Meta-Wealth). The focus of this training is on learning how to think like a millionaire, to develop the mind and meta-mind of someone who is structured and programmed to create wealth economically, personally, mentally, emotionally, relationally, etc. As a Meta-States Application Training, Wealth Building Excellence began as a modeling project and seeks to facilitate the replication of that excellence in participants.

Selling and Persuasion Excellence (Meta-Selling). Another Meta-States Application Training, modeled after experts in the fields of selling and persuasion and designed to replicate itself in participants. An excellent follow-up training to Wealth Building since most people who build wealth have to sell their ideas and dreams to others. This training goes way beyond mere Persuasion Engineering as it uses the Strategic Selling model of Heiman also known as Relational Selling, Facilitation Selling, etc.

Mind-Lines: Lines for Changing Minds. Based upon the book by Drs Hall and Bodenhamer (1997), now in its third edition, Mind-Line Training is a training about Conversational Reframing and Persuasion. The Mind-Lines model began as a rigorous update of the old NLP "Sleight of Mouth" Patterns and has grown to become the persuasion language of the Meta-State moves. This advanced training is highly and mainly a linguistic model, excellent as a follow-up training for Wealth Building and Selling Excellence. Generally a two-day format, although sometimes three and four days.

Accelerated Learning Using NLP and Meta-States (Meta-Learning). A Meta-State Application training based upon the NLP model for "running your own brain" and the Neuro-Semantic (Meta-States) model of managing your higher executive states of consciousness. Modeled after leading experts in the fields of education, cognitive psychologies, this training provides extensive insight into the Learning States and how to access your personal learning genius. It provides specific strategies for various learning tasks as well as processes for research and writing.

Defusing Hotheads: A Meta-States and NLP Application training for handling hot, stressed-out, and irrational people in Fight/Flight states. Designed to "talk someone down from a hot angry state," this training provides training in state management, first for the skilled negotiator or manager, and then for eliciting another into a more resourceful state. Based upon the book by Dr Hall, *Defusing Strategies (1987)*, this training has been presented to managers and supervisors for greater skill in conflict management, and to police departments for coping with domestic violence.

Advanced NLP Flexibility Training Using General Semantics. An advanced Neuro-Semantics training that explores the riches and treasures in Alfred Korzybski's work, *Science and Sanity*. Originally presented in London (1998, 1999) as "The Merging of the Models: NLP and General Semantics," this training now focuses almost exclusively on *developing Advanced Flexibility* using tools, patterns, and models in General Semantics. Recommend for the advanced student of NLP and Meta-States.

Meta-States Trainers Training. An advanced training for those who have been certified in Meta-States and Neuro-Semantics (the seven-day program). This application training focuses the power and magic of Meta-States on the training experience itself—both public and individual training. It focuses first on the trainer, to access one's own Top Training States and then on how to meta-states or set the frames when working with others in coaching or facilitating greater resourcefulness.

Instant Relaxation. Another practical NLP and Meta-States Application Training designed to facilitate the advanced ability to quickly "fly into a calm." Based in part upon the book by Lederer and Hall (*Instant Relaxation*, 1999), this training does not teach NLP or Meta-States, but coaches the relaxation skills for greater "presence of mind," control over mind and neurology, and empowerment in handling stressful situations. An excellent training in conjunction with Defusing Hotheads.

Other titles from
Crown House Publishing
www.crownhouse.co.uk

Figuring Out People
Design Engineering With Meta-Programs
L. Michael Hall, Ph.D. & Bob G. Bodenhamer, D.Min.

This book contains all you ever wanted to know about Meta-programs, the tools by which we can evaluate how people function! First it provides an in-depth explanation of the Meta-programming technique, and then furnishes fifty-one examples of Meta-programs. It thus provides clear insight into our own behaviour as well as that of other people, challenging us to understand how people operate and how to change our behaviour accordingly in order to communicate with them successfully. An essential addition to any NLP library.

"Unique … an outstanding contribution to this area which lies at the heart of NLP"
—*Wyatt Woodsmall, Ph.D.*

Paperback　　　　　*320 pages*　　　　**ISBN: 1899836101**

Instant Relaxation
How To Reduce Stress At Work, At Home And In Your Daily Life
Debra Lederer & L. Michael Hall, Ph.D.

This is the last word in quick effective NLP and yoga techniques to reduce stress at work and at home. Debra has been utilising and teaching these techniques for many years and sums them up as her state-of-the-art methods for 'flying into a powerful and resourceful state of calm.' The book offers a seven-day program of instruction into the methods, following which the reader will be able readily to access their "relaxed core state." Michael Hall contributes by drawing on his vast knowledge of NLP to explain why Debra's methods are so powerful. Contents include: breath exercises, breath walking exercises, posture exercises, focused eye movements, affirmations, visualisations, pattern interrupts. Unlimited web support provided.

"This is an exciting and innovative book. A masterpiece of its kind."
—*The Hypnotherapist.*

Paperback　　　　　*136 pages*　　　　**ISBN: 1899836365**

The Sourcebook Of Magic
A Comprehensive Guide To The Technology Of NLP
L. Michael Hall, Ph.D. & Barbara P. Belnap, M.S.W.

The Sourcebook Of Magic is an encyclopedic resource for everyone wishing to gain an understanding of how to practice NLP effectively, both on themselves and with others. Divided into three main sections, it covers:

▲ the underlying model and strategies of NLP
▲ the seventy-seven main change patterns of NLP
▲ the application of the patterns with specific reference to NLP in education, business, therapy, sports, health and relationships

This is the first book to integrate all NLP technologies and to describe the individual patterns in detail, whilst providing guidance as to their use. Packed with strategies and skills that will bring pleasure and power to your life, *The Sourcebook Of Magic* is a truly practical, comprehensive NLP resource. Another of our very popular bestsellers.

"I promise you that this is a book you will refer to again and again and it will become a mainstay in your library of NLP reference sources. I expect to have my copy dog-eared in about a month!"
—*Judith E. Pearson, Ph.D., Psychotherapist and Certified NLP Trainer/Practitioner,* Anchor Point.

Paperback   **336 pages**   **ISBN: 1899836225**

The Spirit of NLP—Revised Edition
The Process, Meaning And Criteria For Mastering NLP
L. Michael Hall, Ph.D.

This fully revised edition of *The Spirit of NLP* represents the core of a brilliant Richard Bandler master training. It also includes significant contributions from other master trainers, including Eric Robbie, Wyatt Woodsmall, Tad James, Christina Hall and the late Will McDonald. Providing a deeper understanding of the true genius of the co-developer of Neuro-Linguistic Programming, it includes mastery of the neurology of NLP, and developmental work associated with sleight of mouth patterns. Systematically tackling the areas of Programming, Linguistics and Neurology, *The Spirit of NLP* is ideal for all those wishing to update and expand their understanding of the subject, or wanting a fresh and exciting new perspective on NLP. An outstanding contribution to its field, this book broadens and develops the existing NLP model, taking it into new and dynamic domains. One of the most advanced NLP books available.

Paperback   **352 pages**   **ISBN: 1899836047**

Time-Lining
Patterns For Adventuring In 'Time'
Bob G. Bodenhamer, D.Min. & L. Michael Hall, Ph.D.

Time is one of the major controlling influences of our lives. This amazing book explores the very many different meanings that time has for us and its impact on the way we run our lives. However, perhaps the most important aspect presented in this book is how we can use our internal representations of time to empower us. Preface by Wyatt Woodsmall.

"[A] provocative, compelling new work about time-lines, NLP, and general semantics. They have based their new work on my original theories, introducing us to their own cutting-edge analysis of 'time'."
—*Tad James, from the foreword.*

Paperback　　　　　　*304 pages*　　　　　**ISBN: 1899836128**

The User's Manual For The Brain
The Complete Manual For Neuro-Linguistic Programming Practitioner Certification
Bob G. Bodenhamer, D.Min. & L. Michael Hall, Ph.D.

This book is the most comprehensive manual to date covering the NLP Practitioner course. A fully revised and updated edition, it contains the very latest developments in Neuro-Linguistic Programming, particularly with regard to the Meta-states model and the Meta-model of language. For all those embarking on Practitioner training or wishing to study to Practitioner level at home, this book is your essential companion. Written and designed by two of the most important theorists in NLP today, *The User's Manual For The Brain* covers every aspect of the Practitioner programme, including the very latest insights. *The User's Manual For The Brain:*

▲ fully explains the NLP model and techniques
▲ systematically examines the NLP Language Model and the NLP Neurology Model
▲ provides an introduction to Advanced NLP

Exquisitely structured and organised, *The User's Manual For The Brain* is written in an inviting manner, punctuated by key points, and packed with useful illustrations and diagrams that make NLP highly accessible. Providing a wealth of exercises and techniques, this guide presents the reader with an excellent opportunity to *get the most out of NLP.*

Hardback　　　　　　*422 pages*　　　　　**ISBN: 1899836322**

USA & Canada *orders to:*
Crown House Publishing
P.O. Box 2223, Williston, VT 05495-2223, USA
Tel: 877-925-1213, Fax: 802-864-7626
E-mail: info@CHPUS.com
www.CHPUS.com

UK & Rest of World *orders to:*
The Anglo American Book Company Ltd.
Crown Buildings, Bancyfelin, Carmarthen, Wales SA33 5ND
Tel: +44 (0)1267 211880/211886, Fax: +44 (0)1267 211882
E-mail: books@anglo-american.co.uk
www.anglo-american.co.uk

Australasia *orders to:*
Footprint Books Pty Ltd.
Unit 4/92A Mona Vale Road, Mona Vale NSW 2103, Australia
Tel: +61 (0) 2 9997 3973, Fax: +61 (0) 2 9997 3185
E-mail: info@footprint.com.au
www.footprint.com.au

Singapore *orders to:*
Publishers Marketing Services Pte Ltd.
10-C Jalan Ampas #07-01
Ho Seng Lee Flatted Warehouse, Singapore 329513
Tel: +65 6256 5166, Fax: +65 6253 0008
E-mail: info@pms.com.sg
www.pms.com.sg

Malaysia *orders to:*
Publishers Marketing Services Pte Ltd
Unit 509, Block E, Phileo Damansara 1, Jalan 16/11
46350 Petaling Jaya, Selangor, Malaysia
Tel : 03 7955 3588, Fax : 03 7955 3017
E-mail: pmsmal@po.jaring.my
www.pms.com.sg

South Africa *orders to:*
Everybody's Books
Box 201321 Durban North 401, 1 Highdale Road,
25 Glen Park, Glen Anil 4051, KwaZulu NATAL, South Africa
Tel: +27 (0) 31 569 2229, Fax: +27 (0) 31 569 2234
E-mail: ebbooks@iafrica.com